BUILDING A MONITORING INFRASTRUCTURE WITH NAGIOS

BUILDING A MONITORING INFRASTRUCTURE WITH NAGIOS

David Josephsen

PRENTICE
HALL

Upper Saddle River, NJ • Boston • Indianapolis • San Francisco
New York • Toronto • Montreal • London • Munich • Paris
Madrid • Cape Town • Sydney • Tokyo • Singapore • Mexico City

The publisher offers excellent discounts on this book when ordered in quantity for bulk purchases or special sales, which may include electronic versions and/or custom covers and content particular to your business, training goals, marketing focus, and branding interests. For more information, please contact:

U.S. Corporate and Government Sales
(800) 382-3419
corpsales@pearsontechgroup.com

For sales outside the United States please contact:
International Sales
international@pearsoned.com

This Book Is Safari Enabled

The Safari® Enabled icon on the cover of your favorite technology book means the book is available through Safari Bookshelf. When you buy this book, you get free access to the online edition for 45 days. Safari Bookshelf is an electronic reference library that lets you easily search thousands of technical books, find code samples, download chapters, and access technical information whenever and wherever you need it.

To gain 45-day Safari Enabled access to this book:

- Go to http://www.prenhallprofessional.com.
- Complete the brief registration form.
- Enter the coupon code MLDJ-CB1E-ZBJF-PAEH-HUNP.

If you have difficulty registering on Safari Bookshelf or accessing the online edition, please e-mail customer-service@safaribooksonline.com.

Visit us on the Web: www.prenhallprofessional.com
    Library of Congress Cataloging-in-Publication Data
Josephsen, David.
    Building a Monitoring Infrastructure with Nagios / David Josephsen, 1st ed.
        p. cm.
    Includes bibliographical references.
    ISBN 0-13-223693-1 (pbk. : alk. paper)
    1. Computer systems—Evaluation.   2. Computer systems—Reliability.
    3. Computer networks—Monitoring.   I. Title.

QA76.9.E94J69 2007

004.2'4--dc22

                        2006037765

ISBN 0-132-23693-1
Text printed in the United States on recycled paper at *R.R. Donnelley & Sons in Crawfordsville, IN* 60#
in *Williamsburg*
Third Printing June 2009

For Cynthia, for enduring and encouraging my incessant curiosity.
And for Tito, the cat with the biggest heart.

CONTENTS

ACKNOWLEDGMENTS

I'm terrified to think of the wrong I might do by leaving someone out of this section. Though I'm tempted to give in to that fear and abandon the endeavor entirely, it wouldn't be fair because the wisdom, encouragement, and time I've received from those around me are gifts that cannot go unacknowledged.

First in line is my lovely wife Cynthia, who has put on hold a year's worth of projects to make time for me to write. She is patient and encouraging and pretty, and I love her.

Para mi familia, Jose, Elodia, Claudia, y Ana, gracias por su apoyo y buenos deseos.

Thanks to my parents for being so thrilled.

Tito, Chuck, Lucas, Gilly, Thunder, Deimos, Phobos, and Gus, who brighten my days and have had to make due with a small house until I could get the time to fix up the new one. And Orejas, who missed out on more than a few afternoon walks.

Jer, the best co-author and friend a guy could ask for.

I owe Todd, my boss at DBG, more than a little time and attention.

The tech reviewers on this project were outstanding. In no particular order: Russell Adams, Kate Harris, Chris Burgess, and Taylor Dondich. I want you guys to know that I'm working on figuring out the difference between "weather" and "whether" and shortly thereafter, I plan to tackle the intricacies of the apostrophe.

Lastly, my editors at Prentice Hall and Deadline Driven have been great. They aren't at all like the editors in Spiderman or Fletch, which is kind of what I was expecting. Catherine Nolan, Raina Chrobak, Mark Taub, Terra Dalton, and Ginny Munroe are an amazingly hardworking, on-the-ball, and clued-in group of professionals. They've been patient and helpful, and I appreciate their time and attention.

Thanks.

David Josephsen is Senior Systems Engineer at DBG, Inc., where he maintains a collection of geographically dispersed server farms. He has more than a decade of hands-on experience with Unix systems, routers, firewalls, and load balancers in support of complex, high-volume networks. Josephsen's certifications include CISSP, CCNA, CCDA, and MCSE. His co-authored work on Bayesian spam filtering earned a Best Paper award at USENIX LISA 2004. He has been published in both *;login* and *Sysadmin* magazines on topics relating to security, systems monitoring, and spam mitigation.

ABOUT THE TECHNICAL REVIEWERS

Russell Adams

Russell Adams (rladams@adamsinfoserv.com) is an enterprise systems consultant. He has been working with Linux since the mid 1990s. Author of the Nagios Automated Configuration Engine (NACE), Russell specializes in high-availability clustering, automated systems management, and network monitoring solutions. He is a member of the Houston Area Linux Users Group and contributes software to the OSS community.

Chris Burgess

Chris Burgess has more than ten years of experience in information technology and currently works as a system administrator for a nonprofit organization in Melbourne, Australia. He also works as a freelance Red Hat Certified Engineer on a broad range of UNIX and Windows systems. Furthermore, Chris has worked as an independent security consultant for several organizations specializing in Internet security. Author of *The Nagios Book* (http:// www.nagiosbook.org), he enjoys making presentations at conferences and providing training sessions on a variety of technologies to IT professionals and end-users. Chris is also the Victorian President of the System Administrators Guild of Australia and regularly coordinates and attends industry and user group meetings.

Taylor Dondich

Previously working in the enterprise network engineering market, Taylor Dondich is now a senior developer at Groundwork Open Source Solutions, a provider of open source IT operations management software and services. Taylor has extensive experience in implementing open source tools to provide the solution to IT management tasks. Taylor is also the author of Fruity, one of the leading Nagios configuration tools available as open source.

Kate Harris

Kate Harris (kate@totkat.org) has been playing with computers since 1980, and despite a master's degree and very nearly a Ph.D. in materials science, she has had the pleasure of being paid to do so for the last ten years. She has brought Nagios into organizations that were paying vast sums of money for less effective solutions. Kate also specializes in herding cats or, in other words, managing system administrators.

INTRODUCTION

This is a book about untrustworthy machines; machines, in fact, that are every bit as untrustworthy as they are critical to our well-being. But I don't need to bore you with a laundry list of how prevalent computer systems have become or with horror stories about what can happen when they fail. If you picked up this book, then I'm sure you're aware of the problems: layer upon layer of interdependent libraries hiding bugs in their abstraction, script kiddies, viruses, DDOS attacks, hardware failures, end-user errors, back-hoes, hurricanes, and on and on. It doesn't matter whether the root cause is malicious or accidental, your systems will fail. When they do fail, only two things will save you from the downtime: redundancy and monitoring systems.

Do It Right the First Time

In concept, monitoring systems are simple: an extra system or collection of systems whose job is to watch the other systems for problems. For example, the monitoring system can periodically connect to a Web server to make sure it responds and, if not, send notifications to the administrators. Although it sounds straightforward, monitoring systems have grown into expensive, complex pieces of software. Many now have agents larger than 500 MB, include proprietary scripting languages, and sport price tags above hundreds of thousands.

When implemented correctly, a monitoring system can be your best friend. It can notify administrators of glitches before they become crises, help architects tease out patterns corresponding to chronic interoperability issues, and give engineers detailed capacity planning information. A good monitoring system can help the security guys correlate interesting events, show the network operations center personnel where the bandwidth bottlenecks are, and provide management with much needed high-level visibility into the critical systems that they bet their business on. A good monitoring system can help you uphold your service level agreement (SLA) and even take steps to solve problems without waking anyone up. Good monitoring systems save money, bring stability to complex environments, and make everyone happy.

When done poorly, however, the same system can wreak havoc. Bad monitoring systems cry wolf at all hours of the night so often that nobody pays attention anymore; they install backdoors into your otherwise secure infrastructure, leech time and resources away from other projects, and congest network links with megabyte upon megabyte of health checks. Bad monitoring systems can really suck.

Unfortunately, getting it right the first time isn't as easy as you might think, and in my experience, a bad monitoring system doesn't usually survive long enough to be fixed. Bad monitoring systems are too much of a burden on everyone involved, including the systems being monitored. In this context, it's easy to see why large corporations and governments employ full-time monitoring specialists and purchase software with six-figure price tags. They know how important it is to get it right the first time.

Small- to medium-sized businesses and universities can have environments as complex or even more complex then large companies, but they obviously don't have the luxury of high-priced tools and specialized expertise. Getting a well-built monitoring infrastructure in these environments, with their geographically dispersed campuses and satellite offices, can be a challenge. But having spent the better part of the last seven years building and maintaining monitoring systems, I'm here to tell you that not only is it possible to get it done right the first time, but you can also do it for free, with a bit of elbow grease, some open source tools, and a pinch of imagination.

Why Nagios?

Nagios is, in my opinion, the best system and network-monitoring tool available, open source or otherwise. Its modularity and straightforward approach to monitoring make it easy to work with and highly scalable. Further, Nagios's open source license makes it freely available and easy to extend to meet your specific needs. Instead of trying to do everything for you, Nagios excels at interoperability with other open source tools, which makes it flexible. If you're looking for a monolithic piece of software with check boxes that solve all your problems, this probably isn't the book for you. But before you stop reading, give me another paragraph or two to convince you that the check boxes aren't really what you're looking for.

The commercial offerings get it wrong because their approach to the problem assumes that everyone wants the same solution. To a certain extent, this is true. Everyone has a large glob of computers and network equipment and wants to be notified if some subset of it fails. So, if you want to sell monitoring software, the obvious way to go about it is to create a piece of software that knows how to monitor every conceivable piece of computer software and networking gear in existence. The more gadgets your system can monitor, the more people you can sell it to. To someone who wants to sell monitoring software, it's easy to believe that monitoring systems are turnkey solutions and whoever's software can monitor the largest number of gadgets wins.

The commercial packages I've worked with all seem to follow this logic. Not unlike the Borg, they are methodically locating new computer gizmos and adding the requisite monitoring code to their solution, or worse: acquiring other companies that already know how to monitor lots of computer gadgetry and bolting those companies' codes onto their own.

They quickly become obsessed with features, creating enormous spreadsheets of supported gizmos. Their software engineers exist so that the presales engineers can come to your office and say to your managers, through seemingly layers of white gleaming teeth, "Yes, our software can monitor that."

The problem is that monitoring systems are not turnkey solutions. They require a large amount of customization before they start solving problems, and herein lies the difference between people selling monitoring software and those designing and implementing monitoring systems. When you're trying to build a monitoring system, a piece of software that can monitor every gadget in the world by clicking a check box is not as useful to you as the one that makes it easy to monitor what you need, in exactly the manner that you want. By focusing on *what* to monitor, the proprietary solutions neglect the *how*, which limits the context in which they may be used.

Take ping, for example. Every monitoring system I've ever dealt with uses ICMP echo requests, also known as pings, to check host availability in one way or another. But if you want to control *how* a proprietary monitoring system uses ping, architectural limitations become quickly apparent. Let's say I want to specify the number of ICMP packets to send or want to send notifications based on the round-trip time of the packet in microseconds instead of simple pass/fail. More complex environments may necessitate that I use IPv6 pings, or that I portknock before I ping. The problem with the monolithic, feature-full approach is that these changes represent changes to the core application logic and are, therefore, nontrivial to implement.

In the commercial-monitoring applications I've worked with, if these ping examples can be performed at all, they require re-implementing the ping logic in the monitoring system's proprietary scripting language. In other words, you would have to toss out the built-in ping functionality altogether. Perhaps controlling the specifics of ping checks is of questionable value to you, but if you don't actually have any control over something as basic as ping, what are the odds that you'll have finite enough control over the most important checks in your environment? They've made the assumption that they know *how* you want to ping things, and from then on it was game over; they never thought about it again. And why would they? The ping feature is already in the spreadsheet, after all.

When it comes to gizmos, Nagios's focus is on modularity. Single-purpose monitoring applets called plugins provide support for specific devices and services. Rather than participating in the feature arms race, hardware support is community-driven. As community members have a need to monitor new devices or services, new plugins are written and usually more quickly than the commercial applications can add the same support. In practice, Nagios always supports everything you need it to and without ever needing to upgrade Nagios itself. Nagios also provides the best of both worlds when it comes to support, with several commercial options, as well as a thriving and helpful community that provides free support through various forums and mailing lists.

Choosing Nagios as your monitoring platform means that your monitoring effort will be limited only by your own imagination, technical prowess, and political savvy. Nagios can go anywhere you want it to, and the trip there is usually simple. Although Nagios can do everything the commercial applications can and more, without the bulky insecure agent install, it usually doesn't compare favorably to commercial-monitoring systems because when spreadsheets are parsed, Nagios doesn't have as many checks. If they're counting correctly, Nagios has no checks at all, because technically it doesn't know *how* to monitor anything; it prefers that you tell it how. How, in fact, is exactly the variable that the aforementioned check box cannot encompass. Check boxes cannot ask how; therefore, you don't want them.

What's in This Book?

Although Nagios is the biggest piece of the puzzle, it's only one of the myriad of tools that make up a world-class open source monitoring system. With several books, superb online documentation, and lively and informative mailing lists, it's also the best documented piece of the puzzle. So my intention in writing this book is to pick up where the documentation leaves off. This is not a book about Nagios as much as it is a book about the construction of monitoring systems using Nagios, and there is much more to building monitoring systems than configuring a monitoring tool.

I cover the usual configuration boilerplate, but configuring and installing Nagios is not my primary focus. Instead, to help you build great monitoring systems, I need to introduce you to the protocols and tools that enhance Nagios's functionality and simplify its configuration. I need to give you an in-depth understanding of the inner workings of Nagios itself, so you can extend it to do whatever you might need. I need to spend some time in this book exploring possibilities because Nagios is limited only by what you feel it can do. Finally, I need to write about things only loosely related to Nagios, such as best practices, SNMP, visualizing time-series data, and various Microsoft scripting technologies, such as WMI and WSH.

Most importantly, I need to document Nagios itself in a different way than normal. By introducing it in terms of a task-efficient scheduling and notification engine, I can keep things simple while talking about the internals upfront. Rather than relegating important information to the seldom-read advanced section, I empower you early on by covering topics such as plugin customization and scheduling as core concepts.

Although the chapters stand on their own and I've tried to make the book as reference-friendly as possible, I think it reads better as a progression from start to end. I encourage you to read from cover to cover, skipping over anything you are already familiar with. The text is not large, but I think you'll find it dense with information and even the most-seasoned monitoring veterans should find more than a few nuggets of wisdom.

The chapters tend to build on each other and casually introduce Nagios-specific details in the context of more general monitoring concepts. Because there are many important decisions that need to be made before any software is installed, I begin with "Best Practices" in

Chapter 1. This should get you thinking in terms of what needs to take place for your monitoring initiative to be successful, such as how to go about implementing, who to involve, and what pitfalls to avoid.

Chapter 2, "Theory of Operations," builds on Chapter 1's general design guidance by providing a theoretical overview of Nagios from the ground up. Rather than inundating you with configuration minutiae, Chapter 2 gives you a detailed understanding of how Nagios works without being overly specific about configuration directives. This knowledge will go a long way toward making configuration more transparent later.

Before we can configure Nagios to monitor our environment, we need to install it. Chapter 3, "Installing Nagios," should help you install Nagios, either from source or via a package manager.

Chapter 4, "Configuring Nagios," is the dreaded configuration chapter. Configuring Nagios for the first time is not something most people consider to be fun, but I hope I've kept it as painless as possible by taking a bottom-up approach, only documenting the most-used and required directives, providing up-front examples, and specifying exactly what objects refer to what other objects and how.

Most people who try Nagios become attached to it and are loathe to use anything else. But if there is a universal complaint, it is certainly configuration. Chapter 5, "Bootstrapping the Configs," takes a bit of a digression to document some of the tools available to make configuration easier to stomach. These include automated discovery tools, as well as graphical user interfaces.

In Chapter 6, "Watching," you are finally ready to get into the nitty-gritty of watching systems, which includes specific examples of Nagios plugin configuration syntax and how to solve real-world problems. I begin with a section on watching Microsoft Windows boxes, followed by a section on UNIX, and finally the "Other Stuff" section, which encompasses networking gear and environmental sensors.

Chapter 7, "Visualization," covers one of my favorite topics: data visualization. Good data visualization solves problems that cannot be solved otherwise, and I'm excited about the options that exist now, as well as what's on the horizon. With fantastic visualization tools such as RRDTool and no fewer than 12 different glue layers to choose from, graphing time series data from Nagios is getting easier every day, but this chapter doesn't stop at mere line graphs.

And finally, now that you know the rules, it's time to teach you how to break them. At the time of writing Chapter 8, "The Nagios Event Broker Interface," it was the only documentation I'm aware of to cover the new Nagios Event Broker interface. The Event Broker is the most powerful Nagios interface available. Mastering it rewards you with nothing less than the ability to rewrite Chapter 2 for yourself by fundamentally changing any aspect of how Nagios operates or extending it to meet any need you might have. I describe how the Event Broker works and walk you through building an NEB module.

Who Should Read This Book?

If you are a systems administrator with a closet full of UNIX systems, Windows systems, and assorted network gadgetry, and you need a world-class monitoring system on the cheap, this book is for you. Contrary to what you might expect, building monitoring systems is not a trivial undertaking. Constructing the system that potentially interacts with every TCP-based device in your environment requires a bit of knowledge on your part. But don't let that give you pause; systems monitoring has taught me more than anything else I've done in my career and, in my experience, no matter what your level of knowledge, working with monitoring systems has a tendency to constantly challenge your assumptions, deepen your understanding, and keep you right on the edge of what you know.

To get the most out of this book, you should have a good handle on the text-based Internet protocols that you use regularly, such as SMTP and HTTP. Although it interacts with Windows servers very well, Nagios is meant to run on Linux, which makes the text Linux-heavy, so a passing familiarity with Linux or UNIX-like systems is helpful. Although not strictly required, you should also have some programming skills. The book has a fair number of code listings, but I've tried to keep them as straightforward and easy-to-follow as possible. With the exception of Chapter 8, which is exclusively C, the code listings are written in either UNIX shell or Perl.

Perhaps the only strict requirement is that you approach the subject matter with a healthy dose of open curiosity. If something seems unclear, don't be discouraged; check out the online documentation, ask on the lists, or even shoot me an email; I'd be glad to help if I can.

For more information, as well as full-color diagrams and code listings, visit http://www.skeptech.org/nagiosbook.

Best Practices

Building a monitoring infrastructure is a complex undertaking. The system can potentially interact with every system in the environment, and its users range from the layman to the highly technical. Building the monitoring infrastructure well requires not only considerable systems know-how, but also a global perspective and good people skills.

Most importantly, building monitoring systems also requires a light touch. The most important distinction between good monitoring systems and bad ones is the amount of impact they have on the network environment, in areas such as resource utilization, bandwidth utilization, and security. This first chapter contains a collection of advice gleaned from mailing lists such as nagios-users@lists.sourceforge.net, other systems administrators, and hard-won experience. My hope is that this chapter helps you to make some important design decisions up front, to avoid some common pitfalls, and to ensure that the monitoring system you build becomes a huge asset instead of a huge burden.

A Procedural Approach to Systems Monitoring

Good monitoring systems are not built one script at a time by administrators (admins) in separate silos. Admins create them methodically with the support of their management teams and a clear understanding of the environment—both procedural and computational—within which they operate.

Without a clear understanding of which systems are considered critical, the monitoring initiative is doomed to failure. It's a simple question of context and usually plays out something like this:

Manager: "I need to be added to all the monitoring system alerts."

Admin: "All of them?"

Manager: "Well yes, all of them."

Admin: "Er, ok."

The next day:

Manager: "My pager kept me up all night. What does this all mean?"

Admin: "Well, /var filled up on Server1, and the VPN tunnel to site5 was up and down."

Manager: "Can't you just notify me of the stuff that's an actual problem?"

Admin: "Those *are* actual problems."

Certifications such as HIPAA, Sarbanes-Oxley, and SAS70 require institutions such as universities, hospitals, and corporations to master the procedural aspects of their IT. This has had good consequences, as most organizations of any size today have contingency plans in place, in the event that something bad happens. Disaster recovery, business continuity, and crisis planning ensure that the people in the trenches know what systems are critical to their business, understand the steps to take to protect those systems in times of crisis, or recover them should they be destroyed. These certifications also ensure that management has done due diligence to prevent failures to critical systems; for example, by installing redundant systems or moving tape backups offsite.

For whatever reason, monitoring systems seem to have been left out of this procedural approach to contingency planning. Most monitoring systems come in to the network as a pet project of one or two small tech teams who have a very specific need for them. Often many different teams will employ their own monitoring tools independent of, and oblivious of, other monitoring initiatives going on within the organization. There seems to be no need to involve anyone else. Although this single-purpose approach to systems monitoring may solve an individual's or small group's immediate need, the organization as a whole suffers, and fragile monitoring systems always grow from it.

To understand why, consider that in the absence of a procedurally implemented monitoring framework, hundreds of critically important questions are nearly impossible to answer. For example, consider the following questions.

- What amount of overall bandwidth is used for systems monitoring?
- What routers or other systems are the monitoring tools dependent on?
- Is sensitive information being transmitted in clear text between hosts and the monitoring system?

If it was important enough to write a script to monitor a process, then it's important enough to consider what happens when the system running the script goes down, or when the person who wrote the script leaves and his user ID is disabled. The piecemeal approach is by far the most common way monitoring systems are created, yet the problems that arise from it are too many to be counted.

The core issue in our previous example is that there are no criteria that coherently define what a "problem" is, because these criteria don't exist when the monitoring system has been installed in a vacuum. Our manager felt that he had no visibility into system problems and when provided with detailed information, still gained nothing of significance. This is why a procedural approach is so important. Before they do anything at all, the people undertaking the monitoring project should understand which systems in the organization are critical to the organization's operational well-being, and what management's expectation is regarding the uptime of those systems.

Given these two things, policy can be formulated that details support and escalation plans. Critical systems should be given priority and their requisite pieces defined. That's not to say that the admin in the example should not be notified when /var is full on Server1;only that when he is notified of it, he has a clear idea of what it means in an organizational context. Does management expect him to fix it now or in the morning? Who else was notified in parallel? What happens if he doesn't respond? This helps the manager, as well. By clearly defining what constitutes a problem, management has some perspective on what types of alerts to ask for and more importantly...when they can go back to sleep.

Smaller organizations, where there may be only a single part-time system administrator (sysadmin), are especially susceptible to piece-meal monitoring pitfalls. Thinking about operational policy in a four-person organization may seem silly, but in small environments, critical system awareness is even more important. When building monitoring systems, always maintain a big-picture outlook. If the monitoring endeavor is successful, it will grow quickly and the well-being of the organization will come to depend on it.

Ideally, a monitoring system should enforce organizational policy rather than merely reflect it. If management expects all problems on Server1 to be looked at within 10 minutes, then the monitoring system should provide the admin with a clear indicator in the message (such as a priority number), a mechanism to acknowledge the alert, and an automatic escalation to someone else at the end of the 10-minute window.

So how do we find out what the critical systems are? Senior management is ultimately responsible for the overall well-being of the organization, so they should be the ones making the call. This is why management buy-in is so vitally important. If you think this is beginning to sound like disaster recovery planning, you're ahead of the curve. Disaster recovery works toward identifying critical systems for the purpose of prioritizing their recovery, and therefore, it is a methodologically identical process to planning a monitoring infrastructure. In fact, if a disaster recovery plan already exists, that's the place to begin. The critical systems have already been identified.

Critical systems, as outlined by senior management, will not be along the lines of "all problems with Server1 should be looked at within 10 minutes." They'll probably be defined as logical entities. For example "Email is critical." So after the critical systems have been identified, the implementers will dissect them one by one, into the parts of which they are composed. Don't just stay at the top; be sure to involve all interested parties. Email administrators will have a good idea of what "email" is composed of and criteria, which, if not met, will mean them rolling their own monitoring tools.

Work with all interested parties to get a solution that works for everyone. Great monitoring systems are grown from collaboration. Where custom monitoring scripts already exist, don't dismiss them; instead, try to incorporate them. Groups tend to trust the tools they're already using, so co-opting those tools usually buys you some support. Nagios is excellent at using external monitoring logic along with its own scheduling and escalation rules.

Processing and Overhead

Monitoring systems necessarily introduce some overhead in the form of network traffic and resource utilization on the monitored hosts. Most monitoring systems typically have a few specific modes of operation, so the capabilities of the system, along with implementation choices, dictate how much, and where, overhead is introduced.

Remote Versus Local Processing

Nagios exports service checking logic into tiny single-purpose programs called *plugins*. This makes it possible to add checks for new types of services quickly and easily, as well as co-opt existing monitoring scripts. This modular approach makes it possible to execute the plugins themselves, either locally on the monitoring server or remotely on the monitored hosts.

Centralized execution is generally preferable whenever possible because the monitored hosts bear less of a resource burden. However, remote processing may be unavoidable, or even preferred, in some situations. For large environments with tens of thousands of hosts, centralized execution may be too much for a single monitoring server to handle. In this case, the monitoring system may need to rely on the clients to run their own service checks and report back the results. Some types of checks may be impossible to run from the central server. For example, plugins that check the amount of free memory may require remote execution.

As a third option, several Nagios servers may be combined to form a single distributed monitoring system. Distributed monitoring enables centralized execution in large environments by distributing the monitoring load across several Nagios servers. Distributed monitoring is also good for situations in which the network is geographically disperse, or otherwise inconveniently segmented.

Bandwidth Considerations

Plugins usually generate some IP traffic. Each network device that this traffic must traverse introduces network overhead, as well as a dependency into the system. In Figure 1.1, there is a router between the Nagios Server and Server1. Because Nagios must traverse the router to connect to Server1, Server1 is said to be a child of the router. It is always desirable to do as little layer 3 routing between the monitoring system and its target hosts as possible, especially where devices such as firewalls and WAN links are concerned. So the location of the monitoring system within the network topology becomes an important implementation detail.

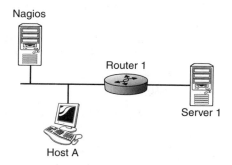

Figure 1.1   The router between Nagios and Server1 introduces a dependency and some network overhead in the form of layer 3 routing decisions.

In addition to minimizing layer 3 routing of traffic from the monitoring host, you also want to make sure that the monitoring host is sending as little traffic as possible. This means paying attention to things such as polling intervals and plugin redundancy. Plugin redundancy is when two or more plugins effectively monitor the same service.

Redundant plugins may not be obvious. They usually take the form of two plugins that measure the same service, but at different depths. Take, for example, an imaginary Web service running on Server1. The monitoring system may initially be set up to connect to port 80 of the Web service to see if it is available. Then some months later, when the Web site running on Server1 has some problems with users being able to authenticate, a plugin may be created that verifies authentication works correctly. All that is actually needed in this example is the second plugin. If it can log in to the Web site, then port 80 is obviously available and the first plugin does nothing but waste resources. Plugin redundancy may not be a problem for smaller sites with less than a thousand or so servers. For large sites, however, eliminating plugin redundancy (or better, ensuring it never occurs in the first place) can greatly reduce the burden on the monitoring system and the network.

Minimizing the overhead incurred on the environment as a whole means maintaining a global perspective on its resources. Hosts connected by slow WAN links that are heavily utilized, or are otherwise sensitive to resource utilization, should be grouped logically. Nagios provides *hostgroups* for this purpose. These allow configuration settings to be optimized to meet the needs of the group. For example, plugins may be set to a higher timeout for the Remote-Office hostgroup, ensuring that network latency doesn't cause a false alarm for hosts on slower networks. Special consideration should be given to the location of the monitoring system to reduce its impact on the network, as well as to minimize its dependency on other devices. Finally, make sure that your configuration changes don't needlessly increase the burden on the systems and network you monitor, as with redundant plugins. The last thing a monitoring system should do is cause problems of its own.

Network Location and Dependencies

The location of the monitoring system within the network topology has wide-ranging architectural ramifications, so you should take some time to consider its placement within your network. Your implementation goals are threefold.

1. Maintain existing security measures.
2. Minimize impact on the network.
3. Minimize the number of dependencies between the monitoring system and the most critical systems.

No single ideal solution exists, so these three goals need to be weighed against each other for each environment. The end result is always a compromise, so it's important to spend some time diagramming out a few different architectures and considering the consequences of each.

The network topology shown in Figure 1.2 is a simple example of a network that should be familiar to any sysadmin. Today, most private networks that provide Internet-facing services have at least three segments: the inside, the outside, and the demilitarized zone (DMZ). In our example network, the greatest number of hosts exists on the inside segment. Most of the critically important hosts (they are important because these are Web servers), however, exist on the DMZ.

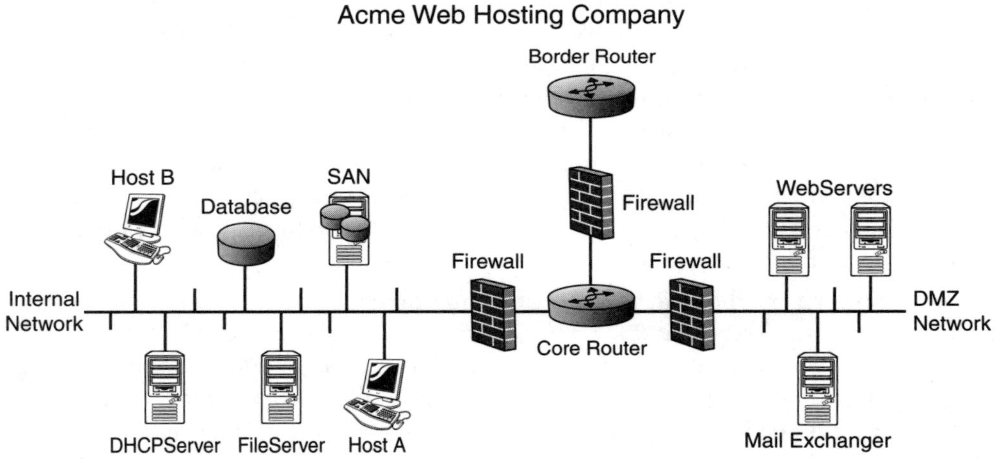

Figure 1.2   A typical two-tiered network.

Following the implementation rules at the beginning of this section, our first priority is to maintain the security of the network. Creating a monitoring framework necessitates that some ports on the firewalls be opened, so that, for example, the monitoring host can connect to port 80 on hosts in other network segments. If the monitoring system were placed in the DMZ, many more ports on the firewalls would need to be opened than if the monitoring system were placed on the inside segment, simply because there are more hosts on the internal segment. For most organizations, placing the monitoring server in the DMZ would be unacceptable for this reason. More information on security is discussed later in this chapter, but for this example, it's simple arithmetic.

There are many ways to reduce the impact of the monitoring system on the network. For example, the use of a modem to send messages via the Public Switched Telephone Network (PSTN) reduces network traffic and removes dependencies. The best way to minimize network impact in this example, however, is by placing the monitoring system on the segment with the largest number of hosts, because this ensures that less traffic must traverse the firewalls and router. This, once again, points to the internal network.

Finally, placing our monitoring system in a separate network segment from most of the critical systems is not ideal, because if one of the network devices becomes unavailable, the monitoring system loses visibility to the hosts behind it. Nagios refers to this as a *network-blocking outage*. The hosts on the DMZ are children of their firewall, and when configured as such, Nagios is aware of the dependency. If the firewall goes down, Nagios does not have to send notifications for all of the hosts behind it (but it can if you want it to), and the status of those hosts will be flagged unknown in availability reports for the amount of time that they were not visible. Every network will have some amount of dependency, so this needs to be considered in the context of the other two goals. In the example, despite the dependency, the inside segment is probably the best place for the monitoring host.

Security

The ease with which large monitoring systems can become large root kits makes it imperative that security is considered sooner, rather than later.

Because monitoring systems usually need remote execution rights to the hosts it monitors, it's easy to introduce backdoors and vulnerabilities into otherwise secure systems. Worse, because they're installed as part of a legitimate system, these vulnerabilities may be overlooked by penetration testers and auditing tools. The first, and most important, thing to look for when building secure monitoring systems is how remote execution is accomplished.

Historically, commercial monitoring tools have included huge monolithic agents, which must be installed on every client to enable even basic functionality. These agents usually include remote shell functionality and proprietary byte code interpreters, which allow the monitoring host carte blanche to execute anything on the client, via its agent. This implementation makes it difficult, at best, to adhere to basic security principles, such as least privilege.

Anyone with control over the monitoring system has complete control over every box it monitors.

Nagios, by comparison, follows the UNIX adage: "Do one thing and do it well." It is really nothing but a task optimized scheduler and notification framework. It doesn't have an intrinsic ability to connect to other computers and contains no agent software at all. These functions exist as separate, single-purpose programs that Nagios must be configured to use. By outsourcing remote execution to external programs, Nagios maintains an off-by-default policy and doesn't attempt to reinvent things like encryption protocols, which are critically important and difficult to implement. With Nagios, it's simple to limit the monitoring server's access to its clients, but poor security practices on the part of admin can still create insecure systems; so in the end, it's up to you.

The monitoring system should have only the access it needs to remotely execute the specific plugins required. Avoid rexec style plugins that take arbitrary strings and execute them on the remote host. Ideally, every remotely executed plugin should be a single-purpose program, which the monitoring system has specific access to execute. Some useful plugins provide lots of functionality in a single binary. NSCLIENT++ for Windows, for example, can query any perfmon counter. These multipurpose plugins are fine, if they limit access to a small subset of query-only functionality.

The communication channel between the remotely executed plugin and the monitoring system should be encrypted. Though it's a common mistake among commercial-monitoring applications, avoid nonstandard, or proprietary, encryption protocols. Encryption protocols are notoriously difficult to implement, let alone create. The popular remote execution plugins for Nagios use the industry-standard OpenSSL library, which is peer reviewed constantly by smart people. Even if none of the information passed is considered sensitive, the implementation should include encrypted channels from the get-go as an enabling step. If the system is implemented well, it will grow fast, and it's far more difficult to add encrypted channels after the fact than it is to include them in the initial build.

Simple Network Management Protocol (SNMP), a mainstay of systems monitoring that is supported on nearly every computing device in existence today, should not be used on public networks, and avoided, if possible, on private ones. For most purposes involving general-purpose workstations and servers, alternatives to SNMP can be found. If SNMP must be used for network equipment, try to use SNMPv3, which includes encryption, and no matter what version you use, be sure it's configured in a read-only capacity and only accepts connections from specific hosts. For whatever reason, sysadmins seem chronically incapable of changing SNMP community string names. This simple implementation flaw accounts for most of SNMP's bad rap. Look for more information on SNMP in Chapter 6, "Watching."

Many organizations have network segments that are physically separated, or otherwise inaccessible, from the rest of the network. In this case, monitoring hosts on the isolated subnet means adding a Network Interface Card (NIC) to the monitoring server and connecting it to the private segment. Isolated network segments are usually isolated for a reason, so at a minimum, the monitoring system should be configured with strict local firewall rules so that they don't forward traffic from one subnet to the other. Consideration should be paid to building separate monitoring systems for nonaccessible networks.

When holes must be opened in the firewall for the monitoring server to check the status of hosts on a different segment, consider using remote execution to minimize the number of ports required. For example, the Nagios Box in Figure 1.3 must monitor the Web server and SMTP daemon on Server1. Instead of opening three ports on the firewall, the same outcome may be reached by running a service checker plugin remotely on Server1 to check that the apache and qmail daemons are running. By opening only one port instead of three, there is less opportunity for abuse by a malicious party.

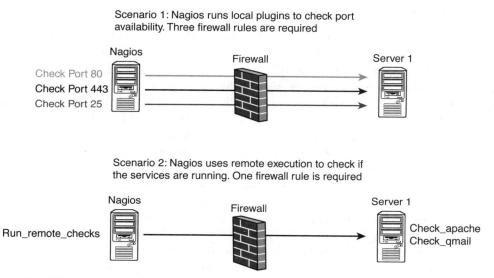

Figure 1.3   When used correctly, remote execution can enhance security by minimizing firewall ACLs.

A good monitoring system does its job without creating flaws for intruders to exploit; Nagios makes it simple to build secure monitoring systems if the implementers are committed to building them that way.

Silence Is Golden

With any monitoring system, a balance must be struck between too much granularity and too little. Technical folks, such as sysadmins, usually err on the side of offering too much. Given 20 services on 5 boxes, many sysadmins monitor everything and get notified on everything, whether the notifications might represent a problem.

For sysadmins, this is not a big deal; they generally develop an organic understanding of their environments, and the notifications serve as an additional point of visibility or as an event correlation aid. For example, a notification from workstation1 that its network traffic is high, combined with a CPU spike on router 12, and abnormal disk usage on Server3, may indicate to a sysadmin that Ted from accounting has come back early from vacation. A diligent sysadmin might follow up on that hunch to verify that it really is Ted and not a teen-ager at the University of Hackgrandistan owning Ted's workstation. It happens more often than you'd think. For the non-sysadmin, however, the most accurate phrase to describe these notifications is *false alarm*.

Typically, monitoring systems use static thresholds to determine the state of a service. The CPU on Server1, for example, may have a threshold of 95 percent. When the CPU goes above that, the monitoring system sends notifications or performs an automatic break/fix. One of the biggest mistakes an implementer can make when introducing a monitoring system into an environment is simply not taking the time to find out what the normal operating parameters on the servers are. If Server1 typically has 98 percent CPU utilization from 12 a.m. to 2 a.m. because it does batch processing during these hours, then a false alarm is sent.

False alarms should be methodically hunted down and eradicated. Nothing can under-mine the credibility of, and erode the support for, a fledgling monitoring system such as people getting notifications that they think are silly or useless. Before the monitoring system is configured to send notifications, it should be run for a few weeks to collect data on at least the critical hosts to determine what their normal operational parameters are. This data, col-lectively referred to as a baseline, is the only reasonably responsible way to determine static thresholds for your servers.

That's not to say our sysadmin should be prevented from getting the most out of his cell phone's unlimited data plan. I'm merely suggesting that some filtering be put in place to ensure no one else need share his unfortunate fascination. One great thing about following the procedural approach outlined earlier in this chapter is that it makes it possible to think about the organization's requirements for a particular service on a specific host *before* the thresholds and contacts are configured. If Alice, the DBA, doesn't need to react to high CPU on Server1, then she should not get paged about it.

Nagios provides plenty of functionality to enable sysadmins to be notified of "interest-ing events" without alerting management or other noninterested parties. With two threshold levels (warning and critical) and a myriad of escalation and polling options, it is relatively simple to get early-and-often style notifications for control freaks, while keeping others abreast of just the problems. It is highly recommended that a layered approach to notifica-tion be a design goal of the system from the beginning.

Good monitoring systems tend to be focused, rather than chatty. They may monitor many services for the purpose of historical trending, but they send fewer notifications than one would expect, and when they do, it's to the group of people who want to know. For the intellectually curious, who don't want their pager going off at all hours of the day and night, consider sending summary reports every 24 hours or so. Nagios has some excellent reporting built in.

Watching Ports Versus Watching Applications

In the "Processing and Overhead" section, earlier in the chapter, we briefly discussed redundant plugins that monitored a Web server. One plugin simply connected to port 80 on the Web server, while the other attempted to login to the Web site hosted by the server. The latter plugin is an example of what is increasingly being referred to as End to End (E2E) Monitoring, which makes use of the monitored services in the same way a user might. Instead of monitoring port 25 on a mail server, the E2E approach would be to send an email through the system. Instead of monitoring the processes required for CIFS, an E2E plugin would attempt to mount a shared drive, and so on.

While introducing more overhead individually, E2E plugins can actually lighten the load when used to replace several of their conventional counterparts. A set of plugins that monitors a Web application by checking the Web ports, database services, and application server availability might be replaced by a single plugin that logs into the Web site and makes a query. E2E plugins tend to be "smarter." That is, they catch more problems by virtue of detecting the outcome of an attempted use of a service, rather than watching single points of likely failure. For example, an E2E plugin that parses the content of a Web site can find and alert on a permissions problem, where a simple port watcher cannot.

Sometimes that's a good thing and sometimes it isn't. What E2E gains in rate of detection, it loses in resolution. What I mean by that is, with E2E, you often know that there is a problem but not where the problem actually resides, which can be bad when the problem is actually in a completely unrelated system. For example, an E2E plugin that watches an email system can detect failure and send notifications in the event of a DNS outage, because the mail servers cannot perform MX lookups and, therefore, cannot send mail. This makes E2E plugins susceptible to what some may consider false alarms, so they should be used sparingly.

A problem in some unrelated infrastructure, which affects a system responsible for transferring funds, is something bank management needs to know about, regardless of the root cause. E2E is great at catching failures in unexpected places and can be a real lifesaver when used on systems for which problem detection is absolutely critical.

Adoption of E2E is slow among the commercial monitoring systems, because it's difficult to predict what customers' needs are, which makes it hard to write agent software. On the other hand, Nagios excels at this sort of application-layer monitoring because it makes no assumptions about how you want to monitor stuff, so extending Nagios' functionality is usually trivial. More on plugins and how they work is in Chapter 2, "Theory of Operations."

Who's Watching the Watchers?

If there is a fatal flaw in the concept of systems monitoring, it is the use of untrustworthy systems to watch other untrustworthy systems. If your monitoring system fails, it's important you are at least informed of it. A failover system to pick up where the failed system left off is even better.

The specifics of your network dictate what needs to happen when the monitoring system fails. If you are bound by strict SLAs, then uptime reports are a critical part of your business, and a failover system should be implemented. Often, it's enough to simply know that the monitoring system is down.

Failure-proofing monitoring systems is a messy business. Unless you work at a tier1 ISP, you'll always hit some upstream dependency that you have no control over, if you go high enough into the topology of your network. This does not negate the necessity of a plan.

Small shops should at least have a secondary system, such as a syslog box, or some other piece of infrastructure that can heartbeat the monitoring system and send an alert if things go wrong. Large shops may want to consider global monitoring infrastructure, either provided by a company that sells such solutions or by maintaining a mesh topology of hosted Nagios boxes in geographically dispersed locations.

Nagios makes it easy to mirror state and configuration information across separate boxes. Configuration and state are stored as terse, clear text files by default. Configuration syntax hooks make event mirroring a snap, and Nagios can be configured in distributed monitoring scenarios with multiple Nagios servers. The monitoring system may be the system most in need of monitoring; don't forget to include it in the list of critical systems.

CHAPTER 2

Theory of Operations

Because the job of the monitoring server is to verify the availability of other systems, and every environment runs a subtly different combination of systems, the monitoring server has to be flexible. It needs to give input to, and understand, the output of every protocol spoken by every system in your specific environment.

Most monitoring programs attempt to provide this flexibility by guessing in advance every possible thing you could ever want to monitor and including it as a software feature. Designing a monolithic piece of software that knows how to monitor everything makes it necessary to modify that piece of software when you want to monitor something new. Unfortunately, this is usually not possible, given the licensing restrictions of most commercial packages. In practice, when you want to monitor something that isn't provided, you're usually stuck implementing it yourself in a proprietary scripting language that runs in a proprietary interpreter, embedded in the monolithic monitoring software. The reasoning goes that, because the program is directly designed for a specific feature set, a special purpose language must be used to extend its functionality.

As you can imagine, this approach presents a few problems. The complexity of the software may be the single largest impact. Many large monitoring packages have GUIs with menus 10 to 15 selections deep. The agent software becomes bloated fairly quickly, often larger than 500Mb per server. Security is difficult to manage because the monitoring program assumes you want the entire feature set available on every monitored host, and this makes it difficult to limit the monitoring server's access to its clients. The package, as a whole, is only as good as the predictions of the vendor's development group. Finally, the unfortunate consequence that comes from using proprietary scripting languages is that it's difficult to move to a different monitoring system because a good amount of your customizations will need to be translated into a general purpose language, or worse, into a different vendor's proprietary language.

Nagios, by comparison, takes the opposite approach. It has no internal monitoring logic, assumes next to nothing about what, or how, you might want to watch, neither requires nor provides agent software, and contains no built-in proprietary interpreters. In fact, Nagios isn't really a "monitoring application" at all, in the sense that it doesn't actually know how to monitor anything. So what *is* Nagios exactly, and how does it work?

This chapter provides some insight into what Nagios does, how it goes about doing it, and why. Various configuration options that are available in Nagios are discussed in this chapter, in the context of subject matter, but this chapter is actually meant to provide you with a conceptual understanding of the mechanics of Nagios as a program. Chapter 4, "Configuring Nagios," covers the configuration options in detail.

The Host and Service Paradigm

Nagios is an elegant program that is quite simple to understand. It does exactly what you would want, in a way that you would expect, and can be extended to do some amazing things. After you grasp a few fundamental concepts, you will feel completely empowered to go forth and build the monitoring system your Openview friends can only dream about.

Starting from Scratch

The easiest way to understand what Nagios is and what it does is to go back to our description of the piece-meal approach to systems monitoring in Chapter 1, "Best Practices." The piece-meal approach usually happens when a sysadmin has just been burned by an important service or application. The service in question has gone down, and the admin found out about it from his customers or manager, creating the perception that he's not aware of what's happening with his systems. Sysadmins are a proactive bunch, so before too long, our admin has a group of scripts that he runs against his servers. These scripts check the availability of various things. At least one of them looks something like this:

```
ping -qc 5 server1 || (echo "server1 is down" | mail dude@domain.org)
```

This shell script sends five Internet Message Control Protocol (ICMP) echo packets to Server1, and if Server1 doesn't reply, it emails the sysadmin to notify him. This is a good thing. The script is easy to understand, can be run from a central location, and answers an important question. But, soon, bad things start to happen.

One day, the router between our admin's workstation and servers 1 through 40 go down. Suddenly, the network segment is no longer visible to the system running the scripts. This causes 40 emails to be needlessly sent to our admin, one for each server that is no longer pinging. Later, another administrator and a few managers want to get different subsets of these notifications, so our sysadmin creates a group of mailing lists. But some people soon get duplicate emails because they belong to more than one list, and each of those lists has received the same notification. Some weeks later, our admin gets a noncritical notification at 3 a.m. He decides to fix it in the morning and goes back to sleep. But when morning arrives, he forgets all about it. The service remains unavailable until a customer notices it and calls on the phone.

Our admin doesn't need better scripts, just a smarter way to run them. He needs a task-efficient scheduling and notification system, which tracks the status of a group of little monitoring programs, manages dependencies between groups of monitored objects, provides escalation, and ensures people don't get duplicate pages, regardless of their memberships. This sums up Nagios' intended purpose.

Nagios is a framework that allows you to intelligently schedule little monitoring programs written in any language you choose. Each little monitoring program, or plugin, reports its status back to Nagios, and Nagios tracks the status of the plugins to make sure the right people get notified and to provide escalations, if necessary. It also keeps track of the dates and times that various plugins changed states and has nice built-in historical reporting capabilities. Nagios has lots of hooks that make it easy to get data in and out, so it can provide real-time data to graphing programs, such as RRDTool and MRTG, and can easily cooperate with other monitoring systems, either by feeding them or by being fed by them.

One of the things about Nagios is that it leverages what you're already good at (individually and organizationally) and doesn't throw your hard work into the "bit bucket." If you are a TCL "Jedi" and your organization values you because of your skills, then it shouldn't be forced to trash the five months you spent on a TCL-based monitoring infrastructure in an effort to better centralize their monitoring tools. Because Nagios has no desire to control your monitoring methodology, it won't attempt to drive your organization's use of tool sets and, therefore, will never force you to re-invent the wheel.

Hosts and Services

As mentioned earlier, Nagios makes few assumptions about what and how you want to monitor. It allows you to define everything. Definitions are the bread and butter of how Nagios works. Every element Nagios operates with is user-defined. For example, Nagios knows that in the event a plugin returns a critical state, it should send a notification, but Nagios doesn't know what it means to send one. You define the literal command syntax Nagios uses to notify contacts, and you may do this on a contact-by-contact basis, a service-by-service basis, or both. Most people use email notifications, and you'll find existing definitions for most of the things you want Nagios to do, so you don't really *have* to define everything, but little of how Nagios works is actually written in stone.

The most important assumption Nagios makes about your environment is that there are hosts and services. The definitions of these two objects are the basis by which all others are defined. You may think of a host in terms of a physical entity. Servers and network appliances are the most common types of hosts, but really, a host is anything that speaks TCP. Certain types of environmental sensors and my friend Chris's refrigerator are also examples of hosts. Services are the logical entities that hosts provide. The Web server daemon that runs on the server sitting in the rack is a service.

Typically, a single host runs multiple applications or at least has multiple elements that bear watching, but the host will either be up or down, available or not. Therefore, Nagios allows you to define a single host check mechanism and multiple service checks for each host. These host and service check definitions are what tell Nagios which plugins to call to obtain the status of a host or service. For example, the check_ping plugin may be defined as the host check for Server1. If the host check fails, then the host is not available. If the host is down, then all of the services on that host are also not available, so it would be silly to send a page for each individual service. It would be silly, in fact, to run the service checks at all, until the host itself becomes available again.

The hosts/services assumption makes it easy for Nagios to track which services are dependent on what hosts. When Nagios runs a plugin on a service provided by a host and that plugin returns an error state, the first thing Nagios will do is run the host check for that host. If the host check also returns an error state, then the host is unavailable and Nagios will only notify you of the host outage, postponing the service checks until the host becomes available again.

Interdependence

This idea of interdependence is pervasive throughout Nagios, which tends to be smart about not wasting resources by running checks on, and sending notifications about, hosts and services that are obviously unavailable. Nagios tracks dependencies between services on different hosts two different ways.

The first is child/parent relationships, which may be defined only for hosts. Every host definition may optionally specify a parent using the parents directive. This works well for hosts behind network gear such as firewalls and even virtualized servers. If the parent of host1 goes down, Nagios considers host1 unreachable, instead of down, which is an important distinction for people with a service level agreement (SLA) to live up to. While a host is in an unreachable state, Nagios won't bother to run host or service checks for it. However, Nagios can be configured to send notifications for unreachable hosts if you want it to.

The second way Nagios can track dependencies between hosts is with dependency definitions. These definitions work for both hosts and services and are used to track more subtle dependency relationships between different hosts, or services running on different hosts. A good example of this type of dependency tracking is a web proxy. In Figure 2.1, the firewalls are configured such that only one host on the secure network is allowed to connect to the Web server's port 80. All other servers must proxy their Web requests through the proxy service on this server. Nagios is no exception; if it wants to check the status of the Web server's port 80, it must do so through the proxy server. Because Nagios doesn't rely on the Web proxy for any other type of network access, a parent/child relationship is not appropriate. What is needed is a way to make the Web server's port 80 dependent on the Web proxy's port 8080. If the Web proxy service goes down, Nagios should not check on, or notify, the Web service. This is exactly what dependency relationships do.

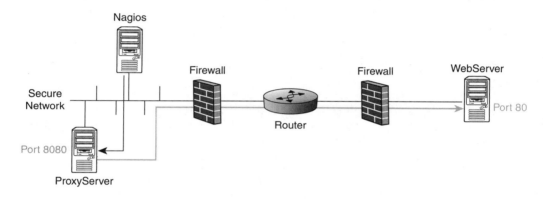

Figure 2.1 Nagios uses dependency definitions to track interdependent services.

The Down Side of Hosts and Services

In my opinion, the manner in which Nagios naturally handles the host and services paradigm is genius. It is simple to understand, always does what you would expect, and makes things generally easy to manage. However, the hosts and services assumption also limits Nagios' functionality, to some degree.

To understand why, consider a large corporate or university email system. Such a system is composed of MXs and border mail systems, internal relay servers, and user-facing groupware. Outages of various services and hosts within the email system affect the entity as a whole but don't necessarily make it completely unavailable. An MX outage (can be multiple MXs), for example, might do nothing at all to affect the flow of mail, whereas a groupware outage might mean that mail is still being delivered to the MXs, but that users cannot interact with it.

Business processes and higher-level entities, such as email, are difficult to capture on a host and service scale, because they are actually an aggregation of many services on many hosts. Nagios provides host and service groups, which can contain individual services from different hosts. So a service group called email can be created, which would summarize the status of each service that corporate email depends upon. But given that post office protocol (POP) on Server1 is unavailable, it is not obvious what effect this outage has on the overall email entity to the uninitiated.

Given that Nagios plugins are user-defined, and in many cases, user-created, an enterprising admin could write a single plugin to check the overall status of the email system piece by piece. But within the hosts and services paradigm, to which host would the service that plugin checks belong? The hosts and services assumption simply makes it a bit difficult to model larger entities, but that's not necessarily game over for those who need to do so. Chapter 7, "Visualization," discusses ways to aggregate service states in ways that help managers to visualize what a given problem means.

Plugins

As discussed, Nagios is a scheduling and notification framework that calls small monitoring programs (plugins). The next section looks at what these plugins are and how they interact with Nagios to provide a fully featured monitoring system.

Exit Codes

The first thing you should probably know is that you don't have to write your own monitoring system from scratch. The Nagios-Plugins project (http://nagiosplug.sourceforge.net) is a collection of user-contributed plugins that contains the functionality you would expect from any monitoring system. These include plugins that run on the monitoring system, such as port scanners and ICMP and SNMP query tools, as well as those designed to be executed remotely, such as CPU and memory utilization checkers. In addition to those included in the plugins project, hundreds of plugins are available from the Nagios Exchange at http://www.nagiosexchange.com.

Eventually, you will want either to write your own plugin or to reuse some existing scripts as Nagios plugins, and doing so couldn't be easier. A Nagios plugin is a program that provides a specific exit code, as defined in Table 2.1.

Table 2.1 *Nagios Plugin Exit Codes*

Code	Meaning
0	Ok
1	Warning
2	Critical
3	Unknown

Providing an exit code is, literally, the sole requirement by which a plugin must abide. Any programming or scripting language that provides an exit code (every programming and scripting language can provide exit codes) can be used to write a Nagios plugin. Typically, a plugin's job is to

- Grab some bit of information from a host, such as its current load, or its index.html page
- Compare that bit of information against an expected state or threshold
- Provide an exit code describing the outcome of that comparison

Plugins are specified in service definitions, along with other details, such as the name of the service and how often to execute a check. Nagios handles the scheduling and execution of the plugin per the service definition and optionally provides it with thresholds to compare against. After the plugin does its thing, it returns one of four exit codes: 0 for ok, 1 for warning, 2 for critical, or 3 for unknown. Nagios parses the plugin's exit code and responds accordingly. In the event Nagios receives a bad code, it updates the service state and may or may not contact people. This is covered later.

Listing 2.1 shows the ping shell script from the starting from scratch section, rewritten as a Nagios plugin.

Listing 2.1 *A ping plugin.*

```
#!/bin/sh
if ping -qc 5 server1
then
  exit 0
else
   exit 2
fi
```

Our ping command still sends five ICMP packets to Server1, but this time, it exits 0 if the command is successful and 2 if it is not.

In addition to the exit code, plugins may also provide a single line of text on standard out, and Nagios will interpret this as a human-readable summary. This text is made available, verbatim, to the Web interface, which displays it in a status field where appropriate. This is handy for passing back information about the service to humans, who aren't big on parsing exit codes. Listing 2.2 is our ping plugin, now modified to give Nagios some summary text.

Listing 2.2 *Ping with summary output.*

```
#!/bin/sh

OUTPUT='ping -c5 server1 | tail -n2'
If [ $? -gt 0 ]
then
    echo "CRITICAL!! $OUTPUT"
    exit 2
else
    echo "OK! $OUTPUT"
    exit0
fi
```

The $OUTPUT variable is used, combined with the tail command, to capture the last two lines of the ping command. Now, when the service is viewed in Nagios' spiffy Web interface, something such as the following text will appear in the Status Information field:

```
5 packets transmitted, 5 packets received, 0% packet loss round-
   trip min/avg/max = 0.1/0.8/3.9 ms
```

One of the many nice things about the way Nagios' plugin architecture works is that, because every plugin is a little self-contained program, it is possible to launch them from the command line. The plugin development guidelines specify that every plugin should have an -h, or help switch, so if you need to find out how a plugin works, you can usually call it from the command line with -h. This also makes troubleshooting plugin problems a snap. If Nagios is having trouble with a plugin, you can just execute the plugin directly from a prompt with the same arguments and see what's happening.

That is all you need to know to modify your existing scripts for use with Nagios. Of course, if you really want to get serious about writing plugins that other people might want to use, you should check out the plugin development guidelines available from the plugin development team at http://nagiosplug.sourceforge.net/developer-guidelines.html.

Remote Execution

As noted earlier, some plugins either run locally on the Nagios server or remotely on the monitored hosts. Given that Nagios has no means of carrying out remote execution, it's important to understand some of the various methods by which it is accomplished in practice.

The easiest way to understand how Nagios launches plugins on remote servers is to revisit sysadmin, now familiar from the previous examples. When he has a need to do remote execution, he turns to SSH. Let's say, for example, that he wants to query the load average of a remote system. This is accomplished easily enough:

```
$ ssh server1 "uptime | cut -d: -f4"
```

The SSH client launches the command uptime | cut –d: -f4 on the remote server and passes back the output to the local client (in our example, this would be something like 0.08, 0.02, 0.01). This is fine, but our sysadmin wants something that will page him if the 15-minute average is above 3, so he writes the script in Listing 2.3 and places it on the remote server.

Listing 2.3 *A remote load average checker.*

```
#!/bin/sh

LOAD='uptime | awk '{print $12}'
if [ $LOAD -gt 1 ]
then
    echo "high load on 'hostname' | mail dude@domain.org"
fi
```

In this script, the output of uptime is filtered through awk, which extracts the last number from uptime's output. This number happens to be the 15-minute load average. This number is compared against 1, and if it is greater, our admin receives an email. After this script is saved as load_checker.sh and placed in /usr/local/bin on the remote server, our admin can execute it with SSH remotely, like so:

```
ssh server1 "/usr/local/bin/load_checker.sh"
```

Well, in reality, he'd probably just schedule it in cron on the remote box, but bear with me for a second. An interesting thing about executing scripts remotely with SSH is that not only does SSH capture and pass back the output from the remote script, but also its *exit code.*

The upshot, of course, is that if our sysadmin were to re-write his script to look like the one in Listing 2.4, he would have a Nagios plugin.

Listing 2.4 *A remote load average checker with exit codes.*

```
#!/bin/sh

LOAD='uptime | awk '{print $12}'
```

(continues)

Listing 2.4 *A remote load average checker with exit codes. (Continued)*

```
if [ $LOAD -gt 1 ]
then
    echo "Critical! load on 'hostname' is $LOAD"
    exit 2
else
    echo "OK! Load on 'hostname' is $LOAD"
    exit 0
fi
```

But how does Nagios execute the remote command, and capture its output and code, when it can only execute programs on the local hard drive? It's simple. Just write a local plugin around the sysadmin's SSH command. This script might look something like Listing 2.5.

Listing 2.5 *A script that calls load_checker and parrots its output and exit code.*

```
#!/bin/sh

#get the ouput from the remote load_checker script
OUTPUT='ssh server1 "/usr/local/bin/load_checker.sh"'

#get the exit code
CODE=$?

echo $OUTPUT
exit $CODE

fi
```

The script in Listing 2.5 doesn't have any conditional logic. Its only job is to execute the remote script, and parrot back its output and exit code to the local terminal. But because it does exit with the proper code and passes back a single line of text, it's good enough for Nagios. It's a plugin that calls another plugin via Secure Shell (SSH), but Nagios doesn't know about this, or care, as long as an exit code and some text are returned.

This methodology is the basis for how any remote execution works in Nagios. Instead of building network protocols into Nagios, the Nagios daemon simply offloads all of that functionality into single purpose plugins, which, in turn, communicate to other plugins through the protocols of their choosing.

The arrangement previously outlined with SSH is not ideal, however. For starters, our remote plugin has a static threshold. It will always check the load average against 1, so if Server2 needs a different threshold because it normally works harder, then Server2 also needs a different plugin. Obviously, this won't scale; you need a way to centrally manage thresholds securely.

The second big problem is SSH authentication. For Nagios to call the remote execution plugin without being prompted for a password, a key is required. Unless some careful configuration is done, this key can be used to execute anything at all on the remote server, which breaks the principle of least privilege. You need to specify exactly what the Nagios server has access to execute on each host.

These problems, and more, are solved by NRPE, the Nagios Remote Plugin Executor. NRPE has two parts: a plugin called check_nrpe, which is executed locally by Nagios, and a daemon, which runs on the monitored hosts. The daemon, run via a super-server, such as xinetd, or as a service in Windows, has a local configuration file, which defines the commands check_nrpe is allowed to ask for. The check_nrpe plugin is configured to simply ask the daemon to execute one of these predefined commands, optionally passing it thresholds. The daemon does so, providing the client output and an exit code, which the client, in turn, passes to Nagios. Any program can be securely executed on the remote server by NRPE, if it's defined in the daemon's configuration file. X509 certificates can be used to authenticate the client to the daemon and encrypt the transmission. NRPE is completely cross platform, so it can handle remote execution for Windows and UNIX clients of all flavors. The installation and configuration of NRPE is covered in Chapter 6, "Watching."

Scheduling

Now that you have a good understanding of what plugins are and how they work, you need to know how Nagios goes about scheduling them. The core of Nagios is a smart scheduler with many user-defined options that allow you to influence the way it goes about its task. Understanding how the scheduler works is imperative to configuring these settings to work with your environment.

Check Interval and States

All internal Nagios processes, including host checks and service checks, are placed in a global event queue. The scheduling of check events is user-defined, but not by using absolute date/ time in the way cron or the Windows Task Scheduler would. Strictly scheduling dates and times for given services is not possible because Nagios cannot control how long it takes a given plugin to execute. Instead, you tell Nagios how long to wait when a plugin has exited before it is executed again. Two options combine to define this time interval.

The interval length defines a block of time in seconds, and the normal check interval is the number of interval lengths to wait. It should be noted that normal check interval applies only to service definitions. Although it is possible to specify a check interval for hosts, it is not required for Nagios to work properly. In general, host checks are carried out as they are needed, usually after a service check on that host fails, so the use of explicit host checks is discouraged. Because the interval length is usually set to 60 seconds, you may think of the normal check interval as the number of minutes to wait between checks.

As depicted in Figure 2.2, events are scheduled by inserting them into the event queue, stamped with the time with which they should be run. After Nagios executes a plugin, it waits for the plugin to return and then adds the check_interval to the last scheduled run time, to decide when the plugin should be run next. It's important to stress that Nagios always uses the time the plugin was originally scheduled to calculate the next execution time, because there are two scenarios where Nagios may need to reschedule a check as a result.

First, if Nagios gets busy and is unable to execute a check at the time it was supposed to, the plugin's schedule is said to have "slipped." Even if slippage occurs, Nagios uses the initially scheduled time to calculate the next execution time, rather than the time the plugin was actually run. If the schedule has slipped so badly that the current time is already past the normal check interval, Nagios reschedules the plugin.

Second, the plugin sometimes takes longer to return than expected, due to network delays or high utilization. In the event that the plugin execution time exceeds the normal check interval, Nagios will reschedule the plugin.

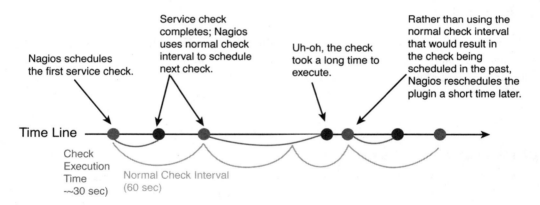

Figure 2.2 Event scheduling.

If you thought the phrase *normal* check interval implied the existence of an abnormal check interval, you're on the right track. If a service check returns a code other than 0 (OK), Nagios reschedules the check using a different interval. This setting, called the retry check interval, is used to do a double take on the service. In fact, Nagios can be configured to do multiple retries of a service, to make absolutely sure the service is down or to ensure the service is down for a certain amount of time, before contacts are notified.

The max check attempts option defines how many times Nagios will retry a service. The first normal check event counts as an attempt, so a max check attempts setting of 1 will cause Nagios not to retry the service check at all. Figure 2.3 depicts the event timeline for a max check attempts setting of 3.

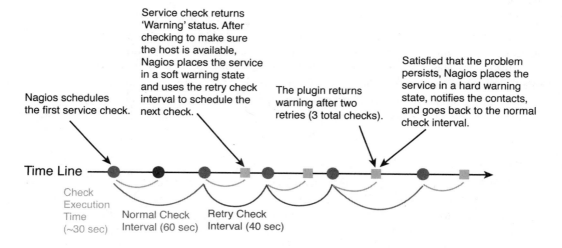

Figure 2.3 Event scheduling during problems.

The time between the service first being detected as down and the time Nagios decides to send notifications can be calculated in minutes as follows:

```
(('retry check interval'*'interval length')*'max check
   attempts')/60
```

In English, that's the number of retries times the number of minutes to wait between retries. Nagios places the service in a soft state while it carries out these retries. After the service is verified as down, Nagios places it in a hard state. Soft states can be one of two types: soft error states, which occur when a service or host changes from okay to something worse, and soft recovery states, when a service or host changes from something bad to something not as bad. Soft states are useful for providing a buffer of time within which to take automatic break-fix steps and because they are logged, they can be useful in detecting services with a tendency to go up and down (or flap) without alerting anyone unnecessarily. The manner in which automatic break-fix is accomplished in Nagios is called an event handler. Event handlers are simply commands that are executed when state changes occur in hosts or services. As usual, the command syntax is, literally, defined by you, so they can do just about anything you want them to do. There are global event handlers, which are executed for every state change, program-wide, as well as event handlers you can define on a host-by-host or service-by-service basis. In addition to break-fix, they are a popular place to hook in custom logging or to communicate changes to other monitoring systems.

Distributing the Load

My description of service scheduling in Nagios presents a problem. Because scheduling is determined based on the last time a service completed, the entire scheduling algorithm is dependent on when the services started. If all services started at the same time Nagios did, then all services with the same normal check interval would be scheduled at exactly the same time. If this were to happen, Nagios would quickly become unusable in large environments, so Nagios attempts to protect the monitoring server and its clients from heavy loads by distributing the burden as widely as possible within the time constraints provided and across remote hosts. Nagios does this through a combination of intelligent scheduling methodologies such as service interleaving and inter-check delay.

When Nagios first starts, it usually does so with a long list of hosts and services. Nagios' job is to establish the status of each element on that list as quickly as possible so, in theory, it could just go down the list item by item until it came to the bottom and then begin again from the top. This methodology is not optimal, however, because working the list from top to bottom puts a lot of load on individual remote hosts. If Server1, at the top of the list, were configured with 18 services, for example, Nagios would demand the status of all 18 immediately. Instead, Nagios uses an interleave factor, as depicted in Figure 2.4.

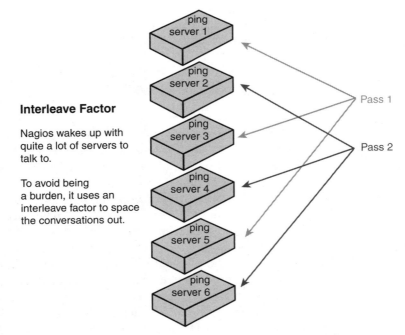

Figure 2.4 With an interleave factor of 3, Nagios checks every third service.

With an interleave factor of 2, Nagios would ask for every other item in the list until it got to the bottom: 1, 3, 5, and so on. Then, beginning from the second to the top, it would ask for every other again: 2, 4, 6, and so on. In this manner, the load is distributed across different servers, yet the overall state of the network takes no longer to discover than with the top down method. The interleave factor is user-definable, but Nagios, by default, will calculate one for you using the following formula, which is optimal in nearly all cases:

```
interleave factor = ( total number of services / total number of
   hosts )
```

Reducing the load on the remote hosts, however, does nothing for the Nagios server, which still needs to process the sending and receiving of large numbers of checks upon startup. To alleviate the intensive burden of the first few minutes after startup and to ensure that cycles are available for important tasks, such as log rotation, Nagios inserts a small amount of time between checks that would otherwise be executed in parallel. This time period, called the inter-check delay, is user-definable, but if set too high, may cause the schedule to slip. Nagios will calculate one for you if the inter-check delay method is set to smart (which it is, by default) using the following formula:

```
inter-check delay = (average check interval for all services) /
   (total number of services)
```

You should be aware that many other options exist to influence the scheduler, especially during startup. For example, a max check spread can be imposed, which limits the amount of time Nagios may take to initially glean the status of each host. Obviously, this option, if set, affects the preceeding inter-check delay formula. To help you sort out some of these settings, execute the Nagios binary with an -s switch to provide scheduling information based on the current configuration.

Reapers and Parallel Execution

The events that are processed in the queue break down into one of two types: those that can be run in parallel and those that cannot. Service checks in Nagios can be run in parallel, so when a service check event is found in the queue, it is forked and Nagios continues on to process the next event in the queue. The service check that was forked will execute a plugin and place its error code and output in a message queue until an event called a *reaper* comes along to collect it.

Reaper events are the heartbeat of Nagios. Their frequency of occurrence in the event queue is a user-defined option and it's an important one. No matter how fast the plugin finishes its work and reports back its status, Nagios will not process it until a service reaper comes along and discovers it in the message queue.

The number of service events Nagios is allowed to execute in parallel is defined by the max concurrent checks option. This variable is also an important one; if set too high, the Monitoring server's resources will be completely consumed by service checks. On the other hand, set it too low, and service check schedules may slip. The Nagios documentation provides a primer about how to optimize the concurrent checks variable, based on the average amount of time it takes for your plugins to execute, at: http://nagios.sourceforge.net/docs/2_0/checkscheduling.html#max_concurrent_checks.

The Nagios Web interface includes tools to quantify the number of checks not meeting their schedules. In practice, users are usually needlessly concerned. Some number of events will inevitably miss their initially scheduled windows because they've been preempted by retry checks for other services that have gone into soft error states, because some checks take longer than others, or because of a plethora of other reasons. So don't worry too much if you see some schedules slip now and again; the Nagios scheduler, in my experience, always does the right thing, given the chaotic nature of its task.

Notification

If you haven't configured it to do otherwise, Nagios will send notifications every time a hard state change occurs or whenever a host or service stays in a bad state long enough for a follow-up notification to be sent. So many options in various object definitions can affect whether notifications are sent that it can be difficult to maintain a mental picture of the overall notification logic. Nagios' notification framework is a welcome surprise to most sysadmins for the robust flexibility it provides, but it is also an often misunderstood subject among neophytes because it is so configurable. See the "Check Interval and States" section for a description of hard states.

Describing the notification logic is a great way to introduce many fundamental concepts. If you can understand how notifications work within Nagios, then you will understand about Nagios. The following sections start from the top and then explain the various levels for which notification options can be configured. It also points out some potential "gotchas" along the way.

Global Gotchas

Nagios, like countless UNIX programs before it, is configured by way of text files. So generally, the definitions in the text files will determine Nagios' state while it's running. However, certain settings can be changed at runtime, so the config file definitions don't necessarily reflect what Nagios is actually doing for a few specific settings. One important example is the global enable notifications setting. This option enables or disables notifications programwide, and it's probably the most dangerous of the runtime changeable configuration options.

It is especially important to be aware of the actual state of enable notifications because Nagios can be configured to use a persistent program state. That is, when Nagios is shutdown, it will write its currently-running configuration state to a file, so when it is started again, it will start right where it left off. When Nagios is started in a persistent program state, via the use retained program option, the settings in the state file override those in the configuration files. This means that if the enable notifications option is set to enable in the config file, but then reset to disable while Nagios is running, it's possible that this setting will persist across application restarts, and someone looking in the configs will believe that it is, in fact, enabled, when it is not.

Always make sure to check the "Tactical Overview" CGI from the Nagios GUI if you have notification problems, to be sure that notifications are globally enabled. If you feel that restarting Nagios may resolve your problem, be sure to disable program state persistence and/or delete the state file before you start Nagios back up. Deleting the state file while Nagios is running is no good; Nagios will simply write a new one when it is shut down. So shut down first, then delete, and then start back up.

Notification Options

Hosts and services each have several options that affect the behavior of notifications in Nagios. The first to be aware of is the notification options setting. Each host or service can be configured to send notifications (or not) for every possible state that Nagios tracks. These states are slightly different for hosts and services, because hosts and services are different in reality. Table 2.2 summarizes the possible host and service states.

Table 2.2 *Host and Service Notification States*

Host States	Service States
Unreachable (u)	Unknown (u)
Down (d)	Critical (c)
Recovered (r)	Warning (w)
Flapping (f)	Recovered (r)
	Flapping (f)

Flapping is the term Nagios coined to describe services that go up and down repeatedly. Nagios can be configured to detect flapping services as a notification convenience, because service flapping can cause many unwanted notifications. The notification options setting should list each state you want Nagios to send a notification for. If critical CPU notifications are wanted, but not warnings, the notification options setting should list only c. If you want to be notified when a service recovers from a bad state, then r must be explicitly listed, as well.

In addition to service and host definitions, contact definitions also have a notification options setting. Contact definitions are used to describe a person who Nagios may send a notification to. In addition to obvious options, such as the contacts' name and email address, each contact definition may contain a host notification options setting, as well as a service notification options setting. Together these options provide you the ability to filter the type of notifications any single contact receives. A programmer, for example, might always want problem notifications for the applications he's responsible for, but never want recovery pages because he knows when the problem is fixed because he's the one fixing it.

Templates

A potential gotcha, with definitions in general, is the concept of definition templates. Because there is a lot to define, Nagios allows you to create generic definitions that list options that certain types of systems have in common. The Web servers may all have common notification contacts and thresholds, for example, so when you go about creating the service definitions for the Web servers, you might create a generic service definition called web-servers first, and refer the individual service definitions to it. This way, you only have to define thresholds and notification contacts once, instead of once per service. These generic definitions are called templates, and they save you a substantial amount of typing.

Options explicitly defined in a service definition take precedence over those set in the template that the definition refers to. However, when the definition inherits its notification options setting from a template, it isn't immediately obvious what states the service is set to notify on. I recommend you always try to explicitly set the notification options. It's common to cut and paste when dealing with Nagios configs, so at least be aware of the notification options setting and know which template it inherits from, if it's not explicitly set. More information on templates can be found in Chapter 4.

Time Periods

Something else that affects Nagios' notification behavior is the configuration setting for time periods. Like many other things in Nagios, time periods are user-defined. They are used to specify a block of time, such as Monday through Friday, 9 a.m. to 6 p.m., which service and host definitions refer to, to derive their hours of operation. Service definitions refer to time periods in two ways. The notification period defines the hours within which Nagios is allowed to send notifications for the service, and the check period defines the period of time Nagios may schedule checks of the service.

Nagios isn't just a monitoring system; it's also an information collection program. Nagios can collect utilization and status information from anything it monitors and pass this information along to other programs for graphing or data mining. Services such as CPU utilization are good candidates for 24 x 7 data collection, but you may not want to send notifications all the time, because CPU intensive things, such as backups, tend to happen at night. This is a perfect example of why you might want to have different settings for the notification period and check period.

If the service breaches its thresholds outside of *either* of these time periods, Nagios will not send a notification. If the threshold breach occurs outside of the notification period, Nagios tracks the state change from OK into Soft Error and into Hard Error, but it will not send notifications because it has been explicitly told not to do so. Alternatively, if the threshold is breached outside the check period, Nagios will simply not notice, because it has been explicitly told not to schedule checks of the service. Like almost every other option within the service definition, the time periods may be inherited from a template, if not explicitly set, so be aware of what time periods are being inherited if you have notification trouble.

As with the notification options setting, time periods may be configured on a contact-by-contact basis, so even if a threshold breach occurs within the time period specified by the service definition, the contact might still filter out notifications.

Scheduled Downtime, Acknowledgments, and Escalations

The last few variables that could affect Nagios' notification decision are escalations, acknowledgments, and scheduled downtime. If planned maintenance must take place on one or more hosts, it is possible to schedule a period of downtime for the host or hosts from the Nagios Web UI. While a host is in a period of scheduled downtime, Nagios will schedule checks as normal and continue to track the host's state, but no notifications will be sent for that host or its services. Further, Nagios distinguishes between actual downtime and scheduled downtime in its various Web reports.

Escalations exist as a means to notify additional contacts if a host or service is down for too long. For example, if Server1 goes down, you may want Nagios to notify the sysadmin, but if Server1 is down for 7 hours, you may want to notify the sysadmin and his manager. Escalations are defined independently, so they are not part of the service definition itself. When Nagios decides the time is right to send a notification, it first checks to make sure there isn't an escalation definition that matches the notification Nagios is about to send. If Nagios finds a matching escalation, it will send it instead of the original notification.

It's important to realize that Nagios will *either* send the notification as defined in the service, *or* the notification defined in the escalation. Normally, this is fine because the escalation and the notification in the service are the same thing, except the escalation has a few extra contacts. However, it is possible to define the escalation with a completely different set of contacts and even a completely different notification command. Be sure to list the original contacts in the escalation definition, along with the upper tier contacts, if you intend for both the sysadmin *and* his manager to be notified.

Acknowledgments are used to silence the re-occurring follow-up pages while you work on fixing the problem. If escalations are configured, it's especially important to tell Nagios that you're aware of, and working on, the problem, so it doesn't get your manager involved.

Acknowledgments can be sent to Nagios by way of the Web interface, along with an optional comment. When an Acknowledgment is sent, Nagios notifies the original recipient list that the problem has been acknowledged and by whom. Follow-up notifications are then disabled until the service goes back into an OK state.

I/O Interfaces Summarized

Nagios is a great monitoring tool, but the area in which it is head and shoulders above any of its commercial brethren is its capability to interact with other external monitoring and visualization tools. Nagios is good at interacting with other systems because this was a design goal of its creators, but also because, as repeatedly stated in this chapter, it has little functionality built into it besides scheduling and notification. Nagios is good at making it easy to get data in and out because it *has* to be good at it, by virtue of its simple, yet elegant, design. This section describes a few of the most common ways to get data into and out of Nagios.

The Web Interface

When you build Nagios, you may also choose to build its Web interface, and I recommend that you do. The main purpose of the Web GUI is to provide you with a window into the current state of the hosts you are monitoring, but it has a lot of functionality beyond that, such as

- Historical reporting and trending tools
- Interfaces for scheduling downtime and providing comments to specific hosts and services
- Interfaces for enabling or disabling service checks and notifications
- Interfaces for examining the current configuration
- Tools for drawing graphical maps of the environment
- Tools for getting information about the Nagios daemon's status

The Web GUI is CGI-based, and the CGI programs are written in C, so they run fast. In general, the CGIs glean their information from several log and state files that Nagios maintains in its var directory. The complete functionality of the GUI is a subject that could fill an entire book, so I'm going to summarize its elements and how they tie together, and I'll also show you some of my personal favorite displays; the ones I find myself revisiting often. With the top-level summary that follows, you should be able to explore the GUI on your own and glean the information you need in no time.

Figure 2.5 shows the Nagios Navigation Bar. The bar is organized into four sections: General, Monitoring, Reporting, and Configuration. The general section has a link to the full

Nagios documentation in HTML. You can use the Configuration section to look at online versions of the configuration files. The two more interesting sections are Monitoring and Reporting.

Figure 2.5 The Nagios Navigation bar.

Monitoring

The monitoring section is intended to provide real-time status displays of the machines you monitor with Nagios. With the exception of the tactical overview, the status map, and the 3-D status map, every display available under the monitoring section is provided by a single CGI: status.cgi. In fact, 90 percent of what you will probably do with the Web interface is interaction with status.cgi and this is a good thing, because status.cgi provides a uniform interface. In general, each screen displayed by status.cgi has four elements in common across the top of the display: a context-sensitive menu of links, the host status table, the service status table, and the display area, as shown in Figure 2.6.

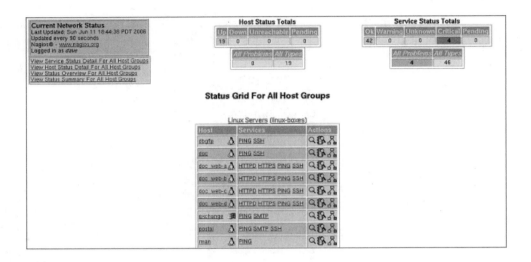

Figure 2.6 The status.cgi display.

The link menu in the upper-left provides shortcut links, which change based on what type of display you look at, and the service and host status tables on the upper-middle portion and the upper-right portion summarize the state of the hosts and services in the display area. It's important to note that the host and service status tables are context-sensitive; that is, they display a summary of the subset of hosts and services you are currently viewing in the display area and *not* the overall status of every host and service in Nagios. Generally, clicking on links in the display area gives you more detailed views. Clicking on a hostgroup gets you a summary display of all the hosts in that group. Clicking on a host gets you the detail display of that host.

Figure 2.7 is a screenshot of the detail display for a host. As you can see, the host and service status displays are gone and the display area contains a table listing the current status of the host, as well as a menu of commands. These commands alter the status of this host. From here, you can schedule downtime for the host, tell Nagios to stop checking it, stop sending notifications about it, acknowledge problems, and so on. If Nagios is configured to use a persistent state, via the retained state option, then these changes will persist even after Nagios is restarted.

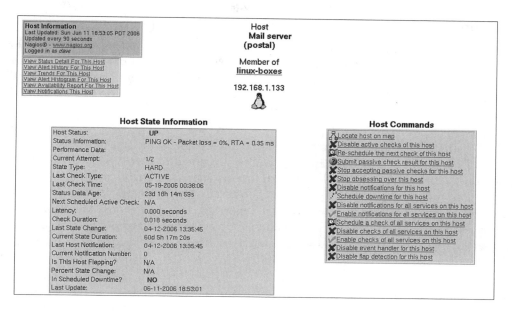

Figure 2.7 Status detail display for a host.

Figure 2.8 is a screenshot of the hostgroup summary display. This is my favorite display; it shows, on a single screen, the state of the entire monitored environment, broken down by hostgroup. No matter how large your environment, you can usually fit the entire summary screen within a 1024 x 768 window. The hostgroup summary is where I go in the morning to see the status of the environment at a glance, and it's also the screen I keep up to glance at throughout the day. From here, you can drill down into any hostgroup, and on down to the host, and because it includes every host and service in the entire environment, the host and service status tables show the current status of the environment as a whole.

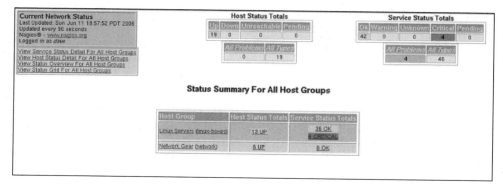

Figure 2.8 Hostgroup summary: my favorite screen.

Reporting

Nagios has some excellent reporting capabilities built in. The Reporting CGIs break down into one of three types: those that just provide log dumps, those that draw graphs, and those that output formatted reports. Alert History, Notifications, and Event Log simply dump the log lines that correspond to their type. Alert Histogram and Trends use the GD library to generate graphs. Availability and Alert Summary generate formatted reports.

All the reporting types that aren't just log dumpers follow the same pregeneration procedure. Click on the report type, and you will be prompted to specify which type of object you want to run the report on. You may run most reports on one or more hosts, services, hostgroups, and service groups. After you choose the type of object, you are prompted to select the specific object you want to run the report on, so if you choose host(s) in the first step, you can specify Server1 in the second. Lastly, you are asked to provide some options, such as the report time period and which state types (hard or soft, error or non-error) you want it to include.

The main difference between a trend graph and a histogram graph is the X-axis. For a period of five days, a trend graph displays each of those five days on the X-axis and plots the service state (unknown, critical, warning, okay) on Y-axis. The trend graph is a straightforward historical representation of the state of the service as a function of time.

The histogram, on the other hand, displays a user-defined breakdown of time intervals (referred to as the breakdown type) on the X-axis, such as hours per day, or days per week. It then plots the number of error states on the Y-axis. For example, a histogram with a period of Last 7 days and a breakdown type of hours per day will plot 24 hours on the X-axis and then plot the number of occurrences of each problem state in the last seven days on the Y-axis, based on the hour it occurred. This is handy for visualizing trends in service outages. A trend graph shows you that the CPU was High on Server1 last Monday at 1 p.m., but the histogram shows you that the CPU is high on Server1 *every* Monday at 1 p.m.

Both the Availability and Alert Summary formatted reports are well done. They are used often. The Availability report is what you look for if you need to prove you're meeting your SLA. Availability reports are color-coded tables that specify the exact amount of availability (as a percentage of three sig-figs for "five nines" people) for any host, service, or collection. The Alert Summary report is great for people who don't want to get paged, but still want a summary of what went on in the last 24 hours or any other user-defined time period. The Alert Summary report can be filtered to exclude soft events, show only host events or service events or both, or display just problem states, just recovery states, and so on. Both the Availability report and Alert Summary report can be easily imported into Excel spreadsheets by saving the report straight out of the HTML frame as nameoffile.xls.

The External Command File

The fact that the Web CGIs are able to do things, such as schedule downtime for hosts and turn off notifications, implies that there is more to the Web interface than a simple CGI wrapper to the log and state files. In fact, the CGIs accomplish command execution by way of the external command file. The command file is a FIFO (or named pipe), which Nagios periodically checks for commands. It can be thought of as a file system entry point to the event queue. The command file isn't just for the Web interface; it can be used by any process with the permissions to do so.

The format for commands is

```
[time] command_id;command_arguments
```

The Time is a timestamp in UNIX seconds since epoch format. To get the current time in seconds on a Unix box, do

```
date '+%s'
```

The command ID is the name of the command you want to execute and each one takes different arguments. As of this writing, there are 131 different commands you can send to the Nagios daemon, by way of the command file, to do things such as turn on and off notifications, acknowledge problems, and provide comments. A listing of these commands, along with their options and sample shell scripts for each one, is available from www.nagios.org/developerinfo/externalcommands/.

Performance Data

Earlier, a plugin was defined as a little program that provides an exit code and optionally some text on stdout. If the optional text contains a pipe character (|), Nagios will treat anything before the pipe as normal summary text and everything after the pipe as performance data. Nagios has specific definitions around what to do with performance data if it exists. Performance data was originally meant to track the performance of the plugin itself. For example, if you wanted to know how long a plugin took to do its job, the plugin could time itself and provide that data back, embedded in the summary text. You could then configure Nagios to do whatever you want with the performance data separately, such as log it to a file or database, for example.

In practice, performance data has become the defacto means to export data from Nagios into graphing programs, such as RRDTool. Most plugins, however, do not support performance data; that is, they have no pipe character in their summary text. This is easy enough to rectify, however, with the check_ wrapper_generic in Listing 2.6.

Listing 2.6 *A performance data wrapper for all plugins.*

```
#!/bin/sh
#a wrapper which adds perfdata functionality to any nagios plugin
#link pluginName_wrapper to this script for it to work
#for example, if you want to enable perfdata for check_mem
#you would 'ln -s check_wrapper_generic check_mem_wrapper'

#get rid of the 'wrapper' on the end of the name
NAME=`echo $0 | sed -e 's/_wrapper//''

#call the plugin and capture it's output
OUTPUT='${NAME} $@`
#capture it's return code too
CODE=$?

#parrot the plugin's output back to stdout twice, seperated with a
pipe
echo "${OUTPUT}|${OUTPUT}"

#exit with the same code that plugin would have exited with
exit ${CODE}
```

This wrapper script is similar to the SSH remote execution plugin in Listing 2.5. It calls another plugin by proxy and parrots back the other plugin's output, this time adding a pipe in the output, thereby adding support for performance data. Chapter 7 discusses performance data and how it can be used to feed visualization programs.

The Event Broker

New to Nagios 2.0 is the Event Broker. The Event Broker is a process that watches the event queue for certain types of events to occur and then notifies one or more Event Broker modules, passing relevent details about the event to the module.

The NEB modules are written in C and linked to the Nagios core process at runtime, at which point they ask the event broker to send them the events they are interested in. These events can be any type that Nagios deals within the event queue. After an interesting event occurs and the module has the relevant details, it may do almost anything it wants, including modifying events in the queue, passing information to other programs, and generally changing the way Nagios operates.

The Event Broker interface is absolutely the most powerful interface to Nagios, for those with some C skills and the inclination to get their hands dirty. In Chapter 8, "Nagios Event Broker Interface," event broker is used to add a file system status interface to Nagios.

CHAPTER 3

Installing Nagios

Nagios is composed of three big chunks: the daemon, the Web interface, and the plugins. The daemon and Web interface make up the tarball available from www.nagios.com, and the plugins must be downloaded and installed separately. (Some distributions include the plugins in their Nagios packages.) Although the Nagios daemon comes with the Web interface, the daemon may be installed alone. Nagios does not require the Web interface to effectively monitor the environment and to send notifications.

After the daemon is installed, most people download and install the plugins tarball. Installing the plugins is technically an optional step; it's entirely possible to run Nagios with nothing but custom plugins, but most people consider that to be a reinvention of the wheel. The plugins provided by the Nagios Plugin Project are well written and contain what you need to monitor an enterprise network. This chapter covers the installation of all three chunks and provides a handy reference to the available configuration options.

OS Support and the FHS

The Nagios daemon was designed for and on Linux, but it is capable of being run by any UNIX-like operating system, including Solaris, BSD, AIX, and even Mac OS X. There are even rumors on the mailing lists of success running the daemon under Cygwin on Microsoft Windows, but I haven't personally seen it done. If you're going to attempt a Cygwin build, be sure to include –enable-cygwin in your configure options. Also note that I run Nagios mostly on Linux, so this discussion is aimed more at Linux.

The main difference between various UNIX environments running Nagios is the file system hierarchy standards associated with each. Unfortunately, different UNIX variants place the same file in different locations, which makes it difficult to predict where particular files might end up. It's a problem that dates back to the BSD split, and no one has come up with a good solution. Even within different distributions of Linux, there may be differences in the file system hierarchy implementation. The only real way to know where all the files will wind up is if you manually install from source.

Aside from some odd constructs, such as the AIX convention of installing everything open source into /opt/freeware, most systems install Nagios in one of two ways: using either FHS or installing into /usr/local. The File System Hierarchy Standard (FHS), is a Free Standards Group proposed standard and describes where files should go in UNIX-like file systems. Most binary Linux distributions I'm aware of, such as Red Hat, Mandrivia, and SuSE, as well as some source-based distributions, such as Sourcemage, use the FHS to some degree. I'd like to place emphasis on the fact that, although the FHS is a good standard, there is still a lot of disagreement and confusion as to how it actually works in practice. So Table 3.1, which shows the FHS Standard file locations for Nagios, should be considered a rough guide.

Table 3.1 *Nagios File Locations in the FHS*

File Type	Location
Configuration files	/etc/nagios
HTML	/usr/share/nagios
CGIs	/usr/share/nagios or /usr/lib/nagios
Program Daemon and other executables	/usr/bin/nagios
LockFiles and FIFOs	/var/lib/nagios or /var/log/nagios
Logs	/var/log/nagios/
Plugins	/usr/libexec/nagios or /usr/lib/nagios

If you use a source-based distribution such as gentoo or manually install Nagios from source on Linux, Solaris, or the BSDs, expect to find everything under /usr/local/nagios or /usr/nagios, unless you specify different locations with options to the configure script. Technically, /usr/local/nagios is consistent with the FHS, which states that locally installed software—that is, software not installed via the system's package manager—should be installed to /usr/local. Table 3.2 lists the file locations for a *local* installation.

Table 3.2 *Nagios File locations for Local Installs*

File Type	Location
Configuration files	/usr/local/nagios/etc
HTML	/usr/local/nagios/share
CGIs	/usr/local/nagios/share
Program daemon and other executables	/usr/local/nagios/bin
LockFiles and FIFO's	/usr/local/nagios/var
Logs	/usr/local/nagios/var
Plugins	/usr/local/nagios/libexec

Installation Steps and Prerequisites

Let's get this show on the road. The high-level steps to install Nagios are

1. Obtain and install Nagios' dependencies.
2. Obtain and install Nagios.
3. Obtain and install the plugins' dependencies.
4. Obtain and install the plugins.

Nagios has only a few dependencies, and most of them are optional. If you want to use the Web front-end, which is the only interactive interface available, you need a Web server with CGI support, such as Apache (see www.apache.org for more information). Three graphics libraries are needed if you want Nagios to display pretty pictures and graphs: libpng, libjpeg, and the gd library. The only required dependency is zlib, and chances are you already have that.

The plugins' dependencies are more of a moving target. You need a ping program, some BIND tools, such as host, dig, or nslookup, the OpenSSL library, and Perl. If you plan on querying network objects with SNMP, you need net-snmp and possibly perl-snmp. Depending on what you need to monitor, packages such as OpenLDAP, Kerberos, and MySQL/pgsql may be needed for special purpose plugins.

On most OSs, the configure script in the plugins package is good at figuring out what packages you have and automatically building plugins for them. If you lack a package, such as OpenLDAP, configure will simply not attempt to build the ldap plugins, rather than generate an error. Solaris has an adept technical reviewer, Kate Harris, who says that she had to comment out the SNMP specific portions of the makefile to get the plugins to compile. The base directory of the plugins tarball contains a REQUIREMENTS file, which lists the requirements of specific plugins, so be sure to check it out before you build.

Installing Nagios

There are currently two branches of Nagios: the 1.x branch and the 2.x branch. This book deals exclusively with the 2.x branch and, at the time of this writing, the current 2.x branch version is 2.5. In this book, I used Nagios 2.1, 2.3, and 2.5 to verify the various commands throughout the chapter.

Most UNIX operating systems I'm aware of ship with prepackaged versions of Nagios or otherwise have them available. In the Linux realm, Red Hat, SuSE, and Mandrivia users find Nagios RPMs on their installation media, Debian and Ubuntu types may apt-get install nagios-text, gentoo pundits can emerge nagios, and even sourcemage...wizards(?) may cast nagios. Red Hat-specific Nagios RPMs are also available straight from www.nagios.com. BSD people can find Nagios in ports, and Solaris folks can pkg-get install Nagios from blast-wave.org. No packages currently exist for AIX. Although manually compiling Nagios on Linux, BSD, and Solaris is straightforward, building it on AIX is not for the faint of heart. If you're going to attempt a local install on AIX, I recommend picking up gcc from bull free-ware rather than using AIX's compiler. If you are an AIX 5L user, the affinity program has made building Nagios on AIX much easier. Consult your local package manager documenta-tion for more information on installing the Nagios package available for your system.

I recommend that you build Nagios from source rather than use packages, unless you plan on making your own packages. Simply put, you know what you get when you take the time to build from source. Further, although I mention that Nagios runs on many different systems, it was written to be run on Linux, so for production systems, I recommend that Linux is what you use.

For manual builds from source, the Nagios tarball may be obtained directly from www. nagios.com. The installation process is a typical configure, make, and make install. Nagios requires a user and group to run, so these must be created first. For the impatient person, Listing 3.1 should be enough to get you up and running.

Listing 3.1 *Iinstalling Nagios for the impatient person.*

```
groupadd nagios
useradd -s /bin/false -g nagios nagios
tar -zxvf nagios-version.tgz
cd nagios-version
./configure
make all
sudo make install
```

As with many great open source applications, configure and build options abound. Let's take a closer look at the three main steps: configure, make, and make install.

Configure

The defaults are sensible and you aren't required to specify anything, but there are a few options you should be aware of. Launch configure with a -h switch for a full list of options. In my experience, you either need to change nearly all of them or few to none. Table 3.3 shows some options you should be aware of, upfront.

Table 3.3 *Important Compile-Time Options*

Option	Description
--enable-embedded-perl	This enables Nagios' embedded Perl interpreter. It is intended to speed up execution of Perl scripts for people who use a lot of Perl-based plugins. I bring it up because it has a reputation for causing segfaults, so turn it on at your own risk. The default is disabled and most people keep it that way.
--with-nagios-user=\<usr>	This is the user that Nagios runs as. It should be created before running configure. The default is nagios.
--with-nagios-group=\<grp>	This is the group that the Nagios user belongs to. It should be created before running configure. The default is nagios.
--with-command-user=\<usr>	The username used to segment access to the Nagios command file, which is described at the end of Chapter 2, "Theory of Operations." It defaults to the nagios-user option.
--with-command-group=\<grp>	This specifies the group used to segment access to the Nagios command file, which is described at the end of Chapter 2. It defaults to the nagios-group option.
--with-init-dir=\<path>	This sets the location that the init script will be installed in, if you use the install-init make target. The default is /etc/rc.d/.
--with-htmurl=\<path>	The CGIs that make up the Web front-end are written in C, so the URL paths in the HTML they generate must be set at compile time. This defaults to /nagios/ meaning that the HTML generated by the CGIs will reference http://localhost/nagios/.
--with-cgiurl=\<path>	Similarly, any CGI URL paths referenced by the HTML that the Web front-end generates must be set at compile time. This defaults to /nagios/cgi-bin/, meaning that the HTML generated by the CGIs will reference http://localhost/nagios/cgi-bin/.

The previous options are good litmus tests for whether you have to specify options to configure. A ./configure with no options at all will get most people a working Nagios implementation, but chances are, if you need to change more than two of the above defaults, you'll have to change something that I haven't listed. Appendix A, "Configure Options," contains a complete list of options for the configure script.

Make

There are, in fact, five make targets to build various pieces of Nagios. A simple make all will build Nagios and the Web front-end. Table 3.4 lists the other build-related make targets.

Table 3.4 *Build-Related Make Targets*

Target	Description
make nagios	Just makes the Nagios Daemon, without the Web interface.
make cgis	Makes only the Web interface, without the daemon.
make modules	Makes the Event Broker Modules. As of this writing, there's only one, helloworld.o, which is really only useful for people who want to learn how to program NEB Modules.
make contrib	Makes various user contributed programs. There are five of these. The more useful ones include a traceroute CGI, a sample apache config file, and a stand-alone version of the embedded Perl interpreter for testing Perl plugins.

Make Install

Executing make install installs the daemon, CGIs, and HTML files. Eight other install-related make targets exist, as defined in Table 3.5.

Table 3.5 *Install-Related Make Targets*

Target	Description
make install-base	Installs only the Nagios Daemon without the Web front-end
make install-cgis	Installs the CGI programs
make install-html	Installs only the static HTML pages
make install-init	Installs the init file (to the directory specified by the –with-init-dir configure option)
make install-config	Installs sample configuration files
make install-commandmode	Creates the external command file (as described at the end of Chapter 2)
make uninstall	Uninstalls Nagios
make fullinstall	Installs the kitchen sink (everything)

Putting it all together, a real Nagios build may look more like Listing 3.2.

Listing 3.2 *A realistic Nagios installation.*

```
groupadd nagios
useradd -s /bin/false -g nagios nagios
useradd -s /bin/false -g nagios nagioscmd
tar -zxvf nagios-version.tgz
cd nagios-version
./configure -with-command-user=nagioscmd
make all
sudo make install install-init install-config install-commandmode
```

After configure finishes running, it provides you a handy summary of what happens if you decide to build. For example, running configure on my Linux workstation with the options in Listing 3.2 gives the summary in Listing 3.3.

Listing 3.3 *Output from configure.*

```
*** Configuration summary for nagios 2.1 03-27-2006 ***:

General Options:
-------------------------
        Nagios executable:  nagios
        Nagios user/group:  nagios,nagios
       Command user/group:  nagioscmd,nagios
            Embedded Perl:  no
             Event Broker:  yes
        Install ${prefix}:  /usr/local/nagios
                Lock file:  ${prefix}/var/nagios.lock
           Init directory:  /etc/rc.d
                  Host OS:  linux-gnu

Web Interface Options:
-------------------------
                 HTML URL:  http://localhost/nagios/
                  CGI URL:  http://localhost/nagios/cgi-bin/
    Traceroute (used by WAP):  /usr/sbin/traceroute

Review the options above for accuracy. If they look okay,
type 'make all' to compile the main program and CGIs.
```

Patches

As of this writing, there are three patches to the Nagios core that you might be interested in. Two of them add new attributes to host definitions, and one makes the "status map" cgi prettier. All patches are available from the Nagios Exchange, which is a Web site dedicated to user-created add-ons and scripts: www.nagiosexchange.org. Specifically, the patches are in the patches section of the Nagios Exchange, under development.

Secondary IP Patch

The first patch, usually referred to as the secondary IP patch, adds a secondary address attribute to the definition, for host objects. The secondary address is intended to provide for hosts with two IP addresses. The specific syntax for object definitions is covered in the next chapter, but I want to mention here that it is not necessary to use this patch to get multiple IP support. You may simply provide a space-separated list of addresses to the built-in address attribute in the host definition, and the check_ping plugin will check each address listed. It is a common misconception that the secondary IP patch is required for multiple IP support. The only real reason to use the second IP patch is when you want to reference the second IP specifically by a macro. Macros are discussed more in Chapter 4, "Configuring Nagios." They can be thought of as variables that are internal to Nagios and used by object definitions. For example, the host definitions built-in address attribute may be referenced by way of the $HOSTADDRESS$ macro. When checks are defined, they point to $HOSTADDRESS$ rather than the hard-coded address of the host. This way, one check definition may be used for any host. If more than one address is defined, then $HOSTADDRESS$ will resolve to more than one IP. The secondary address patch is only required if you want to specifically refer to the two addresses individually, by separate macros. This is not a common requirement.

SNMP Community String Patch

The SNMP community string patch is similar to the secondary IP patch, in that it adds an attribute and macro to the host definition. The attribute—which as you might guess, is the SNMP community string for the host in question—is useful in cases in which you have many different hosts in different SNMP communities. Again, it is possible to support hosts in different SNMP communities without patching Nagios by defining separate checks for each community. The patch makes it possible to use a single check definition for any host by adding the capability to query each host's SNMP community, via a macro. If you use multiple SNMP community strings, I recommend applying this patch.

Colored Statusmap Patch

Finally, the colored statusmap patch adds colors to the status map cgi (the graphical map drawn by the Web front-end), which correspond to the status of hosts therein. Hosts in healthy states show up in green, whereas hosts in degraded or down states show yellow or red, respectively.

All three patches may be applied from inside the source directory with the –p1 switch to patch. Listing 3.4 shows a complete Nagios install, including the application of the patches listed previously.

Listing 3.4 *Installing Nagios with patches.*

```
groupadd nagios
useradd -s /bin/false -g nagios nagios
useradd -s /bin/false -g nagios nagioscmd
tar -zxvf nagios-version.tgz
cd nagios-version
patch -p1 </path/to/second_ip.patch
patch -p1 </path/to/snmp_string.patch
patch -p1 </path/to/statusmap.patch
./configure -with-command-user=nagioscmd
make all
sudo make install install-init install-config install-commandmode
```

Installing the Plugins

After Nagios is installed, it's time to install the plugins tarball so that Nagios can actually run some checks. The plugins tarball, as well as RPMs, are available from the downloads section of www.nagios.com. Typically, UNIX distributions that have a Nagios package also have a Nagios-plugins package of some description.

Manual installation from source code of the plugins is easier than Nagios itself. The configure script figures out the paths to important binaries such as ping and Perl. If it can't find something, you may have to specify the location, but this is unlikely. If you specified custom options to Nagios, you may also have to specify them to the plugins. These include any of the default install directories you may have changed, as well as those listed in Table 3.6.

Table 3.6 *Configure Options for the Nagios Plugins*

Option	Description
--with-cgiurl=<path>	If you specified a custom cgiurl in the Nagios build, you need to tell the plugins about it here.
--with-nagios-user=<user>	If you are running Nagios with a nonstandard username, specify it to the configure script for the plugins.
--with-nagios-group=<group>	Likewise, if you changed the group away from the default during the Nagios build, change it for the plugins as well.
--with-trusted-path=<colon:delimited:list:of:paths>	This very cool option lets you specify a custom PATH for the environment the plugins run in. This increases the security of the system by limiting where the plugins may go to execute other programs.

Call configure with a -h to get a full list of options if, for example, you need to specify the location of the ping command because configure was unable to find it. For most environments, configure can be run with default settings. Similar to the main program, the plugins configure script generates a handy summary like the one in Listing 3.5, which was the result of calling configure on my Linux workstation with no options specified.

Listing 3.5 *Output from plugins configure.*

```
               --with-perl: /usr/bin/perl
             --with-cgiurl: /nagios/cgi-bin
        --with-nagios-user: nagios
       --with-nagios-group: nagios
       --with-trusted-path: /bin:/sbin:/usr/bin:/usr/sbin
       --with-ping-command: /bin/ping -n -c %d %s
      --with-ping6-command:
               --with-lwres: no
                --with-ipv6: yes
             --with-openssl: yes
--enable-emulate-getaddrinfo: no
```

If the summary looks good, a simple make && make install will build and install the plugins to the appropriate place. Not installed, however, are the contents of the contrib directory in the base directory of the plugins tarball. The contrib directory is a gold mine of special purpose and architecture specific plugins. It contains checks for everything from netapp appliances to Sybase databases and everything in between. I highly recommend that you take a look in contrib before developing anything on your own, even if you don't find what you're looking for; it's a great place to go for code to repurpose.

Installing NRPE

After Nagios and the plugin tarball are installed, you probably want to skip ahead to Chapter 4 and get them configured. After you have a fully functional Nagios server, however, the next step is remote execution. As described at the end of Chapter 2, the Nagios Remote Plugin Executor (NRPE) provides Nagios with the capability to execute plugins located remotely on the monitored hosts. As shown in Figure 3.1, NRPE consists of two pieces: a plugin, which resides on the Nagios server, and a daemon, which runs remotely on each monitored host. Nagios uses the check_nrpe plugin to ask the NRPE daemon to run a check on the remote host. If NRPE on the remote host is configured to allow this, it runs the plugin and passes the results back to check_nrpe on the Nagios server.

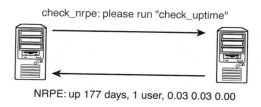
check_nrpe: please run "check_uptime"

NRPE: up 177 days, 1 user, 0.03 0.03 0.00

Figure 3.1 Remote execution with NRPE.

The NRPE daemon can run under a superserver, such as inetd/xinetd, or it can be run as a stand-alone daemon. It is configured by way of a config file, called nrpe.cfg, which is usually located in /etc/. The nrpe.cfg defines a list of the plugins that the check_nrpe client is allowed to request. There is also a version of the NRPE daemon available for Microsoft Windows. Check Chapter 6, "Watching," for more information about how to use NRPE to check services on remote hosts.

To install the Linux version of the daemon, first obtain it from

```
http://prdownloads.sourceforge.net/nagios/nrpe-2.5.1.tar.
gz?download
```

Then, untar it and do ./configure followed by make all. For the Nagios server, simply copy check_nrpe to the plugins directory and you're done. For the monitored hosts, copy nrpe to somewhere like /usr/sbin and then grab the sample config file from the sample-configs directory and put it in /etc/. Modify the config file to suit your needs; it's heavily commented, so it should be self-explanatory. Finally, nrpe –c /etc/nrpe.cfg –d will launch the NRPE daemon in stand-alone mode. The sample-configs directory also contains inetd/xinetd configs, if you want to use a superserver instead.

For Microsoft Windows users, grab the binary NRPE-NT package from

```
www.miwi-dv.com/nrpent/
```

After unzipping it, edit the nrpe.cfg file and type nrpe.exe –i to install. The NRPE daemon then appears as a service in the services.msc. I've always had a hard time dealing with version mismatches between NRPE-NT daemon and the UNIX check_nrpe client. Depending on how far off the versions are, you may experience trouble getting SSL to run or getting them to work at all. I recommend you check the NRPE-NT forums for information about which versions of check_nrpe are compatible with the current NT daemon.

CHAPTER 4

Configuring Nagios

After installation, you need to configure Nagios before it can start. Nagios is configured by way of text files that contain directives and definitions. It can be a beast to configure for the first time because the definitions are self-referential and there's a lot to define.

To get started, Nagios needs to call plugins during a time period against hosts and services and send notifications to contacts if a check returns a bad status, so you need to define the checks, time periods, hosts, services, notification commands, and contacts (and that's all mandatory). Because so many objects refer to so many other objects, it can be hard to know where to begin to explain it all. Don't be discouraged; Nagios comes with options to generate sample configuration files, and further, there are a few shortcuts you can take to bootstrap the configuration process (see Chapter 5, "Bookstrap the Configs"), but first you need a good understanding of what a configuration looks like.

Hosts and services are the core objects. They are the objects that refer to most others, so most of the documentation that has been written about Nagios begins with them. I'm going to take more of a bottom up approach. I'll start by describing the daemon configuration files and then work my way up from commands and time periods, through services and hosts to groups, and then, finally, to optional definitions such as escalations and extended information. Each group of objects is referred to by the objects above them, so by explaining things this way, whenever you come to an attribute in a definition that references another object, you will have already looked at what that object consists of. I find that it's easier to get a grasp of the whole picture by explaining it this way.

Objects and Definitions

In Nagios, there are two types of configuration files: those that contain directives and those that contain definitions. Technically, only two configuration files are needed: nagios.cfg and an object configuration file. The nagios.cfg file contains directives that affect the operation of the Nagios daemon, for instance, where and how to write logs and the name of the object config file, global settings, and things of that nature. The object configuration file defines the various objects that Nagios deals with.

There are quite a few different types of objects (as outlined in Table 4.1), so, although it's possible to just lump all their definitions into a single file, most people prefer to group the object definitions by type and to keep a different file for each type. Because this makes writing about and learning about object configuration easier, that is the convention I follow throughout this chapter. While nagios.cfg will always be named nagios.cfg, the object configuration filenames are user-defined, so the filenames I use throughout the chapter are not written in stone. It's entirely possible that you might inherit a Nagios implementation that groups object definitions by network subnet, OS, or even physical proximity to the Pepsi machine.

Table 4.1 *A Brief Summary of Nagios Objects*

Object Name	Description	Recommended Filename
timeperiod	This is the defined block of time that other objects use to determine their operational hours and blackout periods.	timeperiods.cfg
command	Command definitions map macros to external programs. Other objects use commands for many things, such as sending notifications and running service checks.	misccommands.cfg and checkcommands.cfg
contact	This defines a notification target, which is usually a human being.	contacts.cfg
contactgroup	Contacts are organized into groups called contactgroups. Objects that send notifications always reference contactgroups and never individual contacts. A contact can be a member of any number of groups.	contactgroups.cfg
host	Hosts are physical entities (or the virtual representation of physical entities if you use virtualizations, such as Xen or VMware), such as servers, routers, or tape drives.	hosts.cfg

Table 4.1 *A Brief Summary of Nagios Objects* (continued)

Object Name	Description	Recommended Filename
service	Hosts provide one or more services. For a web server, httpd or IIS would be a service. The majority of Nagios configuration is made up of service definitions.	services.cfg
hostgroup	Hosts may belong to any number of user-defined hostgroups. Names and methodology are up to you, for example: servers-with-blue-LEDs or routers-my-boss-refuses-to-upgrade.	hostgroups.cfg
servicegroup	Like hosts, services may belong to any number of user-defined groups. Servicegroups are a feature unique to Nagios 2.0 and above.	servicegroups.cfg
hostdependency	Dependencies filter out checks and notifications for objects, based on the status of other objects. Be sure you read and understand the section, "Servicegroups," before using these.	dependencies.cfg
servicedependency	This works the same way the hostdependency does.	dependencies.cfg
hostescalation	Escalations provide Nagios the capability to notify additional contacts, such as managers, if a problem persists without being acknowledged past a given number of notifications.	escalation.cfg
serviceescalation	These work the same as hostescalations.	escalation.cfg
hostextendedinfo	Extendedinfo objects map titles and graphics to host and service objects for the Web interface. These definitions are entirely optional and cosmetic in nature.	hostextinfo.cfg
serviceextendedinfo	This works the same way the hostextendedinfo does.	serviceextinfo.cfg

The nagios.cfg file is required. If you use the Web interface, another configuration file, cgi.cfg, is also required. The cgi.cfg file contains configuration directives for the CGIs and is where most of the UI security is configured. The cgi.cfg and the nagios.cfg files contain configuration directives rather than object definitions. The directive syntax should be familiar to anyone who has configured software on a UNIX system. There is one directive per line, followed by an =, followed by the value of the directive. Whitespace is optional and comments begin with a pound (#).

Definitions, no matter the type, use a common syntax that resembles a function in C or Perl. The definition is composed of a block of directives surrounded by curly braces ({}) and beginning with a define keyword, followed by the object type. Directives within the definition block are whitespace-separated, unlike their nagios.cfg counterparts, which use an =. All object definitions have one directive in common: <objecttype>_name. For example, a host object has a host_name directive, whereas a servicegroup has a servicegroup_name directive. Most also have an alias directive. Comments begin with a pound (#). Listing 4.1 is an example host definition, to give you a feel for the syntax.

In Nagios 2.0 and above, it is possible to use regex syntax in place of static text in any directive that accepts a comma-separated list of values. (This option is disabled by default and must be enabled by setting the use_regexp_matching directive to 1 in the nagios.cfg.) For example, specifying simply * in the host_name directive of a service definition causes that definition to apply to all hosts.

Listing 4.1 *A sample host definition.*

```
#A comment about myHost
define host{
    host_name                   myHost
    alias                       My Favorite Host
    address                     192.168.1.254
    parents                     myotherhost
    check_command               check-host-alive
    max_check_attempts          5
    contact_groups              admins
    notification_interval       30
    notification_period         24x7
    notification_options        d,u,r
}
```

nagios.cfg

Required for daemon start
Refers to: everything
Referred to by: cgi.cf

If you run install-config during installation, a nagios.cfg-sample file is written for you. It's specific to the configuration directives you provided, so it should already have the correct locations for lock files, log files, and the sort. In fact, for first time installs, there is usually little you have to change in the nagios.cfg. I recommend you start with an existing nagios.cfg and modify it to suit your needs.

Two things you want to change in the nagios.cfg are the location of your object config files and the check_external_commands directive. There are two ways to specify the location of your object configs. You may either list each object definition file specifically with a cfg_file directive, as shown in Listing 4.2, or you may specify a directory with the cfg_dir directive, as shown in Listing 4.3. If you specify a directory, Nagios parses every file that ends in .cfg in the specified directory.

Listing 4.2 *Specifying object config files individually.*

```
cfg_file=/usr/local/nagios/etc/contactgroups.cfg
cfg_file=/usr/local/nagios/etc/contacts.cfg
cfg_file=/usr/local/nagios/etc/dependencies.cfg
cfg_file=/usr/local/nagios/etc/escalations.cfg
cfg_file=/usr/local/nagios/etc/hostgroups.cfg
cfg_file=/usr/local/nagios/etc/hosts.cfg
cfg_file=/usr/local/nagios/etc/servicegroups.cfg
```

Listing 4.3 *Specifying object config files by directory.*

```
cfg_dir=/usr/local/nagios/etc/
```

Next, if you wish the CGI commands in the web interface to work, or you want to use external commands in general (as described in Chapter 2, "Theory of Operations"), you should tell Nagios to accept external commands from the command file with the following line:

```
check_external_commands=1
```

For external commands to work, the command file must exist in the location specified in the nagios.cfg, and its permissions must be set correctly. This is all taken care of by make if you run make install-commandmode at install time.

Although those two changes get you up and running, there are a few directives in nagios.cfg you should be aware of. These break down into two types: global enablers and global time-outs. Table 4.2 describes the global enablers. You should remember these because they enable or disable important features, programwide.

Table 4.2 *Global Enablers in the nagios.cfg*

Name	Description
execute_service_checks	Setting this to 0 turns off service checks programwide. Defaults to 1 (on).
accept_passive_service_checks	Setting this to 0 turns off passive service checks. Defaults to 1 (on). For a detailed discussion of passive checks, refer to Chapter 2.

(continues)

Table 4.2 *Global Enablers in the nagios.cfg (continued)*

Name	Description
execute_host_checks	This enables/disables host checks. Defaults to 1 (on).
accept_passive_host_checks	This enables/disables checks of hosts. Defaults to 1 (on).
enable_notifications	This setting controls whether Nagios will send notifications. Defaults to 1 (on).
enable_event_handlers	Event handlers may be globally enabled or disabled. Defaults to 1 (on).
process_performance_data	This determines whether Nagios will check for and handle performance data from plugins. Defaults to 0 (off).

Table 4.3 describes the time-outs, which control how long Nagios allows various commands to execute. When a command in the queue is executed, Nagios allows it to run for a user-defined period of seconds. Commands that take longer than that amount of time are killed, so it's important to remember these timeouts if you have a problem with custom checks or event handlers unexpectedly dying. When Nagios kills a command due to a timeout, it logs a warning message.

Table 4.3 *Global Time-Out Values*

Objective Name	Description
service_check_timeout	The length of time Nagios waits for a service check plugin to return its status. Defaults to 60 seconds.
host_check_timeout	The length of time Nagios waits for a host check plugin to return its status. Defaults to 60 seconds.
event_handler_timeout	The length of time Nagios waits for an event handler to finish execution. Defaults to 30 seconds.
notification_timeout	The length of time Nagios allows a notification command to run. Defaults to 30 seconds
perfdata_timeout	The length of time Nagios allows a perfdata handler to run. Defaults to 5 seconds.

There's a lot of stuff in nagios.cfg that I didn't mention here, including many of the directives referred to by Chapter 2, which tweak various operational parameters used by the scheduler. Appendix B contains a comprehensive list of the configuration options available in the nagios .cfg and cgi.cfg files.

The CGI Config

Not required for daemon start
Refers to: nagios.cfg
Referred to by: nagios.cfg

The cgi.cfg file is the only file, other than nagios.cfg, that contains directives instead of definitions, and unless you are using the Web interface, it is optional. The Nagios Web interface is very much a separate entity from the Nagios daemon. The daemon has no real knowledge of the existence of the Web interface, so it communicates with the daemon via the same mechanisms any other program would: It sends commands to the command file and parses logs and state files for the current state of hosts and services. Therefore, a large part of the directives in the cgi.cfg are there to give the CGI programs that make up the Web interface the information they need to send commands to and get information from the Nagios daemon.

Like the nagios.cfg, most of the directives in cgi.cfg shouldn't need to change if you specified them correctly at compile time and built the sample config with make install-config. The directives you want to modify center around the Web interface security model, which is quite simple. The CGI's rely on the Web server to handle authentication, so any Web server can be used to serve up the Web interface, and there is no configuration required for specific users outside of the Web server configs.

When a user successfully authenticates, the Web interface attempts to correlate the username passed from the Web server with a contact in the contacts.cfg. After contacts.cfg is set up, and the Web server is configured to authenticate users, the CGIs allow you to get information about the hosts and services for which you are a contact. This works well for large sites that want least-privilege style security. If you get paged when it goes down, you are allowed to see it in the Web interface, without touching anything whatsoever in the cgi.cfg.

For smaller sites, however, it may be preferable to let everyone see everything; nearly all sites will want to have a few users, such as the Nagios administrator, who can see everything, whether they are configured as a contact for the host or service in question. Table 4.4 shows the directives in the cgi.cfg that make these configurations possible. Most directives take a comma-separated list of users. Each directive that supports a comma-separated list also supports the use of an asterisk (*) to mean all users.

Table 4.4 *Security-Related cgi.cfg Directives*

Object Name	Description
use_authentication	This directive, set to 1 (on) by default, tells the CGIs to use authentication information from the Web server. Because the Web interface can control how Nagios operates, turning authentication off is a bad idea. If you want everyone to see everything, use default_user_name instead.
default_user_name	Usually set to guest, the default_user_name can be granted permissions that will be inherited by all other users. For example, if jdoe doesn't explicitly have access to see information on a service, but the default user does, jdoe can see the service because all users can see what the default user can. If you want everyone to see all hosts, uncomment this directive and list the default user in authorized_for_all_hosts.
authorized_for_system_information	A comma-separated list of users who are allowed to see information related to the Nagios daemon.
authorized_for_configuration_information	A comma-separated list of users who are allowed to see the contents of the configuration files via the Web interface.
authorized_for_system_commands	A comma-separated list of users who are allowed to execute commands relating to the Nagios daemon, such as shutdown and restart.
authorized_for_all_services	A comma-separated list of users who are allowed to see information related to any service that Nagios is monitoring.
authorized_for_all_hosts	Like the preceding definition, except for hosts.
authorized_for_all_service_commands	A comma-separated list of users who are allowed to execute commands related to services, such as rescheduling checks and disabling notifications.
authorized_for_all_host_commands	Like the preceding definition, except for hosts.

Templates

The brunt of Nagios configuration consists of object definitions as described in the "Objects and Definitions" section. Object definitions come in varying degrees of complexity. Command definitions, for example, are normally composed of no more than two or three lines of text. Service definitions, on the other hand, may contain 31 directives, 11 of which are mandatory. For 100 hosts with 1 service each, that's 1,100 lines of configuration just for service definitions, most of which are redundant. Thankfully, Nagios has a few built-in features that mitigate the need for most of the typing. For example, any of the definitions that refer to hosts may refer to a list of comma-separated hosts instead. Nagios 2.x allows you to specify a hostgroup instead of a host for some definitions that refer to hosts. These two features alone bring our 1,100 lines back to 11.

Another wrist-saving feature is template-based configuration. Templates capture redundant directives inside special definitions. Normal objects can then refer to the template and inherit directives instead of specifying them explicitly. Template definitions look and act exactly like their counterparts with two exceptions: the register directive and the name directive. Listing 4.4 is a template version of the host definition from Listing 4.1.

Listing 4.4 *A host template and consumer definition.*

```
# This is my template
define host{
    name                  hostTemplate
    check_command         check-host-alive
    max_check_attempts    5
    contact_groups        admins
    notification_interval 30
    notification_period   24x7
    notification_options  d,u,r
    register              0
}

# myHost is shorter now that it inherits from hostTemplate
define host{
    host_name     myHost
    alias         My Favorite Host
    address       192.168.1.254
    parents       myotherhost
    use           hostTemplate
}
```

As you can see, both definitions define objects of type host. The host template, however, has a name directive (instead of a host_name directive) and a register directive, which is set to 0. Both name and register are specific to templates despite the object type, so any other type of template (like a service template) is defined the same way. The name directive is self-explanatory; it gives the template a name other objects can refer to. Setting the register directive to zero tells Nagios not to treat the object as a host object (don't register it), but rather let other objects inherit settings from it (make it a template).

By adding a use directive to myHost's definition, I instructed Nagios to let myHost inherit settings from the template. The host object inherits anything that is specified in the template. The host object overrides any directives it has in common with the template. Templates may, in turn, inherit properties from other templates, so it's quite common practice with host definitions to define a global host template, then several OS-specific templates, and then hosts that refer to them. Technically, any object can inherit properties from any other object of the same type, registered or not (I don't recommend having normal objects inherit from other normal objects. Stick to dedicated templates or things can get muddled), to an infinite degree via the use directive. I highly recommend the template-based configuration; it's very flexible, saves lots of redundant configuration, and makes for readable config files.

Timeperiods

Required for daemon start

Refers to: none

Referred to by: host, service, contact, hostescalation, serviceescalation

---

Listing 4.5 *Timeperiod example.*

```
define timeperiod{
    timeperiod_name      nonworkhours
    alias                Non-Work Hours
    sunday               00:00-24:00
    monday               00:00-09:00,17:00-24:00
    tuesday              00:00-09:00,17:00-24:00
    wednesday            00:00-09:00,17:00-24:00
    thursday             00:00-09:00,17:00-24:00
    friday               00:00-09:00,17:00-24:00
    saturday             00:00-24:00
}
```

Timeperiods define blocks of time that many other objects reference in the context of operational hours or blackout periods. The timeperiod definition is agnostic; the period of time it defines is not specific to any particular purpose, so two different objects may refer to the same time period for completely different reasons.

Time periods have one directive for each day of the week. Omitting a day altogether means the entire day is not included in the time period. Like all other objects, time periods may inherit directives from other time periods or timeperiod templates. Multiple blocks of time in the same day may be specified by separating them with commas.

Commands

Required for daemon start

Refers to: none

Referred to by: host, service, contact

Listing 4.6 *Command example.*

```
define command{
    command_name      check_ping
    command_line      $USER1$/check_ping -H $HOSTADDRESS$ -w $ARG1$ -c
$ARG2$ -p 5
```

Though composed of only two directives, command definitions are central to the functionality of Nagios. Commands are the solitary means by which Nagios may call external programs, and as we'll see in other definitions throughout the chapter, Nagios calls external programs often.

The most common use of the command object is for calling plugins. As previously mentioned, there are only two directives: command_name, which gives the object a name that other objects can reference, and command_line, which defines the shell syntax of the command.

Command objects don't just refer to external programs; they capture the command syntax of external programs. The uppercase words surrounded by dollar signs are called macros. Macros are context-specific internal variables that Nagios replaces at runtime. The HOSTADDRESS macro, for example, refers to the host address of whatever host Nagios happens to be running this plugin on. See the "Services" section for a description of the ARG macros. This makes it possible to use one command definition for any host. Nagios forks an exec of command_line exactly as it's written in the definition; but just before executing the command, Nagios replaces all of the macros with their actual values.

To avoid unintended shell interpretation and injection attacks, Nagios strips certain characters out of the actual values before it replaces the macro keywords in the commands in some contexts (host and service notifications and escalations, but not host and service checks). For the same reasons, Nagios also prevents you from using special characters in host and service names. These characters are user-definable via directives in the nagios.cfg, and you should be aware of them so that you avoid using them in your definitions. As of the time of this writing, the illegal name characters are

```
'  ~  !  $  %  ^  &  *  |  '  "  <  >  ?  ,  (  )  =
```

...and the illegal macro output commands are

```
'  ~  $  &  |  '  "  <  >
```

Different macros are available in different contexts, so it can be hard to know what macros you can use in every situation. For example, email-related macros, such as CON-TACTNAME, are available to commands being run for notifications but not commands being run for service checks. Check the online documentation at http://nagios.sourceforge. net/docs/2_0/macros.html for a complete matrix of available macros and the contexts they are available in.

In the nagios.cfg file, there is a directive called resource_file, which allows you to specify a file to create your own macros. This file is usually called resources.cfg or resource.cfg, and within it, you may define up to 32 macros. The resources.cfg usually contains at least one macro, USER1, which resolves to the location of the installed plugins. Because resources.cfg is owned by root and read-only, it's a better place to define any usernames or passwords than the checkcommands.cfg, which is world-readable. When set up in resources.cfg, your command objects can refer to the passwords by macro, thereby keeping them safe from prying eyes.

In Nagios 2.0, Macros are exported as environment variables, so any macro available to a command definition is also available to the program called by that definition.

Contacts

Required for daemon start

Refers to: command, timeperiod, contactgroup

Referred to by: contactgroup

Listing 4.7 *Contact example.*

```
define contact{
    contact_name                        dave
    alias                               dave josephsen
    host_notification_period            24x7                        (continues)
```

Listing 4.7 *Contact example.* *(Continued)*

```
    service_notification_period        work-hours
    host_notification_options          d,u,r,f
    service_notification_options       w,u,c,r,f
    host_notification_commands         host-email, send-sms
    service_notification_commands      service-email
    email                              dave@skeptech.org
    pager                              555-1024
    address1                           dave_josephsen@gmail.com
    address2                           cn=djosephs,ou=foo,dc=bar,dc=
com
}
```

The contact object defines everything Nagios needs to know about a person. The name and alias directives provide the usual. Two timeperiod objects may be specified: the hours during which the contact wants to be notified of host problems and those during which the contact wants to be notified of service problems. Each contact can filter the types of alerts it receives for host and service problems (as discussed in Chapter 2) with the notification_options directives. The notification_commands refer to command definitions that perform notification actions, such as sending emails or controlling armies of semi-autonomous messenger robots. Notification commands usually look something like the ones in Listing 4.8. Several addresses can be defined, all of them optional. These include an email address, a pager address, and any number of addressX directives.

Listing 4.8 *A notification command definition.*

```
define command{
    command_name    host-notify-by-email
    command_line    /usr/bin/printf "%b" "***** Nagios   *****\n
    nNotification Type: $NOTIFICATIONTYPE$\nHost: $HOSTNAME$\
    nState:         $HOSTSTATE$\nAddress: $HOSTADDRESS$\nInfo:
    $HOSTOUTPUT$\n\nDate/Time: $LONGDATETIME$\n" | /usr/bin/mail
-s
    "Host $HOSTSTATE$ alert for $HOSTNAME$!" $CONTACTEMAIL$
    }
```

Nagios has no real concept of what these addresses mean; it simply makes them available to the notification commands via Macros, as shown in Listing 4.8. It's up to the notification command definition to do something useful with them.

Contactgroup

Required for daemon start

Refers to: contact

Referred to by: host, service, contact, hostescalation serviceescalation

---

Listing 4.9 *Contact example.*

```
define contactgroup{
    contactgroup_name    admins
    alias                The Administrators
    members              chris,dave,jason,jer,kelly
}
```

Contacts are organized into groups, and host and service checks refer to the groups rather than individual contacts. The only objects that refer directly to contacts are contactgroups. The group definition is straightforward, containing the usual name and alias directives, as well as the members directive. In Nagios 2.0 and above, you may specify contactgroup membership by adding a contactgroups directive to a contact definition. If you use both a members directive in the contactgroup definition and a contactgroups directive in the contact definition, Nagios merges the two; however, I recommend you pick one or the other and stick with it.

Hosts

Required for daemon start

Refers to: timeperiod, contactgroup, command

Refered to by: service, hostgroup, hostdependency, hostescalation, hostextinfo

---

Listing 4.10 *Host example.*

```
define host{
    host_name            myHost
    alias                My Favorite Host
    address              192.168.1.254
    parents              myotherhost
    event_handler        ups-reboot
    check_command        check-host-alive
    max_check_attempts   3
    contact_groups       admins
    notification_interval 30
    notification_period  24x7
    notification_options d,u,r
}
```

Because hosts and services are the central objects in Nagios, their definitions are more involved than most. You may specify 28 different directives within a host definition, but only nine of them are mandatory. (All of the directives in Listing 4.10 are mandatory, except for event_handler and parents.) See the Nagios documentation at http://nagios.sourceforge.net/docs/2_0/xodtemplate.html#host for a complete list of the available directives. The directives in Listing 4.9 are probably all you'll need.

The address directive tells Nagios how to find the host. You may specify either an IP address or a hostname for the address directive, and this is an important decision. If you specify hostnames, DNS problems will cause host failures, because Nagios cannot resolve the hostname. On the other hand, if you specify an IP address, you have to remember to change the definition if the IP of the host changes. In large environments, this may happen quite often and without your knowledge. I prefer to specify hostnames and to run a local DNS name server service, such as tinydns (see www.tinydns.org for more information), locally on the Nagios box. Using a local name cache solves most DNS-related issues because Nagios uses itself as a nameserver, but it also necessitates some type of replication with the real nameservers.

The parents directive tells Nagios where in the network topology the host resides. Parents are defined from the perspective of the Nagios server. If the Nagios server is connected to a router, which also connects to a separate subnet containing 4 hosts, then each of those hosts should be defined with a parents directive listing the router. The router does not need a parents directive, because it is on the same subnet as the Nagios server. Each host may list one or more parents. As described in Chapter 2, Nagios uses parent/child relationships to treat outages on remote subnets differently than those on local subnets. If a host with children, such as a router or switch, goes down, Nagios considers the router down and its children unavailable. This is an important distinction for reporting and notifications. As shown in the section, "Contacts," the contact may filter out the unavailable notifications via its notification options directives.

The event_handler and check_command directives both specify command objects. Event handlers, as described in Chapter 2, are usually commands that launch scripts in an attempt to rectify simple problems automatically. When a host changes state, Nagios executes the host's event_handler before sending notifications. The check_command is the command Nagios uses to check that the host is available. Nagios does not wait for the event handler to return before it sends notifications. However, because event handlers are executed at soft state changes, they usually have a window of time to do their work before notifications are sent, while Nagios retries the checks. See Chapter 2 for a discussion of hard versus soft states. The command definition usually points to the check_ping plugin. As described in Chapter 2, Nagios runs only the check_command if a service check fails on the host, so while directives exist to enable regularly scheduled checks of the host, these are discouraged. By design, Nagios runs check_command automatically as needed. Check Appendix C, "Command-Line Options," for a complete list of command-line switches available to the Nagios binary.

If Nagios runs the check_command and it fails, then it will place the host in a soft down state, and retry the check_command as many times as specified by max_check_attempts. If the check_command fails each time, then the host is placed in a hard down state, notifications are performed, services on the host are assumed down, and service-related checks and notifications on the host are postponed until the host check_command returns an okay state. Setting max_check_attempts to effectively disables soft states for the host. If the check_command fails once, it is immediately placed in a hard down state and notifications are sent.

The last four directives are notification-related and answer the questions "Who?," "What?," "When?," and "How often?" If the host changes into one of the hard states specified by the notification_options directive, and that change occurs during the time period specified by the notification_period, then notifications will be sent to the groups specified by the contact_groups directive. For problem states, follow-up notifications will be sent every so often until the host recovers. Exactly how often is specified by the notification_interval. Technically, the notification_interval specifies the number of time units to wait between notifications. The interval_length directive in the nagios.cfg specifies the number of seconds in a time unit. The default is one minute, so a notification_interval of 30 equates to 30 minutes, unless you've changed it.

Services

Required for daemon start

Refers to: host, timeperiod, contactgroup, command

Referred to by: servicegroup, servicedependency, serviceescalation, serviceextendedinfo

Listing 4.11 *Service example.*

```
define service{
    host_name                myServer
    service_description      check-disk-sda1
    check_command            check-disk!/dev/sda1
    max_check_attempts       5
    normal_check_interval    5
    retry_check_interval     3
    check_period             24x7
    notification_interval    30
    notification_period      24x7
    notification_options     w,c,r
    contact_groups           admins
    }
```

Service objects glue it all together. They refer to every mandatory object that ties together the specifics of how you want to run a given plugin, where you want to run it, how often, and whom to call when things go wrong. A whopping 31 directives may be specified in a service definition. The 11 shown in Listing 4.11 are mandatory. The remaining 20 can be found in the online documentation at http://nagios.sourceforge.net/docs/2_0/xodtemplate. html#service.

The host_name directive specifies a comma-separated list of hosts on which this service runs. The service definition breaks with the name/alias convention in favor of a single service_description directive. This is because, unlike the other objects, services aren't required to have unique names; they need to only specify a unique set of hosts. So it's perfectly fine to create multiple service objects with the same name but completely different settings, if they don't share a reference to the same host object. This is handy, for example, when more than one host needs the same service except for a different retry interval. In this situation, the service can be copied en masse and only the host_name and interval need to differ from the original.

Like host objects, the check_command directive specifies the command object used to check the service. It's common for plugins to provide a subset of functionality (it's also common for command objects to provide a subset of functionality); for example, instead of having two plugins called check_sda1 and check_sda2, the plugins tarball has a single plugin called check_disk, which is capable of checking any disk. The check_disk plugin simply takes the name of the disk as an argument on the command line and checks it.

Service objects, on the other hand, tend to be single purpose and the service in Listing 4.10 is no exception. It uses the check_disk command to check a single disk, namely /dev/sda1. Because command syntax may contain whitespace, an exclamation mark is used to separate the command name from the arguments you want to pass to it. Each argument is made available to the command object via a numbered ARG macro. In the previous example, when Nagios dereferences the check_disk command, it replaces the command definition's $ARG1$ macro with /dev/sda1, and exec the resulting command. Any number of exclamation mark-separated arguments are supported.

Service notifications are a bit more straightforward than host notifications, but they follow the same basic pattern. Service checks that return bad statuses are retried a number of times to ensure they are down and remain down. While Nagios is verifying the state of a service with retries, the service is placed in a soft state. When the service is verified to be down, it is placed in a hard state and notifications are sent. Follow-up notifications are sent every so often until the service recovers.

All _interval type directives in Nagios refer to a number of time units to wait before doing something. A time unit means is user-definable via the interval_length directive in the nagios.cfg. By default, this directive is set to 60 seconds, so, in general, any interval definition is going to refer to the number of minutes to wait before doing something.

max_check_attempts is the number of times Nagios will retry a service. normal_check_interval is the number of minutes to wait between service checks. retry_check_interval is the number of minutes to wait between checks when the service is in a soft state and Nagios is trying to verify the service state. The timeperiod within which checks may be scheduled is given by the check_period. The notification_interval specifies the number of minutes to wait between follow-up notifications. notification_period defines the timeperiod within which notifications may be sent. notification_options filters the type of notifications this service will send and, finally, contact_groups specifies to whom the notifications should go.

Based on the preceding information, it should be obvious that the amount of time a service spends (the possible states are: warning, unknown, critical, recovered, and flapping for services) in a soft state is a function of max_check_attempts and retry_check_interval. If you aren't getting notifications quickly enough, you can either retry less or lessen the amount of time between retries.

Hostgroups

Required for daemon start
Refers to: host
Refered to by: host, hostescalation

Listing 4.12 *Hostgroup example.*

```
define hostgroup{
   hostgroup_name          oracle-servers
   alias                   Servers Running Oracle
   members                 server1,server2
   }
```

Identical in syntax to contactgroups, hostgroup objects exist to ease administration and reporting. Hosts may belong to multiple hostgroups. Membership may be defined in the host objects via the hostgroup directive instead of using members in this object. A unique feature of hostgroups is that multiple members' directives may be defined.

Servicegroups

Not required for daemon start

Refers to: service

Referred to by: service

Listing 4.13 *Servicegroup example.*

```
define servicegroup{
    servicegroup_name     disks
    alias                 Disks
    members               myServer,chk-disk,server1,chk-disk
    }
```

Completely optional and very similar to hostgroup definitions, servicegroups are new to Nagios 2.0 and are mostly used by the CGIs of the Web interface. The syntax of the members directive is different than the other group types, listing first a host object followed by the corresponding service object, separated by commas.

Escalations

Not required for daemon start

Refers to: host, service, hostgroup, contactgroup, timeperiod

Referred to by:

Listing 4.14 *Serviceescalation example.*

```
define serviceescalation{
    host_name              myServer
    service_description    check-disk-sda1
    first_notification     4
    last_notification      0
    notification_interval  30
    contact_groups         admins,themanagers
    }
```

Listing 4.15 *Hostescalation example.*

```
define hostescalation{
    host_name              router-34
    first_notification     5
    last_notification      0
    notification_interval  60
    contact_groups         routeradmins,admins
    }
```

It's possible to configure Nagios to involve managers or other technicians, if a problem persists beyond a certain number of notifications without being acknowledged. Nagios does this by way of escalation definitions. Escalations can be configured for hosts or services, and the definition syntax is nearly identical for each. The two main differences are that host escalations may specify hostgroups instead of hosts, and service escalations must specify the host and the service.

Each time Nagios decides to send a notification, it first checks to see if any escalation definitions match the notification it is about to send. If an escalation definition matches the notification Nagios wants to send, then Nagios sends the escalation instead. It's important to note that it is an either/or proposition, meaning that if the service definition specifies that the admins contactgroup be notified and the escalation specifies that the managers be notified, the escalation will win and the admins contactgroup will get nothing, so be sure to include everyone that needs to be notified in the escalation definition. The first_notification directive specifies the notification number for which the escalation is first enabled. For example, Listing 4.14 will match the fifth notification of a host down alert for router 34. The first four notifications will be sent as normal, but the fifth will be an escalation. Escalation notifications continue to be sent until the number specified by last_notification. If the last_notification directive is set to 0, escalations continue until the host becomes available again.

It is possible to have multiple escalations that match the same notification. If this happens, Nagios sends both escalations, so if two escalations match the same notification and have different contact_groups directives, all the contacts are notified.

Escalations may specify a custom notification_interval, which defines the amount of time to wait between notifications. This interval takes precedence over the interval originally specified in the service definition. If two escalations match one notification and the escalations contain different notification_interval settings, Nagios picks the smallest interval and use it.

Dependencies

Not required for daemon start

Refers to: host, service

Referred to by:

Listing 4.16 *Hostdependency example.*

```
define hostdependency{
    host_name                       myHost
    dependent_host_name             server1
    notification_failure_criteria   d,u
    }
```

Lisiting 4.17 *Servic dependency example.*

```
define servicedependency{
    host_name                          NAS1
    service_description                PING
    dependent_host_name                myServer
    dependent_service_description      check_httpd
    execution_failure_criteria         w,u,c
    notification_failure_criteria      w,u,c
    }
```

Dependencies exist to capture services and hosts that rely on each other. If, for example, you have some Web servers using a network-attached shared storage back-end, you can make the Web server services dependent on the NAS server's ping service. If the NAS box becomes unavailable, Nagios handles the notifications accordingly and reports reflects the outage in the context of the Web servers. Whereas host and service dependencies may be defined, it is almost always preferable to use parent/child relationships to capture interdependencies between hosts. Only host definitions may contain parents directives, so defining interdependent services requires a service dependency object.

Host dependencies require only host_name, which specifies the host that is depended upon, and dependent_host_name, which is self-explanatory. Service dependencies obviously must specify the hosts and services in question. The services are specified by way of the service_name and dependent_service_name directives.

Before Nagios checks the state of a service, it first checks the state of all the services that the service depends upon (its parents). If all of those services are okay, Nagios proceeds to check the child service. If any of the parent services are down, Nagios assumes the child service is down as well and stops checks and notifications on the child. It's possible to modify this behavior by way of the execution_failure_criteria and notification_failure_criteria directives. These directives can be confusing because they specify when something should *not* happen.

The execution_failure_criteria directive specifies the situations in which the child service should *not* be checked. For example, specifying a w for warning here means Nagios should not schedule checks of the child service when the parent is in a warning state, which is probably what you want. Setting this to n for none would mean that active checks always take place, no matter the state of the parent service. Setting an o for okay here would mean that active checks would not take place, even if the parent is in an okay state.

Similarly, the execution_failure_criteria directive specifies the situations for which notifications should *not* be sent out for the child service. Like execution_failure_criteria, the options specify states of the parent host. Setting c, for example, means that notifications for the child should not be sent if the parent is in a critical state. The same options are available to both directives: okay, warning, critical, unknown, pending, and none, for services; okay, down, unreachable, pending, and none, for hosts.

Extended Information

Not required for daemon start

Refers to: host, service

Referred to by:

Listing 4.18 *Hostextendedinfo example.*

```
define hostextinfo{
    host_name       myServer
    notes           this is my server.. many like it.. yadda yadda
    notes_url       http://foo.com/hostinfo.pl?host=myServer
    icon_image      linux40.png
}
```

Extended information can be defined for hosts and services. This is optional information that is used by the CGIs of the Web interface to do things, such as draw pretty icons. All directives are optional, except for host_name, which can be a comma-separated list of hosts. The notes_url provides an easy way to link from the Web interface to external sites for host information. The icon_image directive specifies a 40x40 pixel image to use to represent this host whenever it appears in the Web interface. Icon sets for this purpose can be downloaded from the Nagios Exchange (see www.nagiosexchange.org for more information). The icons are expected to be in the webroot/images/icons directory.

Apache Configuration

After Nagios has been configured, the Web server must be configured to serve up the Web interface's content. The majority of Nagios installations use the Apache Web server to serve up the interface, so the configs in Listing 4.17, shamelessly stolen from the official Nagios documentation, are for the Apache Web server.

Listing 4.19 *Apache sample VirtualHost config.*

```
ScriptAlias /nagios/cgi-bin /usr/local/nagios/sbin

<Directory "/usr/local/nagios/sbin">
    Options ExecCGI
    AllowOverride None
    Order allow,deny
    Allow from all
    AuthName "Nagios Access"
    AuthType Basic
    AuthUserFile /usr/local/nagios/etc/htpasswd.users
    Require valid-user
</Directory>                                          (continues)
```

Listing 4.19 *Apache sample VirtualHost config. (Continued)*

```
Alias /nagios /usr/local/nagios/share

<Directory "/usr/local/nagios/share">
    Options None
    AllowOverride None
    Order allow,deny
    Allow from all
    AuthName "Nagios Access"
    AuthType Basic
    AuthUserFile /usr/local/nagios/etc/htpasswd.users
    Require valid-user
</Directory>
```

The directives beginning in Auth provide simple login functionality via a text file called htpasswd.users, which resides in /usr/local/nagios/etc/. The htpasswd program, provided with Apache, can be used to create the htpasswd.users file like so:

```
htpasswd -c /usr/local/nagios/etc/htpasswd.users dave
```

After the file is created (the specific init syntax for your system may vary but it will be something similar to /etc/init.d/nagios start), more users can be added in the same manner, but be sure to drop the –c switch after the first user, as it is used to create the file and will overwrite any files that already exist. As described in section, "The CGI Config," users who authenticate through the Web server via the htpasswd.users file are matched with contacts in the contacts.cfg that have the same name.

It's very common for people to get the Web interface working but then to have trouble with the CGI commands. For the CGI commands to work, the user ID used by Apache must be a member of the group used for Nagios commands. This group is specified to the configure script at compile time and defaults to nagios. An excellent primer on configuring Apache with Nagios can be found at http://nagios.sourceforge.net/docs/2_0/cgiauth.html.

GO!

At this point, Nagios is ready to start. You can call Nagios with a -v switch to check the config files for errors like so:

```
/usr/local/nagios/bin/nagios -v /usr/local/nagios/etc/nagios.cfg
```

The Nagios daemon will start in interactive mode, check the config files for errors, and provide a helpful summary screen. If no errors are present, Nagios may be started via its init script. Congratulations! That wasn't such a chore, now was it?

CHAPTER 5

Bootstrapping the Configs

Everyone seems to have a different idea of what makes for ease of use when it comes to configuration, but most seem to agree that Nagios isn't it. Although I've yet to meet anyone who enjoys configuring Nagios from scratch, it's also surprising to me what people think will rectify the situation. Many people on the Nagios-Users list, for example, believe that placing the configuration information in databases will make Nagios easier to configure, whereas others swear by PHP-based graphical user interfaces. The nice thing about this difference of opinion is that many people have acted upon it, producing a wealth of tools to make configuration easier. So many so, in fact, that I would be remiss if I didn't include a chapter on making configuration easier.

Depending on the size of your environment, there is a point of diminishing returns where learning and configuring the configuration tool are more trouble than it would be to just manually edit the Nagios config files. In this chapter, I cover three increasingly complex methodologies to help you bootstrap the configuration process. I start with simple scripting templates, then move on to automatic discovery and configuration generation tools, and finally cover two graphical configuration frontends.

The tools all have their good sides and bad; for example, some might feel the shell scripts lack user friendliness, but on the other hand, PHP raises the vulnerability footprint of the Nagios server. I don't cover database back-ends, because I personally haven't dealt with them, but I do talk about two PHP-based configuration tools that I've grown rather fond of, as well as some old-fashioned shell techniques. None of these tools are mutually exclusive, and it's common practice to mix and match them to get what you want.

Scripting Templates

Many Nagios admins I know (myself included) maintain a set of what some refer to as boot-strap templates. These aren't object templates of the type discussed in Chapter 2, "Theory of Operations," and Chapter 4, "Configuring Nagios." They are skeleton config files that can easily be combined with lists of hosts to create valid Nagios configurations. To avoid confusion with object templates, I refer to them as skeletons for the remainder of the chapter.

With this methodology, all that's needed in practice is a plaintext list of hosts. After the skeletons are created, we simply loop through the host list, using sed to inject the hostnames into the skeletons, thereby creating valid definitions.

There are usually two skeletons for each type of object: an object template skeleton and an object definition skeleton. The template skeleton is a Nagios object template that encompasses as much general information as possible. The definition skeleton has just enough information to define an object and relies on the template for everything else. We can then specify more information, on a per object basis, to override the overly general template as necessary. Listing 5.1 is an example of a host template for use with a definition skeleton.

Listing 5.1 *A host template skeleton.*

```
define host{
name                            generic_host
max_check_attempts              2
notification_interval           60
check_period                    24x7
notification_options            d,u,r
check_command                   check-host-alive
contact_groups                  admin
register                        0
}
```

As you can see, the host template skeleton is just a normal object template in Nagios. The only arguably odd thing about it is that contact_groups is a directive people usually assign on a per host basis. Take this template and put it in a file called hosts.cfg. Listing 5.2 shows the second half of the equation, the definition skeleton.

Listing 5.2 *The host definition skeleton.*

```
define host{
use                 generic_host
host_name           NAME
alias               NAME
address             NAME.DOMAIN
}
```

So, given those listings, you probably have a pretty good idea of how this is going to shake out. The skeleton host object will inherit everything it needs from the generic_host template, except for the name and address of the host. Save the object skeleton in a file such as hosts.skel. All that's missing is a hostname and domain name. We can easily fill this in with a list of hosts, such as the one in Listing 5.3.

Listing 5.3 *A list of hosts.*

```
Host1.mydomain.com
Host2.mydomain.com
Host3.mydomain.com
```

Finally, the shell script in Listing 5.4 ties it all together. It's little more than a one-liner while loop that takes a list of hosts from standard input. Lines 5 and 6 extract the host and domain names from each element of the list, and line 7 simply replaces the keywords NAME and DOMAIN in the skeleton file with their actual equivalents.

Listing 5.4 *A shell script to create a hosts.cfg from the skeletons and host list.*

```
#!/bin/sh

while read i
do
    NAME='echo ${i} | cut -d. -f1'
    DOMAIN='echo ${i} | cut -d. -f2-'
    cat hosts.skel | sed -e "s/NAME/$NAME/" -e "s/DOMAIN/$DOMAIN/"
>> hosts.cfg
done
```

You can do the same thing with the services.cfg and hostgroups.cfg. Services.cfg will probably specify little other than a ping service. The template would look something like the one in Listing 5.5.

Listing 5.5 *A services template for use with a definition skeleton.*

```
define service{
    name                    generic-service
    active_checks_enabled           1
    passive_checks_enabled          1
    parallelize_check               1
    obsess_over_service             0
    check_freshness                 0
    notifications_enabled           1
    event_handler_enabled           1
    flap_detection_enabled          0
    process_perf_data               1
    retain_status_information       1
```

(continues)

Listing 5.5 *A services template for use with a definition skeleton. (Continued)*

```
    retain_nonstatus_information    1
    check_period                    24x7
    max_check_attempts              2
    normal_check_interval           5
    retry_check_interval            1
    notification_interval           60
    notification_period             24x7
    notification_options            w,u,c,r
    contact_groups                  admin
    register                        0
}
```

With so much defined in the template, the same shell script in Listing 5.4 can be used with the definition skeleton in Listing 5.6 to create valid ping services for each host.

Listing 5.6 *A services definition skeleton.*

```
define service{
    use                     generic-service
    host_name               NAME
    service_description     PING
    notification_options    c,r
    check_command           check_ping!500.0,20%!1000.0,60%
    }
```

Hosts and service definitions are the hard part. After you are done with those, you can define the admin group in contactgroups.cfg, define the members of the group in contacts.cfg, create a hostgroup with all the hosts, and you're ready to go. Of course, each of those files can be scripted with skeletons in much the same way for larger installs.

I once worked with someone who told me that I was the type of person who liked to "cut metal." What he meant by that was that I wanted to begin implementing before the planning was done. Although I'm familiar with several ways to bootstrap the Nagios configs, I always seem to come back to using skeletons, because they allow me to get some work done and adhere to the "Procedural Approach to Systems Monitoring" I describe in Chapter 1, "Best Practices," at the same time.

In fact, I use Nagios templates and skeletons to document business requirements during the planning process. By the time implementation time rolls around, I usually have some complex configuration out of the way and just need a list of hosts and a few shell scripts. I find this makes implementation a breeze, gets everyone what they expect from the beginning, and most importantly, allows me to at least "put chalk lines on the metal." So, if you have itchy tin-snip fingers, like me, and you're taking Chapter 1 seriously, you can't go wrong with scripting skeletons.

Auto-Discovery

Skeletons are all well and good if you have a list of hosts upfront; however, what if your network is so large, or changes so often, that getting a list of hosts is a problem in itself? Enter auto-discovery. In this section, I present a couple tools I use to automatically detect and write configuration files for hosts and services on the network.

Be careful! Nothing can give your monitoring system a bad rap more quickly than overzealous, automated scanning and discovery tools. The traffic generated from these sorts of tools may appear malicious in nature to intrusion detection systems or rude to people who are unaware of your effort. Before you use any of these tools, make sure you've read their documentation and understand how they work, so you don't generate more traffic than necessary. Also, be sure that you've notified the relevant people at your organization before you set these loose on your network.

Nmap and NACE

My personal favorite auto-discovery tool is the Nagios Automated Configuration Engine, or NACE. Written by Russell Adams, one of this book's technical reviewers, NACE is a set of slick Perl scripts that work together to detect hosts and write configuration files for them. NACE uses input from SNMP queries and the network scanner Nmap, and is capable of writing configuration files for hosts, hostgroups, and services. The current release consists of 11 scripts and a library. The scripts are designed to be tied together by UNIX pipes and understand a common, colon separated input syntax. I won't document all 11 commands here. Instead, I'll give you a rough idea of how NACE might be used in the real world, and if you like what you see, you can grab a copy from www.adamsinfoserv.com/AISTWiki/bin/view/AIS/NACE.

Like scripting skeletons, NACE needs a list of hosts to get started. To do this, the ever-popular network scanner, Nmap, may be employed. For example, the following command generates host definitions for every host that responds to a ping on the 192.168.5.0 network:

```
nmap -sP -oG - 192.168.5.0/24 | grep 'Status: Up' | cut -d\ -f2
   | WriteHosts.pl
```

Nmap is a great tool. By way of a description, here's a quote from its author, Fyodor.

"Nmap ("Network Mapper") is a free open source utility for network exploration or security auditing. It was designed to rapidly scan large networks, although it works fine against single hosts. Nmap uses raw IP packets in novel ways to determine what hosts are available on the network, what services (application name and version) those hosts are offering, what operating systems (and OS versions) they are running, what type of packet filters/firewalls are in use, and dozens of other characteristics."

Let's break the syntax down, in case you aren't familiar with Nmap. The sP switch tells Nmap which type of scan to run. In our case, an ordinary ping scan will suffice. In this mode, Nmap will go no further than simply noting whether the host is up. The oG switch specifies that Nmap should use a grepable output style, which is perfect for the way we use it. Example output from the Nmap scan appears in Listing 5.7.

Listing 5.7 *Grepable Nmap output.*

```
Host: 192.168.5.1 ()      Status: Up
Host: 192.168.5.2 ()      Status: Up
Host: 192.168.5.31 (host.foo.com)       Status: Up
Host: 192.168.5.32 (host1.foo.com)      Status: Up
Host: 192.168.5.33 (host2.foo.com)      Status: Up
Host: 192.168.5.34 (host3.foo.com)      Status: Up
```

We grep this output for lines that contain Status: Up, filter everything but the IP address, and pipe the IPs to NACE's WriteHosts.pl script. WriteHosts writes a cfg file for each host using the IP as its name, alias, and address. You can use –d to add directives to the definition; for example, –d HT=generic_host adds a use directive, which points the definition at a host template. This is certainly easier on the wrists than writing your own skeletons. But wait, that's not all: WriteHosts.pl is only one script. NACE has 10 more where that came from.

Let's say we want to use something more descriptive than an IP address for the host_ name directive. Here's a command that uses the DNS name of the host for the host_name directive and the IP address for the address directive:

```
Nmap -sP -oG - 192.168.5.0/24 | grep 'Status: Up' | sed -e
   's/.*(\(\([^)]\+\)).*/\1/' | NormalizeHostNames.pl -s .foo.com |
   WriteHosts.pl
```

This time, instead of extracting the IP addresses from the Nmap command, we've used sed to extract the hostname, which we then pass on to the NormalizeHostNames.pl script from NACE. NormalizeHostNames.pl takes a domain suffix as an argument. It uses this suffix, which is actually a regular expression, to distinguish the hostname from the domain. NormalizeHostNames.pl will do DNS lookups, if necessary, to determine the IP address of the host. It passes the correctly formatted hostname and IP address of the host to WriteHosts. pl, which, in turn, writes the configuration files.

All manner of specific information can be extracted from network queries and formalized into Nagios configuration files with NACE, which even contains several of its own SNMP query tools, which can be used to assign hosts to hostgroups and write services configs. Other tools exist for extracting info from existing Nagios configs.

NACE, in my opinion, is a category killer for scripted, automatic Nagios configuration; whether you want to bootstrap a large number of hosts quickly or you have a need for ongoing systematic auto-discovery and configuration, I highly recommend you give it a look.

Namespace

Namespace is probably the easiest to use command-line auto-discovery and configuration tool for Nagios that I have come across. Given a range of IP addresses, Namespace simply queries the information it needs from DNS and writes a host config definition for each host it encounters to standard out. Because it uses DNS to get its information, you need to have a reverse-lookup capable DNS infrastructure in place. Namespace can generate host and hostgroup entries and is mostly useful for initial installs rather than ongoing scripting or maintenance. Namespace is a C program and is available in source and binary from www. uni-hohenheim.de/~genzel/.

The following command creates the host definition in Listing 5.8.

```
namespace -h -d1 -c admin -G boxen -x "use generic-template"
192.168.5.1 192.168.5.254
```

Listing 5.8 *Output from the namespace command.*

```
define host{
    use                     generic-host

    host_name               myhost

    alias                   myhost

    hostgroups              boxen

    contact_groups          admin

    address                 192.168.5.201

    check_command           check-host-alive

    max_check_attempts      10

    notification_interval   60

    notification_period     24x7

    notification_options    d,u,r

    use                     generic-template
}
```

Contact and host group directives can be added with –c and –G, as you can see. The –h switch tells Namespace to create a host entry, as opposed to a hostgroup entry or simply dumping domain names. The –x switch can be used to add any number of custom directives. In the preceding example, I use it to add a host template. The final argument is a range of IPs given by the beginning and ending address. Namespace creates a host definition for every host it comes across in the IP range and dumps them all to standard out. It's a lightweight and straightforward tool, especially useful to people working with Nagios for the first time.

Namespace and NACE work well together. For example, Namespace could be used to create the initial host config file, and then NACE's ReturnHostsFromConfig.pl script could read out the hosts and use SNMPServiceQueryKey.pl to create a services file for them.

GUI Configuration Tools

There is a dizzying array of graphical configuration front-ends for Nagios. The two most promising are open source projects managed by a company called Groundwork. Groundwork has spent the last few years extending Nagios into a commercial monitoring application, called Groundwork Foundation, which directly competes with the big four monitoring applications: Openview, Patrol, Unicenter, and Tivoli. Fruity and Monarch are both free, open-sourced GUI front-ends to Nagios, which are managed by folks at Groundwork. Both tools have a polished look and work well.

It should be noted that GUI configuration tools, in general, don't necessarily make things easier for people who haven't dealt with Nagios before. For example, prompting someone with a check box labeled enable flap detection won't be any more meaningful than the same thing in a text file. So don't make the mistake of substituting a GUI for training; it won't get you what you expect.

Fruity

Fruity was written by Taylor Dondich, who works for Groundwork full time and was very helpful as a technical reviewer of this book. Fruity is a PHP application, accessible via a Web browser, and uses MySQL to store its own copy of the Nagios configuration. Fruity is written for Nagios 2.x and is quite simple to install. Just untar it into your Nagios base directory and edit the includes/config.inc file. Of course, as Fruity is a PHP/MySQL application, you'll need PHP on your Web server with MySQL support and MySQL. After all that is installed, you have to manually create a database for Fruity and import the tables from a file included in the tarball.

Figure 5.1 is a screenshot of a host in the Fruity interface. Fruity is a pretty straight-forward GUI; the interface design, however, hides some powerful functionality, such as the ability to set up templates that inherit other objects. Fruity is a good tool for bringing junior admins up to speed and distributing the configuration load amongst people who are otherwise textfile challenged. Fruity can import existing configs and doesn't write the changes to the configs until you tell it to. When it does write files, it backs up the existing configuration first.

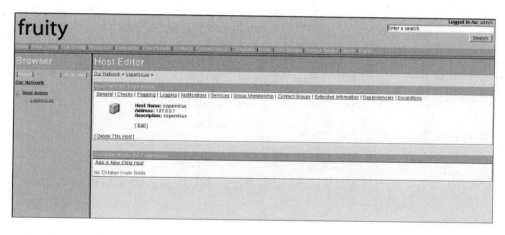

Figure 5.1   More on SNMP in Chapter 6, "Watching." A host definition in the Fruity GUI.

Monarch

Monarch, short for "Groundwork Monitor Architect," is a Perl/CGI/AJAX[7] Application. It is the same configuration engine used by the commercial Groundwork Foundation program. Monarch runs from a web browser and supports both Nagios 2.x and 1.x. Monarch also stores Nagios configs in a MySQL database and includes an installer script that configures the database and puts everything where it needs to go. Monarch is a bit more of a handful than Fruity in the installation department. It has some prerequisites that must be installed before the setup script can be run, including 11 Perl modules.

Figure 5.2 is a screenshot of the same host in Monarch. Note the Profile tab. Monarch adds the concept of profiles to Nagios configuration, and this is a welcome addition in my opinion. Monarch profiles are like super templates; they capture hosts in terms of a role. By way of an example, a Web server can be thought of as a collection of services, hostgroup memberships, contacts, and escalations. A Monarch profile gives a name to a particular combination of services, group memberships, contacts, and pretty much anything else. The profile is then assigned to one or more hosts. This role-based approach to Nagios configuration is very cool and can save a lot of time for those with large environments. Configuring a new host becomes as simple as telling Monarch its name, alias, and address, and assigning the host to a pre-existing profile.

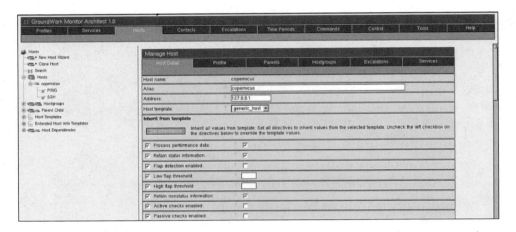

Figure 5.2 More on SNMP in Chapter 6. A host definition in the Monarch GUI.

Like Fruity, Monarch can import existing configs and won't modify the Nagios configs until you tell it to. It's also possible to kick off a backup of the Nagios configs on command, via Monarch, which is helpful.

This chapter was by no means an exhaustive list of automated configuration tools. Many other excellent tools exist, which may play into your particular skill-set quite well. For example, if you are adept at Perl, I'd suggest that you take a look at the configuration modules for Nagios available at CPAN (www.cpan.org). Perhaps the best thing about Nagios is the wealth of great tools surrounding it. Check out the configuration section on the Nagios Exchange (www.nagiosexchange.org) for more information.

CHAPTER 6

Watching

Welcome to where the rubber meets the road. Until now, I've talked a lot about how Nagios works and how it is installed and configured. This chapter ties together the theoretical work of the previous chapters and the details of performing systems monitoring. As pointed out throughout this book, Nagios is a scheduling and notification framework. Small, single-purpose programs called plugins do the monitoring. So an in-depth discussion about monitoring is mostly a discussion about plugins.

Nagios is limited only by the availability of plugins for a given task. Writing your own plugins, as described in Chapter 2, "Theory of Operations," is trivial and highly encouraged, so hundreds of them are available. This chapter gives you a good basis to understand what types of plugins are available, how to use them, and where to begin when you need to start making your own. The chapter is broken into four parts, along architectural lines, with a section about local queries, Microsoft Windows, UNIX, and "other stuff," which includes networking gear and environmental sensors.

Local Queries

There are three primary ways to monitor hosts and services with Nagios. Nagios can use various remote execution techniques to connect to remote hosts and to run plugins. Nagios can wait in a passive mode for remote hosts to notify it of trouble by defining passive checks. Finally, Nagios can launch plugins locally to query the availability of various hosts and services from afar. Let's start by checking some of the things Nagios can do without leaving home.

Pings

By far, the most common service check in any monitoring program is the classic ICMP echo request, more commonly known as the ping. Although pings are easy to set up in Nagios, they can be somewhat confusing to first-time users because, at first glance, they appear to be overused or redundant.

At a minimum, Nagios requires that there be at least one service per host. The most common service to set up first is a ping service because it is a simple definition, and if you're using the example configs, there is already a ping check defined for you. As discussed in Chapter 4, "Configuring Nagios," each host definition also contains a check_command directive that specifies the command to use to verify that the host is operational. This usually defaults to the check_host_alive command, which, in turn, uses ping. So why have two ping checks per host? It's important to remember that, as described in the "Scheduling" section in Chapter 2, host check commands are not scheduled unless they are needed. In practice, the host check command is not run until a service check has already failed. Thus, although the definitions may seem redundant, the checks exist for different purposes.

Let's walk through setting up a simple ping check. Assuming the hosts and contacts are already defined, the first step is to define the command in the check_commands file. Command definitions, as described in Chapter 4, glue service definitions to external monitoring programs. The purpose of the check command is to tell Nagios what external command to launch and how. A command definition for ping might look like Listing 6.1.

Listing 6.1 *Check_ping command definition.*

```
define command{
    command_name    check_ping
    command_line    $USER1$/check_ping -H $HOSTADDRESS$ -w $ARG1$ -c
$ARG2$ -p 5
    }
```

Listing 6.1 is a classic example of a Nagios command definition. They do get simpler than this, but not by much. The –H switch is nearly always used to specify the hostname or IP of the box against which to run the plugin. Likewise, -w and -c nearly always specify the warning and critical thresholds. The check_ping plugin uses the -p switch to specify how many ping packets to send.

The words surrounded by dollar signs are macros. Macros are described fully in Chapter 4. When Nagios actually calls check_ping, it first replaces the macro names with real values from various places. For example, the numbered ARG macros will be replaced with values from arguments in the service definition. Speaking of which, a service definition such as the one in Listing 6.2 is the next step in setting up your ping check.

Listing 6.2 *Check_ping service definition.*

```
define service{
      host_name                      Server
      service_description            check_ping
      check_command                  check_ping!500.0,20%!1000.0,60%
      max_check_attempts             5
      normal_check_interval          5
      retry_check_interval           3
      check_period                   24x7
      notification_interval          30
      notification_period            24x7
      notification_options           w,c,r
      contact_groups                 admins
      }
```

This service defines that the check_ping command is run against the server every 5 minutes, for 24 hours a day, 7 days a week. If something goes wrong, Nagios verifies that the problem persists by rechecking the service four more times, 3 minutes apart. After verified, Nagios begins notifying the admins group every 30 minutes, for 24 hours a day, 7 days a week, until the service comes back online.

Many of the options in Listing 6.2 are better specified inside a template, so in the interest of brevity, the rest of the service definitions in this chapter assume that you use a template, such as the one in Listing 6.3. See the "Templates" section in Chapter 4 for a discussion of templates and how to use them.

Listing 6.3 *The template used by the rest of the examples in this chapter.*

```
define service{
      name                           chapter6template
      max_check_attempts             5
      normal_check_interval          5
      retry_check_interval           3
      check_period                   24x7
      notification_interval          30
      notification_period            24x7
      contact_groups                 admins
      register                       0
}
```

What comes after check_ping in Listing 6.2's check_command directive is a list of arguments. Arguments in service definitions usually specify thresholds and are separated by exclamation points, so there are two arguments here. The first, 500, 20 percent, says that Nagios should generate a warning if the ping packets round-trip time is greater than 500 milliseconds, or if the packet loss is greater than 20 percent. (The argument doesn't explicitly state that it is the warning threshold but, because the $ARG1$ macro is the argument to the -w

switch in the check_ping command definition, the first argument listed in the service definition defines the warning threshold.) I know this because I ran the command /usr/local/nagios/
libexec/check_ping –h on the command line and read the helpful syntax description. Check
Appendix C, "Command-Line Options," for a list of command-line options for common
plugins.

Port Queries

After ICMP echoes, port queries are the next most common service check performed by most
monitoring servers. These plugins attempt to open a TCP or UDP connection to a given port
on a given host. Port queries are performed by either the check_tcp or check_udp plugins.
The command definition looks like the one in Listing 6.4.

Listing 6.4 *The generic check_tcp definition.*

```
define command{
    command_name      check_tcp
    command_line      $USER1$/check_tcp -H $HOSTADDRESS$ -p $ARG1$
}
```

Unlike ping commands, where a warning may be generated, the result of a port query is
usually an XOR. Either the port is available or it isn't. Because there just isn't much room
for ambiguity, no -w or -c is necessary. All that needs to be specified are the hostname and
port number. The "all or nothing" nature of the port check effects the notification options,
as well. There is no point in specifying that Nagios should send notifications on warnings
when warnings cannot occur. Accordingly, the accompanying service description in Listing
6.5 is different from the check_ping service definition in Listing 6.2 in that it specifies different notification options and contains no threshold options.

Listing 6.5 *Check_http service definition.*

```
define service{
    host_name             jkwebServer
    service_description   check_http
    check_command         check_tcp!80
    notification_options  c,r
    use                   chapter6template
}
```

Note also that the service description in Listing 6.5 is check_http, rather than check_tcp.
This is because the service description will appear as the name of the service in the Nagios
Web UI, and check_tcp is not that useful a description of what is actually being monitored.

There are two ways people commonly use check_tcp in practice. The first is to use a single check_tcp command definition and to specify the port and service description in the service definition, as we did in Listings 6.4 and 6.5. The other way is to write a specific command definition for the service you want to monitor. This way, you can add some protocol-specific options to check_tcp, you don't have to specify the port in the service check, and the service description name can match with the check command name.

Redo the check_http service in Listings 6.4 and 6.5; it will give you an idea of what protocol-specific command definitions mean. Listing 6.6 is a check_http command definition that uses check_tcp but is hard-coded to check the HTTP port.

Listing 6.6 *A protocol-specific check_tcp command definition.*

```
define command{
    command_name    check_http
    command_line    $USER1$/check_tcp \
                    -H $HOSTADDRESS$ -p 80 -s 'GET / HTTP/1.0
' -e 'HTTP/1.0 200 OK'
    }
```

Our new command definition makes use of -s (send) to actually send some text to the specified port on the given host. The line wrap is there because the HTTP protocol expects this. The command then uses -e (expect) to specify what we expect to get back from the server. Obviously, the text is protocol-specific and won't work with anything other than HTTP or HTTPS services, and, although these options might have been specified as arguments to a generic service definition, doing so would mean that every service you checked with the generic definition would need to specify send and expect options. So the moral is, when you really must do protocol specific stuff, it's often cleaner to do so with a new command definition.

An interesting side effect of doing protocol-specific queries such as this is that warnings can creep back in. For example, if the service was available, but replied with HTTP/1.0 302 (an HTTP redirect), then check_tcp considers this "unexpected output" and generates a warning. Listing 6.7 is a service definition to go with the shiny new check_http command.

Listing 6.7 *Shiny new check_http service definition.*

```
define service{
    host_name               webServer
    service_description     check_http
    check_command           check_http
    notification_options    c,w,r
    use                     chapter6template
}
```

Although the new check_http has more functionality, the service definition in Listing 6.7 is even simpler than that in Listing 6.5. The second methodology is preferred because when you find a specific check_command with a simple service definition, it scales better than the other way around. It's also easier to get exactly what you want this way. Reusing command definitions tempts you to compromise functionality that you consider nifty, but that is extraneous. This is bad because services have a tendency to fail in ways you don't expect.

An HTTP 404 or 500 error would have been overlooked by the definitions in Listings 6.4 and 6.5, but not by the more specific command in 6.6. Usually, when unexpected failures happen, they are subtler, but they are accounted for more often if you make a habit of writing a specific command definition instead of reusing an existing generic one.

Querying Multiple Ports

As was implied in Listing 6.6, check_tcp has a lot of cool functionality, but one thing that it cannot do is scan multiple ports. Many applications listen on more than one port, and having a single service check to query them all is a common requirement. Whenever I run into a limitation in a plugin, the first question I ask myself is whether a wrapper might help.

Writing shell wrappers around Nagios plugins is a long and honored tradition. The term wrapper, in this context, refers to a program that calls another program or collection of programs to accomplish its intended purpose. Since there have been Nagios plugins, administrators have been extending their functionality with shell wrappers. For more information about how plugins work and a walkthrough of the process of creating wrappers, see the "Plugins" section in Chapter 2. Listing 6.8 is a shell wrapper around check_tcp and check_udp that allows you to query the availability of multiple ports in a single command definition.

Listing 6.8 *A check_tcp wrapper.*

```
#!/bin/bash
#call check_tcp once for each port; aggregate the result

HOME='/usr/local/nagios/libexec' #path to the plugins
PROTO='Nullz0r' #default protocol to use

# a function for printing the help info
printusage ()
{
echo "this plugin calls check_tcp once for each port"
echo "usage:"
echo "check_multi_tcp -H host -u|-t -p \"port [port] ...\""
echo "-h : print this message"
echo "-H hostname: The hostname of the box you want to query
     (default localhost)"
```

Listing 6.8 *A check_tcp wrapper. (Continued)*

```
echo "-p port number: A space separated list of port numbers"
echo "-t wrap around check_tcp"
echo "-u wrap around check_udp"
exit ${EXITPROB}
}

#parse the arguments
while getopts ":hH:utp:" opt
do
        case $opt in
                h )     printusage;;
                H )     HOST=${OPTARG};;
                p )     PORT=${OPTARG};;
                u )     PROTO='udp';;
                t )     PROTO='tcp';;
                ? )     printusage;;
        esac
done

#sanity check
if echo "${PROTO}" | fgrep -q 'Nullz0r'
then
    echo "ERROR: either -u or -t required"
    echo
    printusage
fi

################### Work starts here ###################

#for each port they give us
for i in 'echo ${PORT}'
do
    #call the real plugin
    ${HOME}/check_${PROTO} -H ${HOST} -p ${i}>/dev/null
    #did it exit happy?
    if [ "$?" -ne 0 ]
    then
        #no it's not a happy camper
        echo "port ${PROTO}/$i is not available"
        exit 2
    fi
done

#everything's okay, mon
echo "all ports are open"
exit 0
```

Housekeeping aside, this is a simple shell script. It calls the real check_tcp plugin on each port you give to it in a list, and if any of them are not available, it exits with a critical code. If it gets through all of the ports without any errors, then it exits with the okay code. Shell wrappers are utterly ubiquitous among Nagios administrators. If you can't find the functionality you need in the plugins directory, before you reinvent the wheel, first check the contrib. directory of the plugins tarball, and then ask yourself whether you might be able to coopt a few existing plugins in a wrapper to get what you need.

(More) Complex Service Checks

The examples to this point have probably inspired little more than a yawn from you, so this section branches out and gives you a couple of examples of real-world monitoring scenarios. Hopefully, these will give you a better feel for the capabilities of plugins.

In my first example, Company B uses a rather unreliable combination of filters to block unwanted email on its public MXes. The problem is that its business partner, Company A, seems to be particularly disliked by the filters for some reason, so every few weeks, the filters arbitrarily decide to block all email originating from Company A. Various meetings have taken place to resolve the problem, but the combination of filters is so complex and Company B is so large that Company B just cannot seem to get it together. Every time the people who meet think the problem is fixed, it happens again; and worse, every time it happens, it takes up to a day to figure out that it's happening because the filters at Company B don't bounce the mail. Instead, they answer, "250 not Okay," and then they silently drop the mail on the floor. (A security consultant told them this was the best thing to do.)

To at least provide timely detection of the problem, the system administrator at Company A defines a command that uses the check_smtp plugin to periodically perform an SMTP handshake with Company B's mail server. This definition is shown in Listing 6.9.

Listing 6.9 *A command to perform an SMTP handshake.*

```
define command{
    command_name    check_spam_block
    command_line    $USER1$/check_smtp -H $HOSTADDRESS$ \
                    -C 'hello companyA.com' -R '250 OK' \
                    -C 'mail from: <alice@companya.com>'\
                    -R '250 OK' \
                    -C 'rcpt to: <bob@companyb.com>' \
                    -R '250 OK'
    }
```

This works well; if Company B answers anything other than "250 okay" to any part of the handshake, then the administrators at Company A are immediately notified. Further, there's no reason this definition cannot be expanded to include the data portion of the SMTP conversation, if it were required.

For the record, you should get permission from someone before you do things such as this. Monitoring things you don't own can get you into trouble. Another thing to keep in mind is that service checks that actually interact with the services they are watching affect things such as logs and connection statistics. If the data portion were included, Bob at Company B would actually get an email message; it's usually advisable to stop short of doing something that directly affects a human being. On the other hand, poorly written daemons might actually have problems with service checks that sever the connection at unexpected times. Finally, administrators on the other end might use filters to block access to your monitoring tools if they think the traffic might be malicious in nature. As I said in Chapter 1, "Best Practices," always put some thought into the things you monitor, especially if those things don't belong to your company or group.

The next example centers on Ted, who is a systems administrator for a moderately sized health care company. Ted is responsible for obtaining SSL certificates from the company's rather shady PKI vendor, VeriSure. Ted is also responsible for registering new domain names, but the company doesn't use VeriSure for this. Recently, Ted's mailbox has been filling up with email from VeriSure. Most of them are marketing emails, offering Ted discounts to move his company's domain registry to VeriSure. Because his company owns a few domains and SSL certificates, Ted is receiving about 20 of these message per day, so he has a dilemma. Ted wants to /dev/null all email from VeriSure, but he also needs to get SSL expiry notifications. Guess what the command in Listing 6.10 does.

Listing 6.10 *A solution for Ted.*

```
define command{
    command_name    check_ssl
    command_line    $USER1$/check_http $ARG1$ -C 10
    }
```

Check_http is a great plugin that can do all sorts of useful things. The job of the -C switch is to check the expiry date of a given Web site's SSL certificate. If the certificate on the Web site expires in less than the number of days given (ten, in this case), the plugin generates a critical error. This solves Ted's problem and is probably a bit more reliable than VeriSure notifications.

This definition is the first we've seen that doesn't use the $HOSTADDRESS$ macro. This is because we're specifying a URL, as opposed to a server address. The URL is passed via an ARG macro, as shown in the service description in Listing 6.11.

An interesting digression is that, because the $HOSTADDRESS$ macro is normally the macro that decides which host the plugin will run on; the host_name directive in the service definition can be whatever you want when that macro isn't used. That is, you can specify an unrelated accounting database server for host_name in Listing 6.11, and the check will work in this example. The only place the host_name directive is used, in the absence of the $HOSTADDRESS$ macro in the command definition, is in the Web UI, which lists the check_ssl service as belonging to whatever host_name references.

Listing 6.11 *The check_ssl service definition.*

```
define service{
    host_name                webServer
    service_description      check_ssl
    check_command            check_ssl!www.myweb.org
    notification_options     c,w,r
    use                      chapter6template
    }
```

E2E Monitoring with WebInject

Hopefully, you are excited about the types of solutions you can build with the built-in plugins. The next example is of "end-to-end" monitoring. Currently, end-to-end, or e2e, is all the rage with the monitoring systems vendors. As discussed in Chapter 1, e2e means that the monitoring system makes use of the service in question in the same way that a user might. This means different things in different contexts; for example, instead of the classic methodology of monitoring port 25 for SMTP, an e2e system attempts to send an email to itself through the mail system.

A favorite Nagios plugins is WebInject, which is a Perl program for performing Web site regression testing. With WebInject, you create test cases in XML, which describe a list of sites to visit. When visiting each site in turn, WebInject can do many useful things, such as parse out and save strings for later use and verify the presence or absence of particular text. Perhaps the best thing about WebInject is the way it seamlessly handles session states and authentication. For example, WebInject handles cookies automatically in the same manner as your Web browser. It saves cookies received from each test case and presents them in the HTTP header of the following test case. For embedded session ID-based (or, if you prefer, cookieless) authentication schemes, WebInject can parse session IDs out of the response text or header of a site and provide it in a variable for later use.

Actually, the best thing about WebInject is that it has a Nagios plugin mode. With a simple configuration parameter in its config.xml, WebInject becomes a Nagios plugin, carrying out its test cases and returning with a Nagios-compatible exit code and output string. It even provides performance data.

All of this combines to make WebInject the perfect end-to-end Web site monitoring plugin. For example, assume you run a Web site with a search entry field and a database back-end. For example, you are probably familiar with www.google.com. In this example, you want to be sure that your Web site operates as expected; that is, not only is it alive, but it's also functional.

In Listings 6.4 and 6.5, you saw that you could monitor port 80 with check_tcp, but this wouldn't catch HTTP errors, such as 404. This was improved in Listings 6.6 and 6.7 by sending an HTTP GET and by parsing the response code. However, an error in the database back-end could still render the Web site useless. Although the HTTP server might run flawlessly, users wouldn't get useful information from the queries. This example uses WebInject to do an e2e check of www.google.com. The new check_http service basically reinvents the feeling lucky button. It goes to the Web site, performs a query, parses the query results to find the first link, proceeds to that link, and verifies that the search text appears. If you can do all that, you know you have a working Web daemon and a working Web site.

The first step is, of course, installing WebInject. It can be obtained from www.webinject.org. Because it's a Perl script, there's not much installing that needs to happen beyond acquiring the various modules it depends upon. By default, WebInject will look for a config.xml file in the present working directory.

As you can see in Listing 6.12, there isn't much to the config.xml used in this example. The reporttype directive specifies what kind of output WebInject provides. I set it to nagios, so that WebInject would operate in Nagios plugin mode. The testcasefile directive specifies the location of the XML file containing the test cases. Finally, the globalhttplog directive enables logging for the tests. By default, logging information goes into http.log in the present working directory. You can set this option to yes to log everything, but here, it is set to onfail, so that it only logs when there are failures in the test.

Listing 6.12 *The config.xml for WebInject.*

```
<reporttype>nagios</reporttype>
<testcasefile>testcases.xml</testcasefile>
<globalhttplog>onfail</globalhttplog>
```

There are two test cases in the testcases.xml file in Listing 6.13. The first test case performs a Google search for the word foo and parses the output to find the first link in the list. The parsing syntax, specifed by the parseresponse directive, is unusual but adequate for the task. It uses a single pipe character (|) to separate everything before the desired text from everything after the desired text. So, to capture the word bar in the string foo bar biz, the parseresponse syntax is be foo | biz.

After the URL of the first hit has been extracted by parseresponse, it is placed in the WebInject variable {PARSEDRESULT}. You can then refer to this variable in test case 2, which is done in the url directive. Test case 2 then proceeds to the Web site pointed to by the results of test case1 and verifies that the word foo exists on that site with the verifypositive directive. Verifypositive supports regex syntax, but you don't need that for this simple example.

Listing 6.13 *The test case file for WebInject.*

```
<testcases repeat="1">

<case
    id="1"
    description1="goto google. search for foo."
    method="get"
    url=http://www.google.com/search?hl=en&q=foo&btnG=Google+Sear
ch
    parseresponse='\<a class=l href="|"'
/>

<case
    id="2"
    description1="goto {PARSEDRESULT} check for foo"
    method="get"
    url="{PARSEDRESULT}"
    verifypositive='foo'
/>

</testcases>
```

You can test the plugin by calling webinject.pl from the command line. If everything goes according to plan, you should get some output such as this:

```
WebInject OK - All tests passed successfully in 0.704 seconds
|time=0.704;;;0
```

If you delete the reporttype directive from the config.xml, WebInject provides more verbose output, as shown in Listing 6.14. The first match from Google was the Official Foo Fighters Web site. This can be helpful for debugging or for the intellectually curious.

Listing 6.14 *Verbose output from WebInject.*

```
Starting WebInject Engine...

------------------------------------------------------
Test:   testcases.xml - 1
goto google. search for foo
Passed HTTP Response Code Verification (not in error range)
TEST CASE PASSED
Response Time = 0.372 sec
------------------------------------------------------
Test:   testcases.xml - 2
goto http://www.foofighters.com/ make sure it says foo there
Verify : "foo"
Passed Positive Verification
Passed HTTP Response Code Verification (not in error range)
TEST CASE PASSED
Response Time = 0.267 sec
------------------------------------------------------

Start Time: Sat Aug 12 21:49:57 2006
Total Run Time: 0.718 seconds

Test Cases Run: 2
Test Cases Passed: 2
Test Cases Failed: 0
Verifications Passed: 3
Verifications Failed: 0
```

All that's left to do now is to create a command and service definitions, such as those in Listing 6.15 and 6.16. Because the query logic is entirely specified within the testcases.xml, there isn't a lot left to define in the command and service definitions. It is possible to give WebInject command-line arguments, telling it where to find alternate config files, but the test cases themselves must be read from files. If you thought to yourself that you could write a shell wrapper to create testcase.xmls on-the-fly from Nagios macros, then you're well on your way to becoming a Nagios administrator.

Listing 6.15 *A WebInject command definition.*

```
define command{
    command_name     check_google
    command_line     $USER1$/webinject.pl
    }
```

Listing 6.16 *A WebInject service definition.*

```
define service{
    host_name                webServer
    service_description      check_google
    check_command            check_google
    notification_options     c,w,r
    use                      chapter6template
    }
```

Hopefully, you now feel good about the remote-querying capability of Nagios. Now it's time to move on to remote execution.

Watching Windows

Windows can be a challenge for administrator-building monitoring systems using Nagios or otherwise because it is a bit more of a black box than most UNIX environments. NSClient, a Windows-specific plugin for Nagios, provides almost all of the functionality you could want, but even it presupposes a knowledge of the current Microsoft scripting environment, especially WMI. In fact, understanding the Windows scripting environment is probably the largest barrier to entry for someone who wants to monitor Windows, so let's tackle that first. If you're already adept at programming and scripting in Windows, feel free to skip ahead to the subsection entitled "Getting Down to Business."

The Windows Scripting Environment

Google "Microsoft Scripting" and you'll get back a dizzying array of acronyms and product names: WSH, OLE, Cscript, WMI, ADSI, JScript, VBScript, and PowerShell to name just a few. If you're wondering, "Whatever happened to batch?", then this section is for you.

Beginning with DOS and OS/2, batch scripts were used to automate tasks. These scripts were little more than lists of DOS commands in a file, which the command.com program could execute. Although they possessed rudimentary functionality and cumbersome syntax, batch scripts managed to scale well for many systems administration tasks. (See Tim Hill's excellent book *Windows NT Shell Scripting*.)

However, something more robust was needed, so around the time Windows 98 was introduced, so was WSH. WSH, or Windows Script Host, is a language-independent execution environment for scripts. For most purposes, you can think of it in the same terms as any interpreter you are familiar with, such as Perl or Python. What makes WSH different is its use of modular engines to provide syntax, so while you speak Perl to the Perl interpreter and

Python to the Python interpreter, WSH has no native syntax. In fact, it's possible to speak both Perl and Python to WSH in the same script. WSH provides the execution environment, some common data structures, and I/O hooks, and it leaves the specific syntax up to the language engine.

WSH, as installed by Microsoft, includes only language engines for VBScript and Jscript and in practice, most people use the VBScript syntax. Because of this, many people refer to scripts executed by WSH, in general, as VBScripts or Visual Basic Scripts.

VBScript, or Microsoft Visual Basic, Script Edition, is a subset of Microsoft Visual Basic programming language, which, in turn, owes its lineage to the original Beginner's All-Purpose Symbolic Instruction Code developed at Dartmouth College. The vbscript.dll script engine interprets code written in VBScript, and it can be used by either the ASP engine in Internet Explorer for Web applications or WSH for systems programming and automation. So, VBScript wears two hats: it is both a Web application language and a general purpose scripting language. In its Web application role, VBScript is embedded into HTML (similar to Javascript) to be interpreted by the Web browser. In its stand-alone or WSH role, VBScript is executed by WSH from a file, usually possessing a .vbs extension. (This is not a requirement. The PATHTEXT environment variable contains a list of extensions to which the script name is appended if the extension is omitted.)

To muddle things further, WSH is composed of two separate execution environments: Wscript and Cscript. These environments, implemented as two separate programs, are identical except that Wscript is GUI-based and Cscript is command-line driven. For example, the following snippet when executed by Wscript opens a new window that contains the words Hello World:

```
Wscript.Echo "Hello World"
```

The same code, executed by Cscript, simply prints Hello World to standard out at the command prompt.

WSH scripts are self-contained files with extensions that denote their syntax. VBScript WSH scripts usually end in .vbs and can be executed with either Cscript or Wscript in the following manner:

```
cscript foo.vbs
```

```
wscript foo.vbs
```

When the execution environment (or host, in Microsoft parlance) is not specified, the default host is chosen. The default host, out of the box, is (of course) Wscript, which is probably not what you want. There are a few other annoyances built into WSH, such as its habit to output a banner that informs you that your script was run by Microsoft's WSH. In Cscript, this banner is actually injected into the output of your program (STDOUT, not STDERR). This is bad if you're writing Nagios plugins because Nagios will only parse the first line of text output by the plugin. Switches exist to change the default behavior. The following is what most people use:

```
cscript //I //nologo //H:cscript //S
```

The I switch specifies interactive mode as opposed to batch mode. Nologo removes the banner. The H switch specifies that Cscript should be the default script host, making it possible to launch foo.vbs without first specifying Cscript. Finally, the S switch saves these settings to the registry, making them permanent.

COM and OLE

Although UNIX relies on small, text-based, single-purpose programs that work together toward accomplishing tasks, Windows, as an environment, tends toward large, monolithic, graphical programs. This poses a dilemma to would-be automators: How do you script a GUI? Enter Component Object Model (COM). Since 1993, COM and related technology have attempted to provide a language-agnostic interface to software that is otherwise immune to automated integration.

Software developers using COM build their applications using COM-aware components. If implemented correctly, these components provide interfaces to the applications' functionality via any other program that speaks COM. These interfaces can be used for any number of purposes, such as interprocess communication or even automation. OLE is COM's object model. OLE gives COM objects their names and specifies things such as object inheritance. Most people associate OLE with embedding an Excel spreadsheet within a word document (the purpose it was originally designed for in 1991), but it is now much more powerful than that.

Because most important applications in Windows expose their functionality via COM, and WSH provides access to any COM object, it is possible to use scripting languages such as Perl and VBScript to automate applications in Windows, including everything from programmatically creating Excel documents to driving Microsoft Management Consoles (MMC). OLE and COM provide the glue with which Nagios may be tied to any application that exports its functionality via COM, which is most applications out there. Scripts that use COM to query information from Windows systems and then exit with the appropriate exit codes are, by definition, Nagios plugins.

WMI

One piece of software that doesn't export its functionality via COM is the kernel. Various flavors of UNIX have their proc or sysfs filesystems, but until recently, this critically important system information was largely unavailable to scripting languages in Windows. The closest thing was perfmon, which is a real-time performance statistics program that didn't lend itself to being driven from scripting languages or the command line. Products such as SNMP Informant could export perfmon information via SNMP, but this is more kludge than solution. Windows Management Instrumentation fills this gap nicely. WMI is like a COM interface to the runtime environment. It can be thought of as another COM interface, but one that provides access to things such as disk and network utilization.

WMI is derived from the Distributed Management Taskforce's CIM concept. CIM, or Common Information Model, is a large database (called a CIM Repository) of objects that represent manageable entities, such as hard drives, entire computer systems, and software packages. WMI is Microsoft's implementation of CIM. The CIM concept encompasses more than what you'd find in /proc. It is a collection of information about computer systems that includes the current memory utilization, as well as things such as the system's serial number and PowerPoint version. As such, many current Windows applications extend the CIM database with their own information. Applications and drivers that provide information to the CIM are called providers.

Because the CIM repository contains a lot of information, it is broken down into namespaces specific to provider types, such as Root\SNMP or Root\MicrosoftIISv2. The built-in OS providers use Root\CIMv2. These namespaces are further broken down into classes, which are functionality-specific objects, such as Win32-Process or DiskObject. Additionally, WMI implements a SQL-like query language called WQL to help you find the specific pieces of information you need. Few people programmatically explore the CIM repository using WQL, however. Most use a GUI browser, such as wbemtest.exe, located in system32/wbem on most Windows systems. WQL is still necessary, however, to instantiate specific class objects in a script.

To give you a feel for the capabilities of WMI/OLE, as well as what a Nagios plugin that uses WMI looks like, look at Listing 6.17, which is a Nagios plugin called check_dllHost. Its purpose is to make sure that no single dllHost process consumes more than a user-specified amount of RAM. It is written in Perl and uses the Win32_Process WMI Class.

Listing 6.17 *Check_dllHost.*

```perl
#!/usr/bin/perl
#a plugin to check whether any dllHost processes are
#eating too much ram
#Blame Dave Josephsen --> Wed Apr 20 13:23:10 CST 2005

#########variable init#########
#we use the win32::ole module to connect to wmi
use Win32::OLE;
use Win32::OLE qw (in);

#our warning and critical thresholds are passed via arguments
$warn=$ARGV[0];
$warn='200000000' unless ($warn);
$crit=$ARGV[1];
$crit='250000000' unless ($crit);

$counter=0;

#########real work begins here#########
#spawn a wmi object
$oWmi = Win32::OLE->GetObject("WinMgmts://./root/cimv2")
        or die "no wmi object";

#this wql query gets all the processes running on the box
$oProcessEnumObj=$oWmi->
               ExecQuery("Select * from Win32_Process ");

#iterate through the process list. Retrieve  'dllHost' procs
foreach $oProcess ( in($oProcessEnumObj) ){

       if($oProcess->Name =~/dllHost.*/i){
       $counter += 1 ; #keep track of how many there are for later

    #are you using up my ram?
       if ( $oProcess->WorkingSetSize >= $crit){

       #you sure are
          print "CRITICAL ". $oProcess->WorkingSetSize .
               "kb in use by ". $oProcess->Name . "\n";
    exit 2;

      } elsif ( $oProcess->WorkingSetSize >= $warn){
          print "WARNING ". $oProcess->WorkingSetSize .
               "kb in use by ". $oProcess->Name . "\n";
    exit 1;
      }
   }
}

#if we made it this far, then everything's all right, mon
if($counter >= 0){
```

(continues)

Listing 6.17 *Check_dllHost. (Continued)*

```
print "OK ". $counter . " dllHosts running,
        none over the limit \n";
    exit 0;

}else{

    print "OK no dllHost processes running\n";
    exit 0;
}
```

Scripts that use WMI almost invariably follow the same pattern. Spawn a WMI object, use WQL to query some subset of information from the object, check the status of that information against thresholds or expected results, and exit. The WMI URL, or class path, if you prefer—WinMgmts://./root/cimv2—is important. It specifies from where in the CIM the WMI object is derived, which limits the kind of information you can use WQL to query. Also important is the WQL query:

```
$oProcessEnumObj=$oWmi->ExecQuery("Select * from Win32_Process ");
```

The syntax "Select * from Win32_Process" is WQL. Its purpose is self-explanatory: it returns all of the currently running processes. The result of a WQL query is always a collection object. A collection object is a fancy sort of array that doesn't behave in the usual Perl manner. To ease iteration across collection objects, the Win32::OLE module provides the in function. The in function makes constructs such as the following two possible:

```
foreach $oProcess ( in($oProcessEnumObj) ){
```

```
@oProcesses=in($oProcessEnumObj)
```

Python treats collection objects as enumerations. The dot (//./) in the URI specifies that the WMI object in question is spawned on the local system. If you replace the dot with the hostname of a remote host, you can consume WMI information from a remote host via RPC over the network. This assumes you had the privileges that you needed on the remote host.

Listing 6.18 is another WMI/Perl Nagios plugin. Although its purpose—to determine if any services in a cluster are not currently online—is different from Listing 6.17, the pattern is nearly identical.

Listing 6.18 *A check_cluster plugin in Perl/WMI.*

```perl
#!/usr/bin/perl
#check_cluster a perl script/nagios plugin to check if any cluster
#resources are in a state other than online.
#blame Dave Josephsen --> Sat Jan 22 17:03:34 CST 2005

#########variable init#########
use Win32;
use Win32::OLE qw (in);

#swap these if you want to take the servername as an arg
$server=".";
#$server="$ARGV[0]";

#unlike most WMI classes, MSCluster is derived from
#/Root/MSCluster, so we have to specify that
#in the class path.
$class = "WinMgmts://"."$server"."/Root/MSCluster";

#the MSCluster provider classes are just barely documented here:
#http://msdn.microsoft.com/library/default.asp?url=/library/en-us/
mscs/mscs/server_cluster_provider_reference.asp
$object_class='MSCluster_Resource';

#possible resource states, from;
#http://msdn.microsoft.com/library/default.asp?url=/library/en-us/
mscs/mscs/clusresource_state.asp
$state{-1}='Unknown';
$state{0}='Inherited';
$state{1}='Initializing';
$state{2}='Online';
$state{3}='Offline';
$state{4}='Failed';
$state{128}='Pending';
$state{129}='Online_Pending';
$state{139}='Offline_Pending';


#########real work begins here#########

#get a wmi object
$wmi = Win32::OLE->GetObject ($class);

#get a collection of resources off the cluster
$resource_collection=$wmi->
     ExecQuery("Select * FROM $object_class");

#how many resources are there?
$max=$resource_collection->{Count};

#the 'in' function comes from Win32::OLE
#it's the same thing as: Win32::OLE::Enum->All(foo)
@collection=in($resource_collection);
```

(continues)

Listing 6.18 *A check_cluster plugin in Perl/WMI. (Continued)*

```perl
#are any resources in any state other than online?
for ($i=0;$i<$max; ++$i){
    if($collection[$i]->{State}!='2'){
        push(@broken,$collection[$i]);
    }
}

#if so, do bad things
if(scalar(@broken)>0){
    foreach $j (@broken){
        print("$j->{Name} is $state{$j->{State}}, ");
    }
    exit(2);
}else{
    #otherwise, do good things
    print "$max resources online\n";
    exit(0);
}
```

To WSH or not to WSH

Although the scripts in my examples run on Windows and consume information from WMI objects, they don't, in fact, use WSH. If you choose to script in any language other than VBScript, you'll have to install the language engine, which means you'll also have a choice of interpreters. ActiveState Perl, for example, installs both the Perl interpreter and the Perl WSH language engine. Scripts with Perl syntax, executed via Cscript and possessing a .pls extension, are executed by WSH, while those with a .pl and called without a script host are executed by the native Perl interpreter, perl.exe.

Within WSH, things are a bit different. For example, you can't use modules and Perl switches, such as -w, don't work. The ARGV array is absent as well, because perl.exe, in one way or another, provides all of these things. The WSH environment instead provides a $Wscript object with which you can parse arguments and make connections to OLE objects. In WSH, $Wscript even supersedes print(), such that

```perl
print("foo $bar");
```

becomes

```perl
$Wscript->Echo("foo",$bar);
```

In Listing 6.17, Win32::OLE CPAN module connects to WMI via COM. Within WSH, this becomes easier.

```
use Win32::OLE;
use Win32::OLE qw (in);
$oWmi = Win32::OLE->GetObject("WinMgmts://./root/cimv2")
        or die "no wmi object";
```

becomes

```
$oWmi = $Wscript->GetObject("WinMgmts://./root/cimv2");
```

The choice is yours. WSH doesn't provide anything that native Perl with Win32:: OLE doesn't, and if you're adept at Perl, you would probably rather use @ARGV than $Wscript->Arguments. The situation is the same for Python and Ruby. If alternate language engines were installed out of the box, then WSH might be a compelling alternative. As it is, most people who don't use VBScript use the native interpreter for their language of choice. For more information on programming with WSH in Perl, Python, Ruby, or even Object REXX, check out Brian Knittel's book, *Windows XP, Under the Hood*.

To VB or Not to VB

The fact that the VBScript language engine is installed by default on all current versions of Microsoft Windows makes it the prevalent scripting language for the platform. The extent to which this is true is difficult to express. VBScript is so popular that it's nearly impossible to find a problem for which three or four scripts have not already been posted on the Internet. So prevalent is sample code that it's not even necessary to know the language at this point. In fact, I've yet to actually meet a Windows administrator who knows the language well enough to write a script from scratch. It's as if every Visual Basic Script currently in existence is a modification of a modification of an original Visual Basic Script that was written from scratch 12 years ago. Microsoft technet boasts a tool it is particularly fond of, called the scriptomatic, that will generate VBScript for you from pull-down menus. Microsoft-hosted courses on the subject of automation, at this point, teach only enough of the syntax to enable students to download and modify existing code. A good friend of mine, while attending such a course, went so far as to temporarily sabotage the instructor's network connection to see what the instructor would do if sample code on the Internet was unavailable. (The instructor quickly reverted to searching his local hard drive for a suitable script to modify.)

Getting back to the point, VBScript is a supportable choice for system automation and monitoring on Microsoft Windows. If you are familiar with Java, you can probably pick up the syntax in a weekend, but its only real advantage is that it is available on all Windows servers out of the box. Its lack of case-sensitivity, unwieldy regex syntax, and strange habit of using list context in inappropriate situations make it unpopular among people who actually enjoy programming, but administrators who might otherwise use another language choose VBScript, so they don't have to install an interpreter on every machine.

For that reason, tools exist for most of the popular scripting languages that make it possible to package scripts in a stand-alone manner. PAR for Perl, py2exe for Python, and rubyscript2exe for Ruby create .exe programs out of scripts. The .exe programs can then be run on Windows machines without the interpreter. The binaries created by these tools can be large (usually between 1–3 megabytes, depending on how many libraries the scripts include), and they don't run any faster in their compiled form than they do in the interpreter. However, they enable you to write scripts and Nagios plugins in the language of your choice and run them on any Windows machine in your environment, without having to install the interpreter on each Windows host.

The Future of Windows Scripting

Currently, in the world of Microsoft, .Net is all the rage. The .Net framework is a large class library of solutions to commonly occurring programming problems. It is meant to eventually supercede many existing Microsoft technologies, including COM and OLE. There is no plan, however, to stop development or support of COM at Microsoft, and .NET does little to address the needs of systems people, so the VBScript/COM/OLE combination will likely remain the systems scripting environment of choice for the foreseeable future.

PowerShell, formerly known as MSH, or Mondad, will probably have a larger impact on scripting on the platform going forward than .Net. PowerShell is a scriptable CLI that is currently available as a download. PowerShell is capable of doing anything WSH can do, while providing a much friendlier interface to systems administrators. Where COM and VBScript provide a scriptable interface to existing GUI tools that support COM, Microsoft claims that future versions of system configuration utilities will actually be written in PowerShell with GUI wrappers, thus ensuring a scriptable interface to the OS going forward.

Although the PowerShell implementation borrows concepts from UNIX, such as passing information between small distinct programs via pipes, PowerShell does this in a much more object-oriented manner. For example, PowerShell programs (called cmdlets) give output to the shell in text, but when the same output is piped to another PowerShell cmdlet, data objects are exchanged instead. Microsoft is fond of saying that this completely eliminates the need for text processing tools such as awk, sed, and grep. To see what they mean by that, consider the list of servers in Listing 6.20.

Listing 6.20 *A list of servers.*

```
Name,Department,IP
frogslime,R&D,12.4.4.17
tequilasunrise,Finance,12.4.5.23
151&coke,R&D,12.4.4.151
theangrygerman,MIS,12.0.0.2
7&7,Finance,12.4.5.77
```

Say you want to extract and print only the machines in the finance department. In UNIX, you'd probably do something such as this:

```
cat list.csv | grep Finance
```

Or if you wanted to be specific, you would use

```
cat list.csv | awk -F, '$2 ~ /Finance/ {print}'
```

In these examples, grep and awk are given the comma-separated list as a text input stream, and they filter their output of the text according to the options given to them. Grep was told to print the lines containing Finance, and awk was told to print the lines with Finance in the second field, where fields were separated by a comma.

PowerShell cmdlets don't receive text input from each other, so while the semantics of the following line of code is similar to the UNIX examples, it operates in an altogether different manner.

```
Import-csv list.csv | Where-Object {$_.department -eq "Finance"}
```

The PowerShell cmdlet Import-csv reads in the contents of list.csv and creates an object of type csvlist (or something similar). This csvlist object is then passed to the Where-Object cmdlet, which uses the department property of the object to extract the records matching Finance. Because the pipeline ends here, the Where-Object cmdlet dumps its findings in plain text to the shell. If the pipeline had continued, however, the Where-Object cmdlet would have provided the modified csvlist object to the next cmdlet in line. The Perl-like $_ object (which represents the current iterator), curly braces, and pipes combine to give the command a very UNIX-ish feel. The syntax is far more appealing to systems-type scripting people than VBScript, which is why PowerShell has a good chance of catching on.

Microsoft has also made the statement that the UNIX pipes model has made sysadmins into expert text manipulators, and this is undoubtedly true. To that point I would add: Along with being expert text manipulators comes the expectation that data will be manipulated and formatted in the manner specified by the person performing the manipulation. Given this, many administrators might hear PowerShell's message as, "Give us your data and we'll tell you what you can do with it." So I see where Microsoft is going when it says that the object model will eliminate the need for text processing, but I humbly predict that the most popular PowerShell site on the Internet, other than Microsoft's, will be the site providing text processing cmdlets for use alongside the official Microsoft ones.

PowerShell is a promising technology whose time is far overdue, and although I'm skeptical that the object model makes a compelling case for the wholesale abandonment of text processing tools, I'm glad that Microsoft is headed in this direction. PowerShell is certainly a net gain, and it will greatly expand the use of scripting and automation among systems professionals on the Windows platform. Although the current VBScript/WSH/COM combination will probably remain the de facto scripting standard for a while because of its overwhelming mindshare and default availability, there's no real reason you can't use PowerShell to get work done right now.

Getting Down to Business

Now that you have a good understanding of the environment and where the good information is, you can check out ways to extract the stats you need and provide them to Nagios. There are two popular ways to glue Windows plugins to Nagios: NRPE_NT and NSCPlus.

NRPE

NRPE, as described in Chapter 2 and Chapter 3, "Installing Nagios," is a lightweight client and server that enables the Nagios server to remotely execute plugins stored on the monitored hosts. NRPE is great when you have existing monitoring scripts that you want to use with Nagios or you have a need for custom monitoring logic. Any scripts you may have written (or downloaded) to monitor your Windows boxes can be defined as a service in Nagios and called via NRPE_NT, the Windows port of NRPE.

For example, to run the check_dllhost plugin from Listing 6.16 with NRPE-NT, first obtain and install NRPE-NT, as described in Chapter 3. After the NRPE service is installed on the Windows host, add the following line to the bottom of the nrpe.cfg file.

```
Command[check_dllhost]=c:\path\to\check_dllhost.pl 200000000
250000000
```

This line tells the NRPE daemon on the Windows host what to do if someone asks it to run check_dllhost. The Nagios server must then be configured to run the check. The first step is to define the command in the commands.cfg, as in Listing 6.21.

Listing 6.21 *Check_dllhost command definition.*

```
define command{
     command_name     check_dllhost
     command_line     $USER1$/check_nrpe -H $HOSTADDRESS$ \
                      -c check_dllhost
     }
```

The command definition in Listing 6.21 makes use of the check_nrpe plugin. As mentioned in previous descriptions of NRPE, check_nrpe is the client portion of the NRPE package. In the previous definition, it is given two arguments: -H, with the hostname of the Windows server, and -c, with the name of the command to be executed on the remote server. After the command has been defined, Nagios can schedule it for execution. This is done with a service check command, so the next step is to define the service, such as the one in Listing 6.22.

Listing 6.22 *Check_dllhost service definition.*

```
define service{
     host_name             windowsServer
     service_description   check_dllhost
     use                   chapter6template
     notification_options  w,c,r
     }
```

After this is done and the Nagios daemon is restarted, Nagios will poll the check_dllhost program on a regular basis. NRPE may be used to execute any script on any Windows host in this manner.

So now that you know how to schedule plugins, the question becomes what to schedule. One popular answer to this question is the basic NRPE plugins for Windows, available at the NagiosExchange here:

```
www.nagiosexchange.org/NRPE_Plugins.66.0.html?&tx_netnagext_pi1
  [p_view]=62
```

This package includes plugins to check the usual metrics: CPU, memory utilization, and disk space. It also contains a plugin to query the state of arbitrary services and an eventlog parser. The basic plugins are DOS programs written in C and satisfy the basic monitoring needs most people have. This has the added bonus of being the closest, methodologically, to remote execution in UNIX, so if you like standardized methodologies, this may be for you.

NSClient/NSCPlus

Another popular Windows plugin is NSClient, which is a monolithic standalone Nagios plugin that comes with its own client. In other words, NSClient is not executed by way of NRPE, but by its own client software on the Nagios server, check_nt. NSClient contains all of the functionality previously mentioned, plus the capability to query any perfmon counter, which makes it a very attractive alternative to NRPE with the basic pack for people who don't have any custom plugins. Running check-nt –h on the Nagios server gives a rundown of NSClients features and use.

NSClient is the plugin used by the majority of people who watch Windows hosts with Nagios. It's very simple to install and contains just about all the functionality that most people want starting out. NSClient cannot run external scripts; it provides only the functionality built into it. This means that if you want to run NSClient and a few custom scripts, such as the ones in Listings 6.16 and 6.17, you need to install two services on each Windows host: the NSClient service as well as NRPE.

Another problem with NSClient is that it doesn't seem to be actively maintained anymore. Many people (myself included) have been using it for years without any problems, but it's understandable that some may shy away from it because of its current (apparently) abandoned status.

NSCPlus aims to replace both NSClient and NRPE by combining their functionality into a single monolithic program. NSCPlus contains all of the query functionality of NSClient, plus a built-in implementation of the NRPE protocol. This means that a single Windows service provides the functionality of both NSClient and NRPE. NSCPlus also has the ability to make WMI queries, though this functionality is currently experimental.

Installing NSCPlus and NSClient is very similar. The package comes with source and binaries for the UNIX and Windows pieces. To install the Windows service, execute the binary with a /i. Then start the service from services.msc or from the command line with a net start command.

To use NSClient or NSCPlus to check the CPU load of a Windows box, define the command in checkcommands.cfg, as in Listing 6.23.

Listing 6.23 *Check_nt_cpuload command definition.*

```
define command{
    command_name     check_nt_cpuload
    command_line     $USER1$/check_nt_wrapper -H $HOSTADDRESS$ \
                     -p 4242 -v CPULOAD -l $ARG1$
}
```

In the preceding example command, the -p switch specifies an alternate listening port. The default NSClient port (1284) conflicts with Microsoft Exchange RPC, so you might want to change it. The -v switch specifies which variable to check. Valid variables include CLIENTVERSION, UPTIME, USEDDISKSPACE, MEMUSE, SERVICESTATE, PROC-STATE, and COUNTER. Each type of variable may take options. These options are specified by the -l. The CPULOAD variable takes a comma-separated triplet in the form <minutes range>,<warning threshold>,<critical threshold>. If I wanted to take a 5-minute CPU average and warn on 80 and alarm on 90, I would specify 5,80,90. Multiple triplets can be specified, so if I wanted a 5-minute average and a 10-minute average with slightly lower thresholds, I could use 5,80,90,10,70,80. The command definition in Listing 6.23 uses the triplet specified by argument macros in the service definition in Listing 6.12.

Listing 6.23 *Check_nt_cpuload service definition.*

```
define service{
    host_name                windowsServer
    service_description      check_nt_cpuload
    check_command            check_nt_cpuload!5,80,90,10,70,80
    use                      chapter6template
    notification_options     w,c,r
    }
```

NSCPlus packs a good deal of functionality into a very small package and, going forward, I don't see many reasons to use anything else. It is an arguably more complex install than NRPE alone, but the install is worth it, for the functionality NSCPlus provides.

Watching UNIX

Compared to Windows, the systems programming and automation scene for UNIX users is straightforward. Most sysadmin tend to use some combination of C, Perl, Python, or shell programming to write automation and glue code and, while these tools continue to evolve and get better, the overall systems programming scene doesn't change a lot from year to year. Further, in contrast to Windows, where using any language other than VBScript means downloading and installing an interpreter, UNIX administrators are far more likely to have more interpreters and compilers installed by default than they have a need for.

Combine a rich assortment of available tools with the fact that Nagios was written to run on Linux and what you get is a plethora of UNIX-based Nagios plugins to monitor all manner of things written in all sorts of languages. In fact, when posting a question, such as"How do I monitor X on my freebsd box?" to the nagios-users list, it's not uncommon for over half of the responses to be written in code of one type or another. This section should give you a good feel for the plugins people frequently use. I'll setup checks for the "big three:" CPU, Disk, and Memory. I'll also cover some of the details of what these metrics mean.

NRPE

By now it should be no surprise that NRPE is the remote execution tool of choice for Nagios plugins on UNIX boxes. Unlike Windows, where some multipurpose plugins, such as NSClient, have implemented their own daemons and protocols, plugins on the UNIX side have stayed single-purpose and assume the use of a remote execution program, such as NRPE or check_ssh. As for the plugins, most people start out with the official plugins tarball that the Nagios daemon uses.

Different hosts will build different plugins from the tarball based on the libraries they have installed. So it's not particularly wasteful to have a single set of plugins for both the Nagios daemon and the hosts it monitors. For example, check_snmp will only compile if the host in question has the net-snmp libraries installed. This is true for quite a few of the plugins in the tarball. Check out Chapter 3 for details on getting and installing the official plugins tarball and NRPE.

CPU

While measuring CPU utilization may seem a relatively straightforward task at first glance, it is, in fact, an intricate and complex problem with no easy solutions. There are two CPU-related metrics that are normally used to summarize CPU utilization. The first is the classic percentage-based metric. This is a number representing the percentage of CPU utilization occurring now. For example, "The CPU is currently 42 percent utilized." This number is how most people who aren't UNIX administrators understand things, so let's look at it first.

If you ask embedded systems or computer engineers, they will tell you that processors in the real world are either utilized or not. There is, in fact, no such thing as 42 percent utilization on a micro-processor. At any given instant, the CPU is computing some bit of machine code or it is idle. So if the only two numbers that exist are 0 percent and 100 percent, what can this percentage number actually mean?

In fact, the CPU is never actually idle; "idle" is just one of many states that the processor spends its time computing. Idle happens to be the lowest priority state, so when the CPU spends its time looping in the idle state, it's still doing work, just low priority, preemptable work.

Therefore, to be meaningful, the utilization percentage must be something akin to an average of processor state versus time. Exactly what is being averaged, and for how long, is a question that is answered in software, so even on the same OS, two separate performance applications can measure it differently. Because all processors have a lowest priority state, a popular methodology for providing a single percentage number is that of measuring the percentage of time that the CPU spends in its lowest priority state and then subtracting this number from 100 to obtain the actual utilization percentage. In other words, the utilization percentage is the percentage of time between two polling intervals that the CPU spends in any state other than idle. There are many other ways. For example, some processors have built-in performance counters that may be queried with system calls, so using these is a popular alternative.

The bottom line is that the classic CPU percentage metric presents all sorts of problems from a monitoring perspective. It is an overly volatile and ambiguous metric that doesn't necessarily reflect the load on a system and, therefore, isn't a good indicator of problems. Even in a capacity-planning context, the number has questionable value. For example, 100 percent CPU utilization can be a good thing if you are trying to optimize system performance for an application that is bandwidth- or Disk I/O- intensive. My advice is to avoid this metric in systems monitoring when you can.

The second metric is that of UNIX load averages. This is a set of three numbers that represent the system load averaged over three different time periods: 1, 5, and 15 minutes. You may recognize them from the output of several different shell utilities, including top and uptime. These load average numbers are exponentially damped and computed by the kernel, so they tend to be less volatile than the CPU percentage metric, and they are always computed the same, no matter whom you ask. Exactly what these numbers represent is a question that is difficult to express without using math. In fact, the deeper one delves, the harder the math becomes, until first order derivative calculus becomes involved. If you're in to that sort of thing, I'll refer you to Dr Neil Gunther's paper here: www.teamquest.com/resources/gunther/display/5/index.htm.

For the rest of us, I'll attempt an explanation in English. The current load average is the load average from 5 seconds ago, plus the *run-queue length*, which is the sum of the number of processes waiting in the run-queue plus the number of processes that are currently executing. To save on kernel overhead, the kernel doesn't actually compute three separate load average numbers. The three numbers in the triplet are actually computed from a common base number. When computing the load average for each time period in the triplet, a different exponential factor is applied to both the 5-second-old average and the current run-queue length to dampen or weigh the values accordingly. The ratio used by the dampening/weighing factor is somewhat controversial, at least in Linux, but the load triplet, in my experience, is a useful metric despite disagreement over exponential dampening ratios.

The load average metric is directly tied to the number of processes waiting for execution. Each new process waiting for execution adds a 1 to the run-queue length, which affects the load average in the manner previously described. This is a much more practical metric of server utilization because it effectively captures how capable the system is of keeping up with the work it is being given. For a single-CPU system, a load of 1 would effectively be 100 percent utilization, but a better way of thinking about it is that the system has exactly enough capacity to handle the current load. A load average of .5 would mean that the system has twice the capacity it needs to handle the current load, and 3 means the system would need three times the capacity it currently has to handle the load. For multi-CPU systems, the load numbers should be divided by the number of CPUs, so a load average of 3 on a four-CPU system means the system is 75 percent utilized or it has a quarter more capacity than it needs to handle the current load.

There are two problems with the utilization triplet that you should be aware of. The first, and probably worst of the two, is that the triplet is not understood by laymen, such as managers and execs, and you have no hope of educating them. The second problem with the triplet is that the run-queue length is not strictly CPU-bound. Bad server problems, such as EXT3 panics, can also cause processes to back up in the run-queue, at least on Linux. In practice, this turns out not to be too bad of a problem because anything that is backing up the run-queue is bad news and bears your attention, anyway.

There are various pearls of wisdom floating around in books and on the Web, which say things such as "load averages above 3 are bad." I would agree that you probably want to upgrade a single-CPU system that is perpetually loaded at 3, but in the context of setting monitoring thresholds, nothing is written in stone. In the real world, I've seen systems go as high as 25 before showing any real signs of latency, and I have several boxes I don't worry about until they get at least that high. Figuring out where your thresholds should be is definitely a job for you, so check out my discussion of baselines in Chapter 1, "Best Practices," and decide accordingly.

The first step in setting up a CPU check is to add the check_load command to the nrpe. cfg file on the monitored host. The command at the bottom of the file should look something like this:

```
command[check_load]=/usr/libexec/check_load -w $ARG1$ -c $ARG2$
```

Notice the macros in the nrpe.cfg definition. In previous examples with the nrpe.cfg file, I've used static thresholds. Static thresholds are generally preferable, from a security standpoint, because potentially dangerous data is not accepted by the NRPE daemon. In practice, most people use tcpwrappers to control access to the daemon and use argument passing to centralize the thresholds on the Nagios server. Static thresholds on a per-host basis quickly become too much for most administrators to manage.

To pass arguments, you must first compile nrpe with enable-command-args, and set dont_blame_nrpe to 1 in the nrpe.cfg. (Because the feature is doubly disabled by default and called "Don't blame us" in the config file should give you pause. Use it at your own risk.)

After this is done, you can send arguments to the NRPE daemon via the command definition on the Nagios server. Listing 6.24 has an example command definition for use with an argument-accepting NRPE daemon.

This command definition picks up the thresholds from the service definition via argument macros and passes them on to the NRPE daemon on the remote host. Newer versions of check_nrpe support two syntaxes for argument passing. The classic way is the command name with exclamation-mark-separated arguments, and the new way specifies space-separated arguments after an -a switch. Although the new way is more readable, I prefer the old way because character escaping is cleaner.

Listing 6.24 *Check_load command definition with argument passing.*

```
define command{
        command_name    check_load
     #old way:
     command_line    $USER1$/check_nrpe -H $HOSTADDRESS$ \
                     -c check_load!$ARG1$!$ARG2$

       #new way:
       #command_line     $USER1$/check_nrpe -H $HOSTADDRESS$ \
       #                 -c check_load -a $ARG1$ $ARG2$
}
```

Listing 6.25 contains the accompanying service definition. This is where the thresholds are actually specified by the administrator. The check_load plugin in our example takes two arguments: one for the warning threshold and one for the critical threshold. Thresholds are specified as UNIX load average triplets. In our example, Nagios will generate a warning for someUnixHost if its 1-minute average goes above 15, its 5-minute average goes above 10, or its 15-minute average goes above 5.

Listing 6.25 *The check_load service definition.*

```
define service{
       host_name               someUnixHost
       service_description     CPU LOAD
       check_command           check_load!15,10,5,!30,25,20
       use                     chapter6template
       notification_options    w,c,r
}
```

Memory

One of the things I like best about UNIX Load Average, as a metric for system performance, is that it is common across all UNIX and UNIX-like systems. Be it Linux, Solaris, or

FreeBSD, the load average numbers are there and are (probably) derived in much the same way. Memory utilization, however, is the opposite. (Check out the Solaris section of the Nagios Exchange [www.nagiosexchange.org] for Solaris-specific plugins.) Unfortunately, user-space tools, such as vmstat, don't provide an insulation layer against the differences in the various UNIX system virtual memory implementations, and other tools, such as free, might not exist on particular platforms at all. This makes it hard to write a single Nagios plugin that accurately tracks memory across all UNIX systems.

Additionally, UNIX systems do a lot of memory caching and buffering, so even if the virtual memory systems were similar enough across the board to take these measurements, the results wouldn't be all that useful. When UNIX systems have X amount of RAM, they'll usually use most of it, and this is a good thing.

So for UNIX systems in general, the question becomes not, "How much RAM am I using?" but, "Is this system running low on RAM?" To answer that question, a much better indicator of unhealthy memory utilization is the way in which the system is using its swap space. Tools like sar, vmstat, and iostat are very useful for querying information about swap space utilization, but again, these tools do not contain common functionality across various flavors of UNIX.

For example, vmstat on Solaris provides a page/sr column that details the page scan rate. This is a great metric for understanding whether a system is out of RAM. No matter how much memory a machine has, if the page-scanning rate is above 200 or so, you know you have a problem. Unfortunately, vmstat on Linux provides no such information, so monitoring memory in your UNIX environment depends on what kind of systems you have and what tools you have available to monitor them.

The official Nagios plugins tarball has a check_swap plugin that can give you information on swap utilization for any Linux host. It is also reported to work well on BSD but is unreliable on Solaris. Check_swap provides basic utilization info, rather than rate information, so although it can't measure things such as pages per second, it can tell you what percentage of swap is in use on a given server. To use check_swap, add the following line to your nrpe.cfg on the monitored host.

```
command[check_swap]=/usr/libexec/check_swap -w $ARG1$% -c $ARG2$%
```

This isn't much different from our check_load command. Check_swap will figure out the total amount of swap space available and then figure out how much is used. Thresholds are expressed as either the percentage of free swap space or the number of bytes of free swap space. The example specifies percentages by adding a percent sign after the arguments. Listing 6.26 is the command definition for the checkcommands.cfg.

Listing 6.26 *Check_swap command definition.*

```
define command{
        command_name       check_swap
        command_line       $USER1$/check_nrpe -H $HOSTADDRESS$ \
                           -c check_swap!$ARG1$!$ARG2$
}
```

Check_swap barely scratches the surface of what you can do with memory utilization monitoring in Nagios. I highly recommend that you check the contrib. directory, as well as the Nagios Exchange, for platform-specific swap and memory utilization plugins.

Disk

The check_disk plugin in the offical plugins tarball is one of my favorite plugins. It's well-designed and easy for lazy people to use. Check_disk can generate warnings or errors based on the free space measured in percent kilobytes or megabytes of a given device, directory, or mountpoint. Perhaps best of all, the less information you provide it, the more information it provides you. For example, here is the output of check_disk –w 10% -c 5% on one of my servers at the office.

```
DISK OK - free space: / 1725 MB (90%); /boot 76 MB (82%); /usr
4383 MB (72%); /var 73444 MB (91%); /srv 9439 MB (94%); /opt
1849 MB (92%); /home 9166 MB (92%);| /=198MB;1730;1826;0;1923 /
boot=16MB;82;87;0;92 /usr=1664MB;5442;5744;0;6047 /var=7191MB;725
70;76602;0;80634 /srv=640MB;9071;9575;0;10079 /opt=166MB;1813;191
4;0;2015 /home=787MB;8957;9455;0;9953
```

If you don't specify any particular mountpoint directory or block device, check_disk simply checks all of them. This is, in my opinion, great user interface design. Performance data is provided, so a pipe splits the output with human readable output first, followed by a pipe, followed by machine parseable output. Although it's probably self-explanatory by now, Listing 6.27 is a check_disk command definition for the chkcommand.cfg file.

Listing 6.27 *Check_swap command definition.*

```
define command{
        command_name       check_disk
        command_line       $USER1$/check_nrpe -H $HOSTADDRESS$ \
                           -c check_disk!$ARG1$!$ARG2$
    }
```

Watching "Other Stuff"

Our discussion, thus far, has focused on traditional computer systems running some form of Windows or UNIX. In this section, I'll take a look at some of the other stuff you can monitor with Nagios, including networking gear and environmental sensors.

SNMP

SNMP was created by the IETF in 1988 as a way to remotely manage IP-based devices. It was originally described in RFC 1157 and, since then, has become as ubiquitous as it is hated by security professionals worldwide, but more on that later. The protocol is actually very large in scope. The IETF clearly did not intend to describe a communication protocol, but rather to provide a standardized configuration instrumentation to all IP-based devices going forward. In doing so, they not only specified strictly-typed variables for configuration settings but also an all-encompassing database for network device configuration settings and status information.

Imagine, for a moment, a single hierarchal structure that gives a unique address to every piece of information and configuration setting on every IP-enabled device in the world. The hierarchy you are imagining is called the SNMP MIB tree (Managed Information Base). Each configuration setting is given an address, called an Object Identifier (OID). The OID address is similar to an IP address, in that it is dot separated and gets more specific from left to right. Each number in the address specifies a node in the MIB. Let's dissect an example OID.

```
.1.3.6.1.2.1.2.2.1.8.1
```

As you can see, the OID is very much like an overly long IPv4 address. Like DNS records, the beginning "." on the left specifies the root of the tree. The first number, 1, belongs to the International Standards Organization, therefore, every node specified in this hierarchy is administered by the ISO. The 3 has been designated by the ISO for use by "other" organizations. The United States Department of Defense owns 6 and its Internet Activities Board owns 1. Every OID you'll come into contact with will probably begin with .1.3.6.1. Figure 6.1 graphically depicts this common hierarchy.

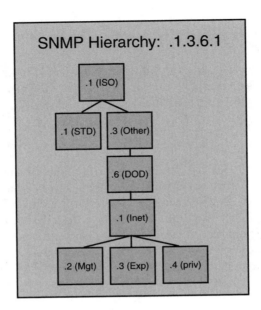

Figure 6.1 The .1.3.6.1 prefix.

From here, the Hierarchy continues to become more specific. The three children of the IAB in Figure 6.1 are all commonly used; the children are management (2), experimental (3), and private (4). The experimental branch is used for nodes that will eventually become IETF Standards. Because RFCs can take a while to become RFCs, the experimental branch enables administrators to use experimental OIDs on production gear without causing conflicts with existing OIDs. The private branch is for private organizations, such as Cisco and Juniper Networks. Private is where you would find information, such as the 1-minute CPU load average on a Cisco Router. Our example OID is in the management branch, which contains IETF Standard nodes. Every node within is described somewhere in an RFC.

The next 1 places our OID within the mib-2 group, meaning that this is an SNMP Version 2 node. SNMP version 1, as first described by the IETF, had two main problems. The first was Moore's Law. When the IETF set out to specify how data could be stored in the MIB, they underestimated the size of the data values that the MIB would need to store. As a result, many of the configuration settings on the network devices quickly outgrew the IETF's strictly typed variables. The second problem, of course, was the lack of security in the SNMP protocol.

SNMP Version 1 uses a shared secret, called the community string, to authenticate peers. Unfortunately, this string is transmitted in clear text between SNMP peers, and there is a nearly universal practice of setting the string to public. This setting is often overlooked by administrators and, in years past, SNMP was enabled by default on many devices, opening them up to remote configuration by possibly malicious entities.

SNMP Version 2 was drafted in 1993 to fix these problems and add some functionality to the protocol, but unfortunately, it died an untimely death when its drafters couldn't agree on the details of the security enhancements. Three years later, a compromise was struck with the release of SNMP Version 2c. V2c took the things the IETF could agree on and combined them with the Version 1 security model. The new standard includes larger data structures, get-bulk transfers, connection-oriented traps, improved error handling, and the same flawed clear-text security model. V2c isn't as widely adopted as V1, but support for it exists on most newer network gear, including Cisco routers with IOS 11.2(6)F and above.

The IETF finished work on SNMP Version 3 in March of 2002. V3, currently a full Internet standard, is described in RFC's 3410-3418. Adoption of V3 seems to be occurring more quickly than did V2c, with many vendor implementations currently available, including Cisco gear running IOS 12.0(3)T and above. V3 supports three security models: no-authnopriv, which sends cleartext SNMP packets and has trivial authentication, authnopriv, which sends cleartext SNMP packets and has strong authentication via MD5 or SHA, and authpriv, which has both encrypted sessions and strong authentication. The use of Version 3, in at least authnopriv, is highly encouraged when it's available.

The next portion of our example OID, 2.2.1, translates to interfaces.ifTable.ifEntry. This means our OID is in reference to a specific interface. The second to last digit, 8, translates to the ifOperStatus node, which is the current operational status of the interface. The very last digit in our OID specifies the interface number, so this OID translates to the current operational status of Interface #1. This value will be one of seven possible values: up, down, testing, unknown, dormant, notPresent, or lowerLayerDown.

Even though the MIB is hierarchal, devices in practice do not implement the entire tree. Devices that support SNMP only contain the subset of the MIB tree that they need. So if a given network device has no configuration settings in the experimental branch of the MIB, they do not implement that portion of the MIB tree. An SNMP device can be either a manager or an agent, or, in some cases, both. Agents can be thought of as SNMP servers; they are devices that implement some subset of the MIB tree and can be queried for configuration information or configured remotely via SNMP. Devices that poll or configure agents are called managers. The snmpget program from the net-snmp project is a manager and my Cisco router is an agent.

SNMP agents don't have to sit by passively and wait to be polled; they can also notify managers of problems using an SNMP trap. SNMP traps use UDP and are targeted at the manager's port 162. Although Nagios has no intrinsic SNMP capabilities (Nagios has few intrinsic capabilities of any type and that is a good thing), the check_snmp plugin, combined with passive alerts and the snmptrapd daemon from the net-snmp project, make it into an SNMP manager that is capable of both polling SNMP devices for information and collecting traps from SNMP agents.

Working with SNMP

Let's get down to business and start monitoring some devices using SNMP. The first step is to get and to install the net-snmp libraries on the Nagios server. The libraries are freely available from www.net-snmp.org. When installed, you may have to rebuild the plugins in order to get check_snmp installed because it won't build unless the net-snmp libraries exist. After everything's installed, you can start poking around your devices with the snmpwalk program from the net-snmp package.

Of course, these days SNMP is probably disabled on your networking gear, so before snmpwalk can see anything, you have to enable SNMP somewhere. The commands in Listing 6.28 should get SNMP working in a relatively safe manner on most modern Cisco routers.

Listing 6.28   *Enabling SNMP on Cisco routers.*

```
ip access-list standard snmp-filter
permit 192.168.42.42
deny    any log
end
snmp-server community myCommunity RO snmp-filter

###########alternatively, if your router supports V3###########

snmp-server view myView mib-2 include
snmp-server group ReadGroup v3 auth read myView
snmp-server user dave ReadGroup v3 auth md5 encrypti0nR0cks
```

Line 1 creates an access list called snmp-filter. The permit line specifies the Nagios server, allowing it to connect. All other hosts are denied and their attempt logged. Finally, SNMP is enabled in a read-only capacity, with the community name of myCommunity, to the hosts allowed in the access list snmp-filter. The SNMP v3 config is outside the scope of this book. Check out what the router has to say for itself.

```
snmpwalk -v2c -c myCommunity 192.168.42.42
```

The -v switch specifies the protocol version; -c is the community string. This command, on my Cisco 2851 router, returns 1,375 lines of output. Most of it looks like Listing 6.29, which is to say it looks like a bunch of unrecognizable SNMP gobbly-gook.

Listing 6.29 *Unrecognizable SNMP gobbly-gook.*

```
SNMPv2-SMI::mib-2.15.3.1.1.4.71.12.23 = IpAddress: 4.68.1.2
SNMPv2-SMI::mib-2.15.3.1.2.4.71.12.23 = INTEGER: 6
SNMPv2-SMI::mib-2.15.3.1.3.4.71.12.23 = INTEGER: 2
SNMPv2-SMI::mib-2.15.3.1.4.4.71.12.23 = INTEGER: 4
SNMPv2-SMI::mib-2.15.3.1.5.4.71.12.23 = IpAddress: 4.71.12.23
SNMPv2-SMI::mib-2.15.3.1.6.4.71.12.23 = INTEGER: 30511
SNMPv2-SMI::mib-2.15.3.1.7.4.71.12.23 = IpAddress: 4.71.12.24
SNMPv2-SMI::mib-2.15.3.1.8.4.71.12.23 = INTEGER: 179
SNMPv2-SMI::mib-2.15.3.1.9.4.71.12.23 = INTEGER: 3356
SNMPv2-SMI::mib-2.15.3.1.10.4.71.12.23 = Counter32: 4
SNMPv2-SMI::mib-2.15.3.1.11.4.71.12.23 = Counter32: 2
SNMPv2-SMI::mib-2.15.3.1.12.4.71.12.23 = Counter32: 147184
SNMPv2-SMI::mib-2.15.3.1.13.4.71.12.23 = Counter32: 147183
SNMPv2-SMI::mib-2.15.3.1.14.4.71.12.23 = Hex-STRING: 00 00
```

It looks like interesting information, if you could somehow figure out what it is in reference to. The problem is that snmpwalk can only resolve the first bit of the OIDs to their English names. This is because I lack what is referred to as an MIB file, which maps numerical OIDs to their ASCII counterparts. Net-snmp comes with MIB files for most of the management mgmt branch of the MIB tree, but you may need to download custom MIBs for OIDs in the private branch, or weirdos in the management mgmt branch, such as the OIDs in Listing 6.28. In order to make sense of things, I need to install an MIB file so that snmpwalk can resolve the rest of the OID. To find the specific MIB file I require, I need to make things more numeric.

```
snmpwalk -v2c -c myCommunity -On 192.168.42.42
```

Adding the -On switch to the command causes snmpwalk to print the full OID instead of printing a partial English name followed by the part of the OID it couldn't resolve. This gets you the output in Listing 6.30.

Listing 6.30 *Even less recognizable SNMP gobbly-gook.*

```
.1.3.6.1.2.1.15.3.1.1.4.71.12.23 = IpAddress: 4.68.1.2
.1.3.6.1.2.1.15.3.1.2.4.71.12.23 = INTEGER: 6
.1.3.6.1.2.1.15.3.1.3.4.71.12.23 = INTEGER: 2
.1.3.6.1.2.1.15.3.1.4.4.71.12.23 = INTEGER: 4
.1.3.6.1.2.1.15.3.1.5.4.71.12.23 = IpAddress: 4.71.12.23
.1.3.6.1.2.1.15.3.1.6.4.71.12.23 = INTEGER: 30511
.1.3.6.1.2.1.15.3.1.7.4.71.12.23 = IpAddress: 4.71.12.24
.1.3.6.1.2.1.15.3.1.8.4.71.12.23 = INTEGER: 179
.1.3.6.1.2.1.15.3.1.9.4.71.12.23 = INTEGER: 3356
.1.3.6.1.2.1.15.3.1.10.4.71.12.23 = Counter32: 4
.1.3.6.1.2.1.15.3.1.11.4.71.12.23 = Counter32: 2
.1.3.6.1.2.1.15.3.1.12.4.71.12.23 = Counter32: 147189
.1.3.6.1.2.1.15.3.1.13.4.71.12.23 = Counter32: 147188
.1.3.6.1.2.1.15.3.1.14.4.71.12.23 = Hex-STRING: 00 00
```

Now that you have a full OID, you can proceed to the Cisco OID Navigator at http:// tools.cisco.com/Support/SNMP/do/BrowseOID.do?local=en, and paste in one of the OIDs shown in Figure 6.2.

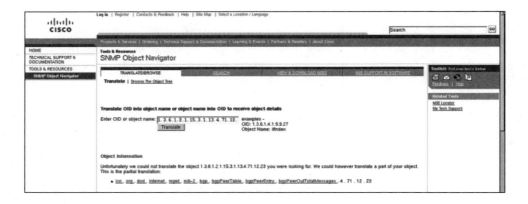

Figure 6.2 Looking up the OID at the Cisco Object Navigator Web site.

Now, you can see the OID that you are missing: bgpPeerIdentifier. Clicking on the MIB name takes you to a page where you can download the MIB as a .my file. Installing the MIB is a snap:

```
cd /usr/share/snmp/mibs && wget ftp://ftp.cisco.com/pub/mibs/v2/
   BGP4-MIB.my
```

This path is probably different for you. Check your net-snmp installation packaging.

After installed, you can force snmpwalk to load it with the -m switch. You can give -m the name of a specific MIB to load or specify the keyword all to load them all.

```
snmpwalk -v2c -c myCommunity -m all 192.168.42.42
```

This makes the output into something you might actually use, as you can see in Listing 6.31. SNMP can be a challenge to use for the first time. There's a lot of data, and it can take some searching to find what you want if you don't know what you are looking for. If you have a load balancer, check out http://vegan.net/MRTG/index.php; it's a sanity-saving collection of often-used SNMP metrics for all types of load balancers. Most administrators go through the process of tracking down the MIBS for their particular combination of network devices once or twice before they begin to carry their SNMP MIB collection with them from box to box, along with their vimrc, muttrc, and assorted other hard-won configuration files. Vendor-specific mailing lists are always a good source of OID tips.

Listing 6.31 *Fully MIB'd snmpwalk output.*

```
BGP4-MIB::bgpPeerIdentifier.4.71.12.23 = IpAddress: 4.68.1.2
BGP4-MIB::bgpPeerState.4.71.12.23 = INTEGER: established(6)
BGP4-MIB::bgpPeerAdminStatus.4.71.12.23 = INTEGER: start(2)
BGP4-MIB::bgpPeerNegotiatedVersion.4.71.12.23 = INTEGER: 4
BGP4-MIB::bgpPeerLocalAddr.4.71.12.23 = IpAddress: 4.71.12.23
BGP4-MIB::bgpPeerLocalPort.4.71.12.23 = INTEGER: 30511
BGP4-MIB::bgpPeerRemoteAddr.4.71.12.23 = IpAddress: 4.71.12.24
BGP4-MIB::bgpPeerRemotePort.4.71.12.23 = INTEGER: 179
BGP4-MIB::bgpPeerRemoteAs.4.71.12.23 = INTEGER: 3356
BGP4-MIB::bgpPeerInUpdates.4.71.12.23 = Counter32: 4
BGP4-MIB::bgpPeerOutUpdates.4.71.12.23 = Counter32: 2
BGP4-MIB::bgpPeerInTotalMessages.4.71.12.23 = Counter32: 147205
BGP4-MIB::bgpPeerOutTotalMessages.4.71.12.23 = Counter32: 147204
BGP4-MIB::bgpPeerLastError.4.71.12.23 = Hex-STRING: 00 00
```

Now that you know what you're looking for, you can use the snmpget program from the net-snmp package to query it directly, like so:

```
snmpget -v2c -c myCommunity -m all 192.168.42.42 BGP4-MIB::bgpPeer
   LastError.4.71.12.23
```

After you've decided on the things you want Nagios to monitor, take note of their OID numbers. I recommend that you use the numerical OID number rather than the name. This is less error-prone because it removes MIB file dependencies. The check_snmp plugin in the official plugins tarball is a reimplementation of the snmpget utility with some output processing functionality and Nagios return codes. Check_snmp can be a complex plugin to use, especially when text comparison becomes involved, but it packs a lot of functionality.

Setup a Nagios check against the SNMP attribute: iso.org.dod.internet.private.enterprises.cisco.local.lcpu.avgBusy1. This is the 1-Minute CPU Utilization Average on a Cisco PIX Firewall. Listing 6.32 is the check_snmp command definition.

Listing 6.32 *The BgpLastError command definition.*

```
define command{
        command_name     check_fwCpu
        command_line     $USER1$/check_snmp -H $HOSTADDRESS$ \
                         -o .1.3.6.1.4.1.9.2.1.57.0 \
                         -C $USER5$ -v 2c -w 0:70 -c 0:100
        }
```

Most of this is pretty self-explanatory. The community name option, -c, from the snmp-get command, became -C because check_snmp needed the lowercase version for the critical threshold. Note the appearance of the $USER5$ macro, which we haven't seen in any previous example. $USER5$ is a variable that is specified in the resources.cfg file, as described in Chapter 4. This file allows you to define your own Nagios macros and the nice thing about the file is its permissions. It's owned by root- and read-only, so it's a safe place to put things, such as community strings and passwords, when you need to use them in object definitions.

The warning and critical thresholds in Listing 6.32 are specified as ranges. This is something common to a few plugins, but this is the first time it's popped into one of the examples. The range is expressed as two numbers separated by a colon. The number on the left side is the minimum value and the number on the right is the maximum. Every time you see this threshold syntax used by a plugin, you may also specify the thresholds in pieces. In other words, it's possible to just specify the min *or* the max, so while 0:5 means "0 to 5," just :5 would mean "5 at the most, with no minimum value."

Environmental Sensors

In the last few years, environmental sensors have been popping up all over the place. With the popularity of the low cost lm78 sensor chip from National Semiconductor, just about anything with a micro-controller or micro-processor in it has some form of onboard environmental monitoring available these days. It's sometimes questionable how sensitive or how well calibrated these sensors are in low-end hardware, but most server-grade equipment possessing these sensors is usable in my experience.

The original lm78 was a special purpose micro-controller with an onboard temperature sensor and inputs for monitoring up to three fans, two voltage sources, and additional external temperature sensors. It supported two different bus architectures for communication with external sensors: i2c (pronounced i squared c) and ISA (IBM's Industry Standard Architecture). The i2c bus, created in the 1980s by Phillips, proved to be a highly successful serial bus for sensor networks because 112 i2c devices can communicate via its simple low cost two-wire interface. Several competing architectures have sprung up since then, including Dallas Semiconductors' 1wire, Motorola's SPI (Serial Peripheral Interface, pronounced Spy)—which, because of the need for a ground wire, actually uses two wires—and Intel's System Management Bus (SMBus).

There are small differences between these bus architectures, but the choice of bus in a given system is usually a function of the brand of micro-controller and sensors involved rather than the inherent superiority of one bus over another. In practice, it's common for a single motherboard to have a combination of several buses and sensors from different vendors. Even when the motherboard only has a single sensor chip, often unexpected components contain their own. Examples include video or TV-tuner cards, battery recharging subsystems, and "backlighting" subsystems for controlling things such as LCD brightness.

If you don't trust the onboard environmental monitoring hardware, the marketplace in the last few years has exploded with stand-alone environmental sensors designed for data center use. It's now possible to spend anywhere from $50 for simple temperature/humidity sensors all the way up to $5,000 for camera-embedded environmental sensor arrays with features such as motion, light, smoke and water detection, and cabinet entry alarms. If you're short on cash, several Web sites sell stand-alone sensor kits for around $20, and there are a few sites that will teach you how to build your own for even less. For the ultimate in DIY hardware-based server monitoring, check out Bob Drzyzgula's work at www.usenix.org/publications/library/proceedings/lisa2000/drzyzgula.html.

Nagios can easily interact with stand-alone sensors, as well as their system-embedded counterparts.

Stand-alone Sensors

Stand-alone sensors are self-contained units that are either dedicated to environmental monitoring or are part of some related piece of server-room hardware. I'm personally enamored with a cool power strip in one of my company's collocation facilities. The PowerTower XL has 32 programmable outlets on two internally redundant, 20-amp busses and two external temperature/humidity probes on 6-foot wires. I especially enjoy telling my friends about how I periodically SSH into my power strip.

These sensors are usually accurate, and the higher-end models have some advanced functionality, such as the capability to communicate with each other to form sensor networks. Most sensors of this type, which are designed for data-center work, have Ethernet hardware and make their data available via some combination of SNMP, SSH, HTTP, and TELNET. SNMP in read-only mode is usually the preferred methodology for interacting with stand-alone sensors.

The first sensor that bears mentioning is, of course, the Websensor EM01B. You can't beat this sensor on Nagios compatibility; the Nagios home page has been linking to it for over 6 years now. The EM01B is a stand-alone sensor that includes temperature, humidity, and illumination levels. It is expandable with external add-ons, such as a cabinet door alarm. The sensor has a 10/100 Ethernet card and communicates via TCP. It even comes with its own Nagios plugins: one written in Perl and the other in C. Expect to pay somewhere around $450.

If you need something more than a single sensor in the rack, you might try APC's EMU, which is a network appliance that resembles a rack-mountable eight port Ethernet switch. Various sensors plug into the EMUs RJ45 jacks, and multiple EMUs can be networked together to form sensor networks. Available sensors include temperature, humidity, motion, smoke, and water. The EMU can also control devices that aren't sensors, such as alarm beacons (literally, police-car-style lights meant to be mounted on the outside of the rack) and sirens. The EMU may be interfaced via a Web interface, TELNET, SSH, or SNMP, so Nagios can monitor it using any of a number of plugins, including check_ssh and check_snmp. The EMU is a bit pricier than the EM01B.

A great place to do some research on stand-alone environmental sensors is Dan Klein's excellent thermd project page. Thermd is a rather complex Perl script intended to collect and plot data from various environmental sensors in your home. Dan has a lot of hands-on experience with many different power and environmental sensors, so you can be sure if thermd supports a given sensor, there's bound to be a way to integrate it with Nagios. The sensors page is at www.klein.com/thermd/#devices.

LMSensors

Using the embedded sensors inside Intel-based servers gives you a better idea of what the temperature is, where it matters the most. The lm-sensors project provides a suite of tools for detecting and interacting with all sorts of server-embedded monitoring hardware. Lm-sensors can be downloaded from the project page at www.lm-sensors.org/. While you're there, you should visit their outstanding Wiki page, which contains all sorts of great information about how to void your PC's warranty.

Users with a 2.4 series kernel may also want to install the i2c package, which is also available from the lm-sensors Web site. If lm-sensors is compiled on a machine with a 2.6 series kernel, it will attempt to use the i2c support included in the kernel. Most current Linux distributions come with a copy of lm-sensors pre-installed, so you might already have it.

After lm-sensors is built, run the sensors-detect program. The sensors-detect program repeatedly warns you about the terrible things that can happen if you decide to continue and, after you repeatedly tell it to continue anyway, detects sensor chips on your motherboard and produces output suitable for appending to your modules.conf file. After you have inserted the drivers that sensors-detect says you need, you can launch the sensors program. The output of the sensors program will look something like Listing 6.33.

Listing 6.33 *Output from the sensors program.*

```
w83627hf-isa-0290
Adapter: ISA adapter
VCore 1:    +1.52 V   (min =   +0.00 V, max =   +0.00 V)
VCore 2:    +3.36 V   (min =   +0.00 V, max =   +0.00 V)
+3.3V:      +3.41 V   (min =   +3.14 V, max =   +3.47 V)
+5V:        +5.05 V   (min =   +4.76 V, max =   +5.24 V)
+12V:      +12.28 V   (min = +10.82 V, max = +13.19 V)
-12V:      -11.62 V   (min = -13.18 V, max = -10.80 V)
-5V:        +0.23 V   (min =  -5.25 V, max =  -4.75 V)
```
(continues)

Listing 6.33 *Output from the sensors program. (Continued)*

```
V5SB:       +5.75 V   (min =  +4.76 V, max =  +5.24 V)
VBat:       +2.11 V   (min =  +2.40 V, max =  +3.60 V)
fan1:         0 RPM   (min =    0 RPM, div = 2)
fan2:         0 RPM   (min = 9926 RPM, div = 2)
fan3:         0 RPM   (min = 135000 RPM, div = 2)
temp1:      +34°C (high = +40°C, hyst = +0°C) sensor=thermistor

temp2:      +25.5°C (high = +40°C, hyst =+35°C) sensor=thermistor

temp3:      +23.5°C (high = +40°C, hyst =+35°C) sensor=thermistor


alarms:   Chassis intrusion detection                      ALARM

beep_enable:
          Sound alarm disabled
```

The sensor chip on this server monitors various voltage levels, including both CPUs, the fan speed of three different fans, and the temperature of three different heat-sensitive resistors. The sensor chip is also tied to a cam-switch to detect when the chassis lid is removed. This is great information and is easily parsed with everyday shell tools. The official Nagios plugins tarball comes with a check_sensors shell script for use with lmsensors and the contrib. directory contains a pPerl script called check_lmmon for BSD users.

IPMI

Intelligent Platform Management Interface (IPMI) is an Intel specification for a hardware-based, out-of-band monitoring and management solution for Intel-based server hardware. Enterprise class servers from the big name vendors ship with integrated IPMI hardware and proprietary client software. IPMI is sometimes offered as an add-on option for commodity server hardware. The Dell OpenManage utility, for example, is a proprietary IPMI client.

IPMI operates independently of the operating system software on the system, which means that IPMI will remain available in the event of a catastrophic system failure or even while the system is powered off. If power is available to the system, IPMI can perform tasks, such as providing system and status information to administrators, rebooting the system, and even blinking LEDs, so that remote-hands personnel can easily find the troubled system in high-density racks. IPMI implementations maintain a ring-buffer, similar to Linux's dmesg, which can provide detailed information about interesting hardware events, such as RAID-card and memory failures. IPMI implementations can even send alerts about problems to SNMP managers using SNMP traps.

Network access to the IPMI hardware is usually available via either by an extra, dedicated network card specific to the IPMI hardware or by sharing a network card with the system. Client software interacts to the IPMI hardware either remotely, using the IPMI-over-LAN interface, or directly, through OS extensions, such as kernel modules.

Many open source tools exist to interact with IPMI hardware including OpenIPMI, which is a kernel module and userspace library for local interaction. Ipmitool and ipmiutil are popular userspace IPMI query tools, which both support IPMI-over-LAN and local IPMI queries via various proprietary and open source drivers. Chris Wilson wrote a check_ipmi Nagios plugin in Perl, which uses ipmitool. This plugin is available from www.qwirx.com/check_ipmi.

Systems monitoring is a fascinating undertaking that introduces an administrator to all kinds of cool technology that, otherwise, would have been overlooked in favor of the more mundane day-to-day tasks. Nagios is one of the few tools whose functionality scales linearly with its administrator's knowledge, so don't think for a moment that this chapter is an all-encompassing Nagios feature list; in fact, it is barely an overview of the tool's capabilities.

CHAPTER 7

Visualization

If you want to summarize the intent of systems monitoring in two words, it would be difficult to do better than increase visibility. There are too many systems doing too many things too quickly for humans to maintain any sense of what's going on at any given moment. The best we can hope for is to tell when something breaks, but a good monitoring system isn't bound by our organic limitations, so it shouldn't stop there. Good monitoring systems act like transducers in electronics, converting the incomprehensibly large number of interactions between systems and networks into an environmental compendium fit for human consumption. Good monitoring systems provide organic interfaces to the network, which allow us to see more, and the extent to which they accomplish this determines their usefulness as tools.

Humans are visual animals, so the best way to understand complex information is to draw us a picture. The importance of data visualization to the success of your implementation and the well-being of your environment cannot be understated. Good visualization solves the visibility problem by effectively communicating the status of the environment, enabling pattern recognition in historical and real-time data, and making propeller-head metrics into indicators laymen can utilize. Good visualization can aid any number of critical undertakings such as capacity planning, forensics, and root cause analysis. Visualization catches problems you didn't tell the monitoring system to look for. On the other hand, absent or poor data visualization severely hinders the usefulness of the system and can render your monitoring system irrelevant altogether.

Out of the box, Nagios doesn't draw very many pretty pictures. The Web interface has good low-level data visualization, but, in general, the Web interface is focused on the now. It lacks long-term or historical data visualization and doesn't provide much in the way of a meaningful services-oriented management interface. However, much like its decision not to build in monitoring logic, the lack of integrated data visualization is to Nagios's favor. By focusing on making the data available to external programs, Nagios arms us with what we need to use the best data visualization software available, rather than forcing us to settle for mediocre built-in functionality. This chapter focuses on bringing your monitoring implementation to the next level by integrating various popular visualization packages. This chapter begins with the tried and true, MRTG and RRDTool, and eventually moves into more uncharted waters.

Foundations, MRTG, and RRDTool

Monitoring systems across the board do much the same thing. They periodically poll systems to retrieve various metrics and compare those metrics with thresholds to determine if there is a problem. This is fine for determining if a service is currently broken, but recording the metric each time it is polled and graphing it over time can solve an entirely different subset of problems. These historical graphs are useful for all sorts of things because they allow us to spot trends over time and tell us what a given service was doing at a particular time in the past. Take the CPU load graph in Figure 7.1, for example.

Figure 7.1   CPU load graph, last 28 hours.

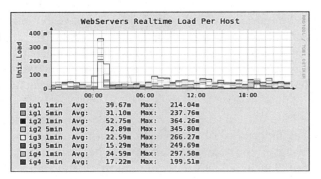

We can clearly see a CPU spike across all servers at approximately midnight in the graph. If we change the time interval on the graph so that it displays a longer period of time, such as Figure 7.2, we can see that this behavior is not typical for these servers; therefore, we may surmise that this behavior constitutes a problem.

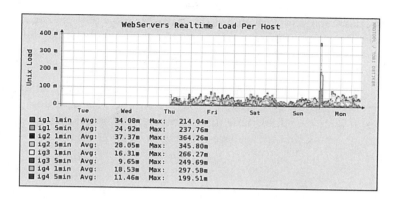

Figure 7.2 CPU load graph, last week.

Time-series graphs are great for visually-stimulated humans; they depict lots of information in a small space and in a way that communicates the subject matter instantly. The simple act of graphing every metric you can helps out in all sorts of situations. You can never graph too much. For instance, if other graphs are available, we can compare them to spot relationships that aid troubleshooting. A comparison of Figure 7.1 to the graph of network utilization on the same servers, in Figure 7.3, shows that the CPU spike coincided with a 6MB/s network spike, implying that the abnormal utilization was somehow related to traffic received by the hosts in question.

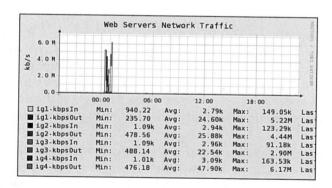

Figure 7.3 Network utilization graph, last 28 hours.

This time-series data is the first, and most important, data visualization you should add to your Nagios Web interface. And there are some important considerations to be made upfront. Because you never know what you might want to compare, how you might want to compare it, or for how long; the manner in which you collect, store, and visualize this data is immensely important. In every case, you want to choose tools that optimize for flexibility, and, unfortunately, the number of tools that actually provide all the flexibility you might want is small.

As depicted in Figure 7.4, there are three pieces to the data visualization puzzle: data collection, data storage, and display. The best way to optimize for flexibility is to get three separate packages to handle each of these three jobs, and the mistake made by most of the software related to graphing time-series data is trying to do too much.

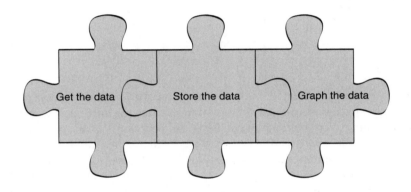

Figure 7.4 Three pieces to the visualization puzzle.

For example, when packages that store data get into the business of collecting data, they make assumptions about what and how you want to collect. Likewise, when display packages get into the business of polling or storing data, they make assumptions about where the data will be and how it will be stored. This makes it difficult to bring together a patchwork of data from all kinds of devices all over the network. Packages that specialize in doing their singular task make fewer assumptions about what you want to do next.

I'm going to choose two of these puzzle pieces for you, right now. Nagios makes a great data collection and polling engine, and RRDTool is the best tool out there for monitoring and performance data storage. You need a glue layer to connect the output of Nagios to RRDTool's input, and you need a flexible front-end to make it easy to draw graphs from data collected by Nagios or any other tools you might have.

To effectively store data from Nagios with RRDTool, you must first understand how it will be stored. With RRDTool's unique storage methodology, this is especially so. Decisions you make about data storage upfront impacts how useful your data is in the long run, because changing the way you store things later is difficult, and not storing enough is something that cannot be remedied after the fact.

MRTG

RRDTool owes its lineage to the ever-popular MRTG. Written by Tobias Oetiker in 1994, MRTG is now the industry standard for graphing utilization data from network gear. Every monitoring system I'm aware of claims support for MRTG in one way or another. Nagios, with two plugins for querying data from MRTG logs and graphs, is no exception. However, for people building monitoring systems, MRTG's usefulness is limited because it does its own polling and data collection.

MRTG, in fact, can really be thought of as a monitoring system. It is a script, run from cron, which periodically polls your SNMP-enabled devices for interesting statistics. It stores these stats in something called a round robin database. An RRD is a circular data structure; a database that, when full, begins overwriting itself. This structure turns out to be perfect for its intended purpose. When allocated, the RRD never grows in size on the disk and allows for fast data retrieval and manipulation. MRTG then uses the data from the RRD to create HTML pages containing time-series graphs.

MRTG is popular because it is a holistic solution. It is easy to implement and, when configured, does everything from the SNMP collection to generate the HTML. Ironically, it is this property that makes it difficult for you to use in a systems-monitoring context. Because it does data collection via SNMP, it assumes all of your data is going to come from SNMP-enabled sources.

You already have a polling engine to collect data, and you want somewhere to store it. Ideally, your storage engine will be flexible about the kind of data it accepts and MRTG is not. Technically, you can implement an SNMP agent on your Nagios server and make your data available to MRTG via SNMP, but this is needlessly complex. The thing that MRTG gets right, from your perspective, is the RRD. If there was a way to extract the RRD from MRTG and use it for arbitrary types of data, your needs would be met perfectly.

RRDTool

In 1999, while MRTG's author Tobias Oetiker was on sabbatical at CAIDA (the Cooperative Association for Internet Data Analysis), he began work on RRDTool, which is exactly what the systems-monitoring community needed for time-series data visualization. By extracting the relevant parts of MRTG into separate utilities and by extending their functionality, Tobias created a category killer for graphing time-series data.

I don't say that lightly. It's difficult to express how perfectly round robin databases solve the problem of storing performance and monitoring metrics. After it is stored in RRDs, the data is available via command-line tools for whatever shell processing you might want to do, but it's the fast and powerful internal processing that makes RRD a net gain.

Storing and graphing time-series data is a more difficult problem than it sounds, and RRDTool is feature-rich, making it one of the most complex and difficult to use pieces of software that systems administrators deal with on a daily basis. It simply isn't feasible to commit RRDTool's command-line syntax to memory, so, in practice, automation is the rule. Most systems administrators use scripts and glue code to hide RRDTool's complexity, but it's tricky to do this without losing flexibility. The more you know about RRDTool, the better off you are in dealing with, and choosing, the scripts you will use to glue RRDTool to other applications like Nagios.

At its most basic level, RRDTool is a database of metrics. These metrics can be anything from the temperature of a room to the throughput of a router interface in bits per second. RRDTool calls these metrics data sources (DS), because that's what they are. Command-line tools are provided to create and periodically update the database. Each data source can be stored in the database as one of several types, including GAUGE and COUNTER, which are the only two types you'll use. To understand why different data types are needed, consider how our example metrics, temperature, and throughput are collected.

RRD Data Types

The temperature measurement comes from some sort of sensor, either inside a server with IPMI or LMSensors, or from a dedicated external sensor via SNMP. When you poll the sensor, you get back a number, such as 42. This number directly corresponds to the temperature, usually in degrees Celsius. This number may increase or decrease, depending on the environment. In the physical world, a gauge with a needle pointing to a number can be used to display the temperature.

Router throughput, on the other hand, normally comes via SNMP from a byte counter on the router. This number is the total number of bytes received by the router. The counter increments only and never decreases. Depending on the size of the memory buffer used, the counter will eventually overflow and return to 0 and then continue incrementing from there. In the physical world, this counter is similar to the odometer in a car. To get an actual throughput measurement, such as 20kb/s, a delta must be taken between the old and new counter values and divided by the polling interval.

For example, let's say that Nagios measures the octets in an SNMP variable of Router7 every minute. The first time Nagios measures the counter, it reads 653,122, meaning that this interface has received 653,122 bytes. One minute later, when Nagios polls it a second time, the counter reads 654,322. At what rate is data flowing through the interface? First, to find out how many bytes were transferred since the first measurement, subtract 653,122 from 654,322. This gives you 1,200 bytes. So 1,200 bytes are transferred to the router while Nagios is asleep. Because Nagios polls every minute, this means that the router receives 1,200 bytes per minute. Dividing 1,200 by the number of seconds in a minute gives us the average number of bytes per second, which in this example is 20 bytes/second.

Deriving rate information from counters is such a common requirement that RRDTool does this math for you. All you need to do is to specify that the number in question is a counter, and RRDTool automatically performs the requisite arithmetic to return your rate information. Of course, if you have something such as a temperature or CPU load, you don't want this math to take place; in that case, you use a Gauge.

Heartbeat and Step

In addition to the type of data source, RRDTool also needs to know how often you poll it. This number is referred to as the step. The step is specified in seconds, so in the previous example, when Nagios is polling every minute, the step is 60. The step is not specific to the data source; it is specified once for the entire round robin database. So, the RRD expects that at least once every 60 seconds, someone will come along and use the command-line tool to give it more data. But what happens when two updates happen in a 60 second window? Or none at all? In a perfect world, the polling engine would always provide the RRD with the data it needed, exactly when it was expected, but because this is the real world, you need to account for oddities. For this reason, you must also specify a heartbeat for the data source.

The heartbeat determines what happens when there is too much or too little data. Literally, it is the maximum number of seconds that may pass before the data is considered unknown for a polling interval. The heartbeat can provide a buffer of time for late data to arrive, if set greater than the step, or it can enforce multiple data samples per polling interval, if set lower than the step. To continue the example, if the router was unreliable for some reason or Nagios had a lot to do, you could set the heartbeat at twice the polling interval: 120. This would mean that two minutes could pass before the data for that interval was considered unknown. In practice, it's common to use a large heartbeat such as this to account for glitches in the polling engine.

Every step seconds, RRDTool takes the data it receives during the step and calculates a primary data point (PDP) from the available data. If the heartbeat is larger than the step and there is at least one data sample in the heartbeat period, RRDTool uses that data. If there is more than one sample, RRDTool averages them. Figure 7.5 shows how RRDTool reacts to glitches when the heartbeat is larger than the step.

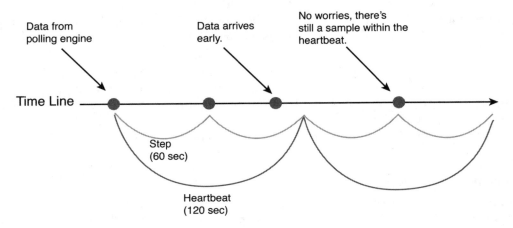

Figure 7.5 Data polling glitches with a large heartbeat.

If the heartbeat is smaller than the step, then multiple data samples per step are required to build the PDP, depending on how much smaller the heartbeat is. When multiple samples are required to create a PDP and enough samples exist, they are averaged into a PDP. Otherwise, the data set for that step is considered unknown. With a small heartbeat, you need more data from the polling engine than would otherwise be necessary to account for glitches. Figure 7.6 depicts a small heartbeat situation.

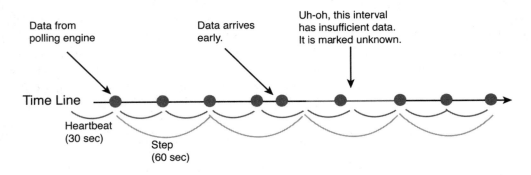

Figure 7.6 Data polling glitches with a small heartbeat.

Min and Max

You may define a minimum and maximum range of acceptable values for your data source, as a sort of sanity check. If the value returned by the polling engine doesn't make sense as defined by the min and max values, the data source value for that polling interval is considered unknown. If you do not want to specify a max or min, you may specify a U (for unknown) instead.

A single round robin database can accept data from any number of data sources. Because the RRD must allocate all the space it needs upfront, the data sources are defined when the RRD is created with the RRDTool create command. This means that you must decide, upfront, how much data you want to keep. Because the data inside the RRD might be useful and disk space is cheap, you should keep as much of it as possible for as long as you think it might be relevant. Keeping data for over a year is quite common in practice. Long-term data is useful for important undertakings, such as convincing management to upgrade hardware.

Round Robin Archives

If you were to poll an SNMP counter on a router every 60 seconds for a year, you would have approximately 525,600 primary data points (PDPs). Storing this much for every metric you monitor, on every server you monitor, quickly adds up to a lot of disk space and can slow down the creation of graphs for large data sets, so RRDTool helps you with its built-in consolidation features. You may tell RRDTool to automatically consolidate your data using a number of different built-in consolidation functions. These functions include AVERAGE, MIN, MAX, and LAST.

For example, if you measure the temperature in your cabinet, and you are interested only in the maximum temperature the cabinet reaches each week, you can tell RRDTool to use the MAX consolidation function on your data every week. RRDTool then creates an archive containing just the highest weekly temperature. This archive of consolidated data is called a Round Robin Archive. You may define as many RRAs as you want, although you must specify at least one. RRAs allow you to consolidate your data in several ways in the same database. This turns out to be a great answer to the space and speed problems associated with keeping large amounts of long-term data.

For example, you might specify three different Round Robin Archives for Router7's octetsIn counter. The first might hold thirty days worth of uncompressed data (43,200 PDPs). The second might store one year's worth of data by using the AVERAGE consolidation function to average the primary data points every 10 minutes. This would keep one data point for every 10 minutes (4,230 averaged PDPs). The third RRA might keep 5 years of data by averaging the data points every 20 minutes (10,800 averaged PDPs).

RRDTool automatically returns the highest resolution data possible. When you graph anything under one month, you get a high-resolution graph because RRDTool returns raw data. Graphing data older than one month, but more recent than one year, yields a lower resolution graph, but more than enough data is available for you to draw the conclusions you need at that scale. Finally, low-resolution graphs are possible on 5 year's worth of data, while the total PDP count remains at only 58,320. That's 5 times as much history, at nearly an order of magnitude less storage space, than if you had kept one year's worth of raw data.

When you consolidate data in a Round Robin Archive from multiple primary data points, it's possible that some of the PDPs may be unknown. So, such as with the heartbeat, you need to tell RRDTool how many of the PDPs can be unknown before the consolidated data point is also considered unknown. This value, called the X-Files Factor, (this does reference the television program *The X-Files*) is a ratio, or if you prefer, a percentage (ranging from 0 to 1) of the PDPs that can be unknown before the consolidated value is also considered unknown.

RRDTool Create Syntax

In concept, it's simple enough. DS definitions describe what and how to store, and RRAs describe how much data to keep and how often to consolidate or compress it. In practice, however, creating RRDs confuses the heck out of people. Listing 7.1 is the literal syntax you might use to create a round robin database to hold a year's worth of data from the inOctets counter on router7.

Listing 7.1 *Creating a single-counter RRD.*

```
rrdtool create Router7_netCounters.rrd \
--start 1157605000 --step 60 \
DS:inOctets:COUNTER:120:0:4294967296 \
RRA:AVERAGE:.5:1:43200 \
RRA:AVERAGE:.5:5:105120 \
RRA:AVERAGE:.5:10:105120
```

Yes, that's a single command, but don't be intimidated; it becomes easier the more you use it, and very few people ever bother to commit the syntax to memory. The RRDTool command works similarly to cvs. There is a single parent command (RRDTool) that operates in a number of modes (create, update, graph, and so on). So the first line puts RRDTool in create mode and tells it to name the RRD you are creating, Router7_netCounters.rrd. The second line gives RRDTool a start date and tells it to expect updates every 60 seconds. The start date is specified in UNIX's seconds-since-epoch style. You may also use an N as a shortcut for now. Specifying a start date is handy if you want to populate an RRD with old data.

In UNIX, epoch is considered to be January 1, 1970 00:00:00 UTC. Tracking seconds in this way makes working with time easier on programmers. You can use the date command to convert into epoch seconds, like this:

```
date +%s
```

You can convert back to a human-readable format, like this:

```
date -d "Jan 1, 1970 UTC + 1157605000 seconds"
```

Because I do a lot of this sort of thing, I find it handy to add the following line to my .bash_profile.

```
export EP='Jan 1, 1970 UTC'
```

That way, I can convert from epoch seconds back to Gregorian, like this:

```
date -d "${EP} + 1157605000 seconds"
```

Getting back to our example, line 3 defines our data source. DS definitions are colon-separated. The syntax is

```
DS:<DS NAME>:<DS TYPE>:<HEARTBEAT>:<MIN>:<MAX>
```

You may name the DS anything you want and, later, you will refer to this name when you graph or export data from the RRD. The DS TYPE is either COUNTER or GAUGE, as already discussed. The heartbeat, minimum, and maximum values should all be self-explanatory by now. I've named the data source inOctets and specified it as a counter. The heartbeat is twice the size of the step, specified in seconds. This means that the polling engine can be late by an entire step before you consider the data for the polling interval unknown.

When you work with counters, it's good form to set minimum and maximum values. These help RRDTool to do some internal sanity checking, thereby ensuring your hard-won data is accurately stored and depicted. My SNMP client informed me that my inOctets counter is of type 32-bit INT, so in this example, I set the minimum value to 0 and the maximum to 4,294,967,295 ($2^{32}-1$). For gauges, no math needs to be done, so if I were working with a gauge metric, I would have specified U:U.

Even if your gauge has a minimum or maximum value, I recommend that you specify U:U, so that the data is stored as it was collected. If you specify minimum/maximum for gauges, you are making a dangerous assumption about your data, namely that it actually behaves the way you expect it should. You could lose interesting data this way. Mucking about with the data during import is bad mojo. You can perform math on the data and enforce limits later during the graphing phase. To paraphrase Kenny Rodgers, there'll be time enough for mucking when the data's stored.

In line 4, you begin to specify Round Robin Archives. These tell RRDTool how much data you want stored and how you would like it to be consolidated. The syntax is

```
RRA:<consolidation function>:<x-files factor>:<PDPs>:<CDP's>
```

The consolidation function will be one of MIN, MAX, LAST, or AVERAGE. The subject of consolidation functions seems to cause a lot of confusion. This is unfortunate and probably because they are more difficult to describe than they are to understand. Simply put, the job of a consolidation function is to take a bunch of data points and to make them into a single primary data point. Each CF accomplishes this task in a slightly different but straightforward manner. Given a group of data points to consolidate, the MIN CF returns the smallest data point, the MAX CF returns the largest data point, the LAST CF returns the most recent data point, and the AVERAGE CF returns the average of all the data points.

For example, let's say I want to consolidate 10 minutes of data down to a single PDP and I am polling the data every two minutes. This means I will have 5 total data points, such as 4,2,12,4,8. Given these 5 points, MIN would return 2, MAX would return 12, LAST would return 8, and AVERAGE would return 6.

As discussed earlier, the X-Files Factor is the number of PDPs that can be unknown before the consolidation function also returns unknown. Most people use .5 (50%) for this, but I like to go a bit higher, such as .8. At least in the context of systems monitoring, overly-averaged data is better than no data at all.

In the RRDTool documentation, the next arguments—the ones I refer to as PDPs and CDPs—are called steps and rows. I hate to possibly cause confusion by calling them something else, but in my experience, most people don't find these names helpful or descriptive, so forgive me for making up my own. The PDPs (or steps) argument defines how many primary data points make up a single consolidated data point. A 10 here consolidates 10 PDPs into a single value, using whichever consolidation function you specify. The CDPs (or rows) argument specifies how many of these newly created consolidated data points to keep.

These two numbers, when combined with the step, work out to the total length of time your data stays in the RRD before it is overwritten. For example, the step in the example is 1 minute, so a PDP value of 10 consolidates 10 minutes' worth of data. Therefore, keeping 5 of these consolidated data points gets you 50 minutes' worth of data. A handy formula for deriving the number of days from these values is

```
(step*PDPs*CDP's)/86400 = x days
```

That's the number of PDPs to consolidate times the number of CDPs to keep times the step, all over the number of seconds in a day. In practice, the polling engine usually dictates the step for you, and you usually know how much you want to consolidate and how many days you want to keep the data. In other words, most people need a formula for deriving the number of CDPs to keep. You can derive this from the last formula by solving for CDPs. This gets you

```
(86400*days)/(step*PDPs)=CDPs
```

In Listing 7.1, I create three RRAs. The first effectively keeps raw data for one month. (The PDPs value of 1 says that I want to average one PDP into a CDP. The average of a single value is the value over one, so nothing is really consolidated.) I keep 43,200 of these points, so using the formula, (1*60*43200)/86400=30 days. Using the first formula, you can easily see what the other two RRAs do. The second consolidates the data into 5-minute chunks and keeps 1 year's worth. The third consolidates even more, keeping 2 years of data consolidated into 10-minute chunks. For homework, create an RRA for Listing 7.1 that keeps 5 years' worth of 1-hour chunks. (This is the type of problem you'll be solving when you work with RRDTool. The second formula makes this problem easy.)

It's possible to store as many data sources as you want in a single round robin database, but new ones can't be added post-creation (easily). In Listing 7.2, I add an additional counter DS for out Octets, so you can track both the bytes coming in and going out of your router in the same RRD.

Listing 7.2 *Creating a multi-counter RRD.*

```
rrdtool create Router7_netCounters.rrd \
--start 1157605000 --step 60 \
DS:inOctets:COUNTER:120:0:4294967296 \
DS:outOctets:COUNTER:180:0:4294967296 \
RRA:AVERAGE:.5:1:43200 \
RRA:AVERAGE:.5:5:105120 \
RRA:AVERAGE:.5:10:105120
```

The step in Listing 7.2 applies to both data sources, meaning that each data source you store in a round robin database must have the same polling interval. However, because the heartbeat is specified in the data source definition, each DS may have a different heartbeat. In Listing 7.1, I specified 180 for outOctets's heartbeat. The RRAs also apply to all data sources. They will consolidate data for each of the data sources, so each data source you add to an RRD must be stored in the same manner.

When you create an RRD, updating it is very simple. Just call RRDTool in update mode, with a filename, date stamp, and colon-separated values. RRDTool derives which values go with which data sources by matching them up in the order they were specified during creation. For example

```
rrdtool update netCounters.rrd N:42:15842
```

The previous updates the netCounters RRD with the current time and a value of 42 for inOctets and a value of 15,842 for outOctets.

Because I have dealt with RRDTool for a number of years, I tend to be shy about putting a lot of data sources in a single RRD. There are two main reasons for this. The first is that I always eventually forget what data is inside an RRD. Although it's easy to derive what's stored inside an RRD by using RRDTool in fetch mode, my problem is that I forget I ever stored the data in the first place, so when I'm looking for data of type X, I'll take a cursory glance at the filenames and end up creating a new, redundant RRD with the data I want.

The second reason is that new DSs sometimes pop up that should go in an existing RRD. For example, if you want to track the utilization of various partitions on your hard drives, you could create a single RRD called disks.rrd with a DS for each partition. Then a year later, when /var runs out of space and you add a new disk and mount it to /var, the RRD will have to be expanded to include an additional DS for the new partition. Adding DSs to an existing RRD is possible, but not fun.

My advice is to create single-DS RRDs with especially descriptive filenames. The filename of the RRD should, at a minimum, contain the name of the server it refers to. If you keep single-DS RRDs, it's also possible to put the name of the DS in the filename, which makes things especially easy if you're a blockhead like me. For example, I can look at a file called router7_inOctets.rrd and know exactly what I can get and how. The various RRDTool scripts are good at insulating you from this sort of thing, which is nice. Finding good scripts can be a problem, however, as you'll see in the next section.

Data Collection and Polling

In the early paragraphs of section, "Foundations, MRTG, and RRDTool," I said that there were three pieces to the visualization puzzle: polling engines, data storage back-ends, and graphing user interfaces. To get the most out of the monitoring system, you want to optimize each of these pieces for flexibility, so you can use any piece of data you may have collected however you want. Because you don't know upfront how you may want to visualize the data, keeping things flexible means that every metric from every server can be made available to any program that might want to consume it.

You have chosen Nagios for your polling engine and RRDTool for your storage engine. Now that you have a handle on how RRDTool works, you can talk about the middle ground between collecting your data and storing it. There are quite a few glue layers to tie RRD-Tool to Nagios, and all of them automatically create the RRDs for you, so in practice, many administrators never need to deal with manual RRD creation.

If nothing else, I hope the section impressed upon you the critical importance of RRAs to your data visualization undertaking. Simply put, if your glue layer doesn't let you define the Round Robin Archives, you can't control how much data you keep, or for how long. I make this point because I'm not aware of a Nagios-RRDTool glue layer that allows you to specify custom RRAs in a configuration file. This is a big problem. You have a super-flexible polling engine and a perfect data storage back-end for your task, but the flexibility of both of them could be severely limited by the capabilities of the glue layer you put between them.

Shopping for Glue

I'm not sure why this RRA problem exists. Either end-user definable RRAs are a difficult hack to pull off (I haven't tried, but it doesn't seem like they would be difficult) or the people coding the various glue libraries think it's more important to insulate you from the inner workings of RRDTool than to provide you the flexibility to define your own RRAs.

The authors are in the business of insulating you from the inner workings of RRDTool, so this is an understandable oversight, but one that makes your task more difficult. You need to choose a glue layer that meets your needs and won't become a liability later. Pick one written in a language you understand so that you can change things, such as the RRAs, in code if you need to or at a minimum, be sure you can, at least, figure out what the RRAs are, so you can plan accordingly.

Another bad habit of the polling and collection scripts is doing too much. Most of the scripts out there that collect data from Nagios and store it in RRDs also contain Web interfaces that actually draw graphs from the data, as well. In concept, it seems like a good idea, but in my experience, scripts that do both tend to lock you in by doing things such as storing the data a certain way because that's what their user interface expects. You should pick a polling engine glue layer that is good at polling and can be used separately from its user interface. Ideally, you should pick one with the polling code and graphing code in separate files.

Some of the glue layers are definition-happy. For example, storing data from the inOctets counter of router6 and router7 requires a separate definition for each host. The point of using the glue layer in the first place is to make things easier. You shouldn't need to remember to reconfigure it when you add new hosts. Choose glue that has services-based configurations. You should only have to define what the output from a particular service check looks like, and the glue code should auto-detect new hosts using that service check.

Finally, the fancier a glue library is, the further you should stay away from it. For your purposes, you want a very small, lightweight wrapper around RRDTool so that the glue layer doesn't limit how much you can store by virtue of it being heavy and slow. Things such as GUI configuration tools, Java, and database back-ends are red flags.

NagiosGraph

I've used a few of the more promising glue libraries from Nagios Exchange over the years, and I've finally settled on a Perl script called Nagios Graph. Simply put, I use Nagios Graph because it is the closest thing to what I would write if I were going to reinvent the wheel. NG is a lightweight Perl script that has many of the beneficial traits previously mentioned.

It comes with two scripts, one for data collection and RRD storage and one for drawing HTML pages with graphs, so you can use just the polling/storage script if you want (which I do). NG uses straight Perl regular expression syntax to define service output and auto-detects new hosts. Alas, you cannot define RRAs in a configuration file, but a simple grep RRA of the insert.pl program (NG's data collection script) yields the output in Listing 7.3.

Listing 7.3 *Modifying RRAs in Nagios Graph.*

```
$ds .= " RRA:AVERAGE:0.5:1:600";
$ds .= " RRA:AVERAGE:0.5:6:700";
$ds .= " RRA:AVERAGE:0.5:24:775";
$ds .= " RRA:AVERAGE:0.5:288:797";
```

It's not a text configuration file, but it's close enough. Even if you aren't familiar with Perl, you can modify those RRAs to get what you want. NagiosGraph is equally easy to install. There are two configuration files, one that sets up NG's defaults and one that maps the text parsed from Nagios via regular expressions into RRD variables. Simply copy the configuration files and insert.pl script to locations that make sense for you. Then edit insert. pl to point to the configuration files and change the configurations according to your tastes. Most people should only need to change the rrddir, which is the directory into which you want insert.pl to put its newly created RRDs. I talk more about the map file in a moment.

Nagios graph uses the RRDTool default step of 300 seconds (5 minutes) and allows you to specify the heartbeat in its configuration file. Four RRAs are created by default, as you can see in Listing 7.3. The default RRDs are a bit conservative, in my opinion. Two days of raw data are kept and then the average CF is applied to store 14 days of 30-minute chunks, 64 days of two-hour chunks, and two years of one-day chunks.

Nagios sends output and performance data to NG by way of the process_performance_ data directive in the nagios.cfg file. This feature is designed to provide performance metrics to external programs. First, enable it by setting process_performance_data to 1 in the nagios. cfg and then add the following line, which configures a global performance data handler.

```
service_perfdata_command=process-service-perfdata
```

Now, when Nagios gets data from a plugin, it executes the process-service-perfdata command. Listing 7.4 contains process-service-perfdata command definition, which belongs in your commands.cfg or misccommands.cfg. It is this command that effectively ties Nagios to NG.

Listing 7.4 *The process-service-perfdata command for use with NG.*

```
define command{
        command_name    process-service-perfdata
        command_line  /usr/bin/insert.pl \
 "$LASTSERVICECHECK$||$HOSTNAME$||$SERVICEDESC$||\
        $SERVICEOUTPUT$||$SERVICEPERFDATA$"
```

NG's map file contains definitions in Perl regular expression syntax. Lines passed from Nagios to NG's insert.pl script that match the regular expressions in the map file are parsed and made into RRDs. If no RRD for a particular service exists, NG creates it; otherwise, NG updates the existing RRD. The map file may be the thing I like best about NG. If you are adept at Perl, the flexibility inherent in this definition style is great. Listing 7.5 is a simple definition for the check_ping process. It matches the output of the check_ping plugin and extracts the round-trip time and loss percentage, adding them both to a single RRD.

Listing 7.5 *NG's check_ping definition.*

```
#   output:PING OK - Packet loss = 0%, RTA = 0.00 ms
/output:PING.*?(\d+)%.+?([.\d]+)\sms/
and push @s, [ ping,
                [ losspct, GAUGE, $1         ],
                [ rta,     GAUGE, $2/1000 ] ];
```

This is straightforward Perl. The object is to build an aoa, or array of arrays. The first value in the top level array is the name of the service. This name, along with the Nagios hostname and service description, will be used in the filename of the RRD. The second and third values in the array are themselves arrays, which house the names, data types, and values of the DS's that populate your RRD.

If you are familiar with regular expressions, you should have no problem setting up new services by simply copying the existing ones. Because the map file is Perl, it gives you the flexibility to accomplish some pretty neat stuff, programmatically, if you have some Perl chops. For example, Listing 7.6 is my NG disk definition. The problem with disk is that various boxes have different numbers of partitions, so a single static regular expression won't capture them all. The definition in Listing 7.6 dynamically detects partitions, creating a new DS for each, so it is a single definition that works with any box using check_disk.

Listing 7.6 *A check_disk definition for NG.*

```
/perfdata:\/=\d+MB;/ and do {
  my @_perf = /(\/\w*)=(\d+)MB;(\d+);\d+;\d+;\d+/g;
  my @_s;
  my $_sref=\@_s;
  $_s[0]='disk';
  while ( my($_name,$_used,$_total) = splice @_perf,0,3 ) {
    my $_free=$_total-$_used;
    if($_name=~/^\/$/){
      $_name=~s/\//disk_root/;
    }else{
      $_name=~s/\//disk_/;
    }
    push @_s,  [ ${_name}."_total", GAUGE, $_total*1024**2  ],
               [ ${_name}."_used",  GAUGE, $_used*1024**2   ],
               [ ${_name}."_free",  GAUGE, $_free*1024**2   ] ;
  }
    $s[0]=$_sref;
};
```

With the configuration files and insert.pl in place and Nagios configured accordingly, RRDs should begin appearing in your rrddir. Because the map file comes with many preconfigured definitions, you'll probably have RRDs for all sorts of metrics without any map file configuration whatsoever. If you have trouble, check out the debugging options in the configuration file.

Nagios Graph is the solution I prefer at the moment, but it may not be your cup of tea (if you do like it, you can get it from http://nagiosgraph.sourceforge.net/), so be sure to check out Nagios Exchange for something that might suit your environment better. I hope the tips I've provided help you narrow the field.

Front-Ends and Dashboards

Now that you have your data collection and storage squared away, you can busy yourself with graphing it. Like polling and storage engines, you want to optimize your front-end for flexibility. You want to draw any combination of metrics in any RRD, and you don't want to lose any of RRDTools functionality along the way. It would also be nice if you didn't have to do a large amount of clicking through Web interfaces to configure things. Looking around at front-end tools (check out www.rrdworld.com), you will find many of the same problems you had with data collection and polling engines. Most of the graphing front-ends try to do too much or are overly complex, both of which breed inflexibility.

RRDTool Graph Mode

Before you can get into what to look for in a graphing front-end, you need to understand a bit about RRDTools graphing mode. Like create and update, RRDTool has a special mode for drawing graphs from the data stored in an RRD. I've sometimes quipped that RRDTool graph is an existence proof of the old adage, "A picture is worth a thousand words," because RRDTools graph mode is, by far, the most complex and confusing aspect of the toolset, possessing a dizzying array of options to specify everything from the height and width of a graph to its background and foreground colors.

Though graph commands are technically one-liners, it's not uncommon for them to span 15 to 20 lines. Most appear to be shell scripts. A good front-end makes the complicated syntax moot, but to get everything you can out of your FE, you need to quickly review a few important concepts, including DEFs and CDEFs, and brush up on your reverse polish notation.

DEFs are the core definitions in graph mode; they tell RRDTool what to graph. A DEF is made up of the filename of the RRD, a DS within that RRD, and a consolidation function for the DS. A DEF refers to one, and only one, Data Source. You may specify any number of DEFs in a graph command. For example

```
DEF:foo=/usr/nagios/rrd/umbra_load:5min:AVERAGE
```

The DEF is given a name, such as a variable; in this case, foo. The foo DEF refers to the 5-minute Data Source in the /usr/nagios/rrd/umbra_load RRD. The average keyword specifies that you want the data from RRAs that use the AVERAGE consolidation function (if you have more than one type).

This DEF can now be graphed with a graph element definition. There are several types of graph elements; the most commonly used ones are AREA and LINE. The LINE graphs look like the graphs in Figures 7.1 through 7.3. AREA graphs look like the graph in Figure 7.7.

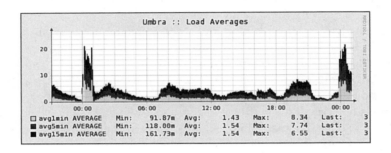

Figure 7.7 Area graph with three data sources.

The only difference between a LINE and an AREA definition is the word LINE or AREA. Lines may be drawn in three thickness levels. LINE1 is the thinnest and LINE3 the thickest. The graphic element definition looks like this:

```
AREA:foo#0000FF:avg5min
```

In this example, foo refers to the DEF that you specified earlier. Following the variable name foo is an RBG Hex color code and then a legend label. The combination of the DEF with the graphical element definition serves to tell RRDTool what and how to graph. Interesting things can be done, however, when CDEFs enter the picture.

A CDEF is a variable, such as a DEF, but instead of being derived directly from a DS in an existing RRD, the CDEF is derived by performing math on one or more DEFs. This real-time number crunching works transparently for the entire time-series and is handy. As an example, check out Figure 7.8, which represents the network throughput of a Web server for the last 18 hours or so.

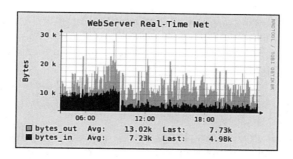

Figure 7.8 A somewhat cluttered network throughput graph.

As you can see, two data sources, one for bytes in and one for bytes out. Although the graph is readable, it has a cluttered appearance, and it's hard to visually correlate the relationship between in and out. If you multiply the bytes_in data source by negative one, however, shown in Figure 7.9, the two counters appear on opposite sides of the Xaxis, making relationships easier to spot.

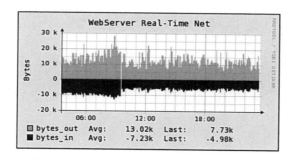

Figure 7.9 Multiplying in_bytes by negative one.

The CDEF makes this possible by creating a virtual DEF derived from operations on values from real DEFs. Listing 7.7 shows the relevant definitions in the graph mode command I used to draw the graph in Figure 7.9.

Listing 7.7 *CDEF syntax.*

```
DEF:out=/usr/nagios/rrd/webServer_bytes_out.rrd:sum:AVERAGE \
DEF:in=/usr/nagios/rrd/webServer_bytes_in.rrd:sum:AVERAGE \
CDEF:negIn=in,-1,* \
AREA:out#FFA500:butes_out \
AREA:negIn#0000FF:bytes_in  \
```

As you can see, the negIn CDEF is a result of a math operation on the in DEF, but the expression (in,-1,*) might look odd to you, unless you've owned a fancy HP Calculator or are otherwise familiar with Reverse Polish Notation. For the uninitiated, I'll provide a brief summary. Feel free to skip ahead if you are already familiar with RPN.

RPN

Traditional mathematical expressions rely on operator precedence to determine the order of operations. You may remember this from grade school as PEMDAS: Parenthesis, Exponent, Multiply, Divide, Add, and Subtract. For example

```
4+5*2
```

The product is 14. First, 5 is multiplied to 2, and then 4 is added. This is because the operator precedence specifies that multiplication must happen before addition. If you want to multiply 2 to the sum of 4 and 5, you must override the operator precedence with parentheses, like this:

```
(4+5)*2
```

In RPN, operator precedence is not necessary because the quantities and operators are specified in the order they are needed. For example, to specify that 5 should be multiplied to 2 in RPN, use

```
5,2,*
```

RPN expressions are never ambiguous about order of operations. They read from left to right, like English, and can be thought of in terms of a horizontal stack. Values are pushed onto the stack and popped off as needed. First, you push a 5 onto the stack, then a 2, and then a multiplication operator. Every time RPN gets a pair of quantities onto the 2 with an operator, it pops them off in order and performs the equation, saving the product back onto the top of the stack. To specify that 2 should be multiplied to the sum of 5 and 4, you could say

```
5,4,+,2,*
```

Because RPN reads left to right, there is no chance that the multiplication could happen first. Here, 5, 4, and + are popped off the stack and evaluated. The sum of 5 and 4 is then pushed back onto the top of the stack. At this point, you can imagine the stack looking like

```
9,2,*
```

Now, 9, 2, and + are popped off the stack and evaluated, returning 18. RPN never evaluates more than 2 quantities at once, so if you prefer, you may stack up all of your quantities and then list out all of your operators. For example, another way to write the previous equation is

```
5,4,2,+,*
```

Here, RPN pops 5 and 4, and then, seeing that the next object in the stack is a quantity instead of an operator, skips over 2 and looks for the next available operator, which is a +. The 5 and 4 are then added, and the sum is pushed back on the top of the stack. From there, execution continues in the same manner as in the last example. Some people find stacking quantities and operators such as this easier to comprehend, especially when the expressions get large.

Now that you know what RPN is all about, take another look at the CDEF in Listing 7.7.

```
CDEF:negIn=in,-1,*
```

Applying what you know about RPN, it's easy to see that you are creating a CDEF called 'negIn, which is the product of the values of in and −1. You may create a CDEF from any number of operations on any number of variables that have been defined. Look at a more complicated CDEF example to give you a feel for what's possible.

Listing 7.8 contains the definitions from a disk utilization graph. The RRDs track the disk metrics megabytes total and megabytes used. Use data from four different Web servers. Graphing the raw data would yield eight lines, one line for Total Megabytes and one line for Used Megabytes, for each of the four Web servers.

In this example, you want to draw a graph for a presentation to management. This graph should depict the month-long history of a single, easily understandable number that quantifies the overall disk utilization on all four Web servers. The best way to show a single disk metric across multiple machines is to show the average disk utilization as a percentage. This puts all the servers on the same scale, regardless of the size of their disks. To do this, you must first convert the raw utilization metrics on each server from megabytes to percentages; then you can average the percentages into a single number. Listing 7.8 shows the RRDTool syntax to accomplish this.

Listing 7.8 *CDEFs for data summarization.*

```
DEF:w1t=/usr/nagios/rrd/web1_disk.rrd:root_total:AVERAGE \
DEF:w1u=/usr/nagios/rrd/web1_disk.rrd:root_used:AVERAGE \
DEF:w2t=/usr/nagios/rrd/web2_disk.rrd:root_total:AVERAGE \
DEF:w2u=/usr/nagios/rrd/web2_disk.rrd:root_used:AVERAGE \
DEF:w3t=/usr/nagios/rrd/web3_disk.rrd:root_total:AVERAGE \
DEF:w3u=/usr/nagios/rrd/web3_disk.rrd:root_used:AVERAGE \
DEF:w4t=/usr/nagios/rrd/web4_disk.rrd:root_total:AVERAGE \
DEF:w4u=/usr/nagios/rrd/web4_disk.rrd:root_used:AVERAGE \
CDEF:pct1=w1u,w1t,/,100,* \
CDEF:pct2=w2u,w2t,/,100,* \
CDEF:pct3=w3u,w3t,/,100,* \
CDEF:pct4=w4u,w4t,/,100,* \
CDEF:M=pct1,pct2,+,pct3,+,pct4,+,4,/ \
```

First, DEFs are created for the requisite metrics on each server. Next, proceed to create a utilization percentage for each server. This is done in RPN by dividing the amount of used space by the amount of total space and multiplying the result by 100, like this:

```
CDEF:pct1=w1u,w1t,/,100,*
```

After you have a utilization percentage for each server, you average the percentages into a single number by adding them up and dividing the result by 4 (the number of servers).

```
CDEF:M=pct1,pct2,+,pct3,+,pct4,+,4,/
```

Note that the percentage variables this CDEF operates on are CDEFs, so you can perform math on CDEF values just like you can on DEFs. If you prefer, you could use value/operator stacking to make this last CDEF a bit neater, like this:

```
CDEF:M=pct1,pct2,pct3,pct4,4,+,+,+,/
```

Shopping for Front-Ends

Because CDEF functionality is so powerful, choosing a graphing engine with fine-grained control over the DEFs and CDEFs is of the utmost importance. There are a lot of graphing front-ends to choose from, and they are not all created equal. Here are some tips that might help you narrow the field.

Look for tools that use configuration templates and filters. With a lot of metrics on a lot of servers, it's a big timesaver to automate some of the configuration with templates or at least to narrow the available options with filters. If the front-end saves its data in text files, all the better; this implies that you can back-end process the creation of some objects, bypassing the user interface altogether. Solutions that do this tend to be written in straight CGI instead of Web application languages, such as PHP, which brings me to my next point....

Look for tools that use straight CGI over tools written in Web application languages, such as PHP. The PHP applications usually have a more polished look, but the CGI applications tend to be more flexible. Linking is critical; you want to link directly to specific graphs or use wget or curl for email reports and custom dashboards. If you choose a PHP application, be sure it can generate reusable links to specific graphs. Tools that generate static graphs every so often with random, unique names should be avoided. Additionally, CGI applications are usually easier to install.

Look for tools that tell you how they created the graph. RRDTools graph mode is tough on administrators who need to do manual graph creation and processing. But many front-ends give you the literal syntax they used to create any graph. This can save you a lot of time.

Beware of graphing tools that do their own polling because they tend to be inflexible. Some assume that you are using their polling engine and, therefore, that the data was stored in a certain way. Many cannot graph metrics that aren't configured for polling, as well. Most of them pay too much attention to either polling or graphing and suffer needless hindrances as a result.

By far the most popular tool in this genre is Cacti (www.cacti.net), so I would be remiss in not mentioning it. Cacti is a great tool. It is written in PHP, is highly configurable, and has a very polished user interface. (I'm especially fond of its zoom feature, which allows you to click-drag to select a portion of a graph to zoom into.) I suspect its user interface has a lot to do with its widespread success. Cacti can be thought of as an MRTG replacement. It does everything from polling the data to storing and graphing it. This shouldn't necessarily preclude its use in your environment, because it remains very flexible in its data handling, and the user interface really does make up for any drawbacks it may have. I won't be covering Cacti in this book because it's much more than an RRDTool front-end, but I highly recommend that you take a look.

drraw

The tool I like the best for Web-based, RRDTool-backed data display is drraw (http://web.taranis.org/drraw/). drraw is the only RRDTool front-end I've found that specializes in data display. In fact, the author clearly states that he feels it is a design flaw for a graphing engine to do things like collection and polling, and I couldn't agree with him more.

drraw is composed of a configuration file and a CGI script written in Perl. It installs in a matter of minutes. Simply copy drraw to your CGI directory and edit it to point it at its configuration file. The only thing you need to change in the configuration file is datadirs, which is a hash of directories where RRDs may be found. There is a lot to configure if you want to customize drraw's look and feel for your site. You can also specify things, such as access rights to various capabilities such as viewing, creating, and deleting graphs.

drraw gets everything right. It is a lightweight wrapper around RRDTool graph, providing all the functionality in a quick, easy-to-use package. Features, such as regular expression-enabled filters, templates, and graph cloning, save your wrists. Additionally, drraw does some very sysadmin-friendly things, such as storing saved configurations as text files, making possible programmatic creation of graphs and dashboards. It also provides a change log so you can see who changed what and when.

Figure 7.10 shows drraw's home page on one of the monitoring systems at my office. You may create graphs by clicking "Create a new graph" or define dashboards by clicking "Define a new dashboard." drraw dashboards are collections of graphs drawn in a user-defined way. For example, you can suppress the graph legends in a dashboard or specify alternative sizes for the graphs.

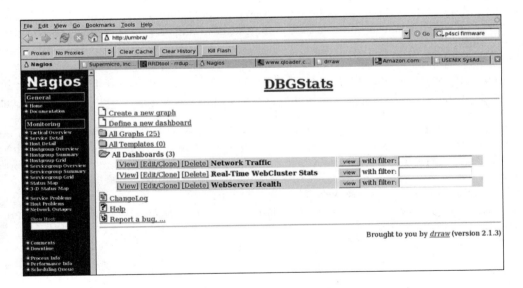

Figure 7.10 drraw's home page.

It's not the prettiest interface out of the box, but just about everything related to aesthetics can be modified in the configuration file. This includes the icons, headers, and footers. You may even specify a custom style sheet. Figure 7.11 is a screenshot of my Network Traffic dashboard.

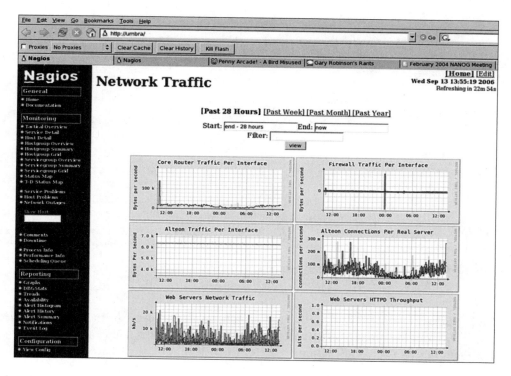

Figure 7.11 A drraw dashboard.

Finally, Figure 7.12 is a screenshot of the drraw data store configuration that was used to create the consolidated disk example in Listing 7.8. You may use regular expression searches to specify RRDs and DSs for use in your graphs. Note the RRA CDEF column. This is where you can type in RPN expressions to create CDEFs.

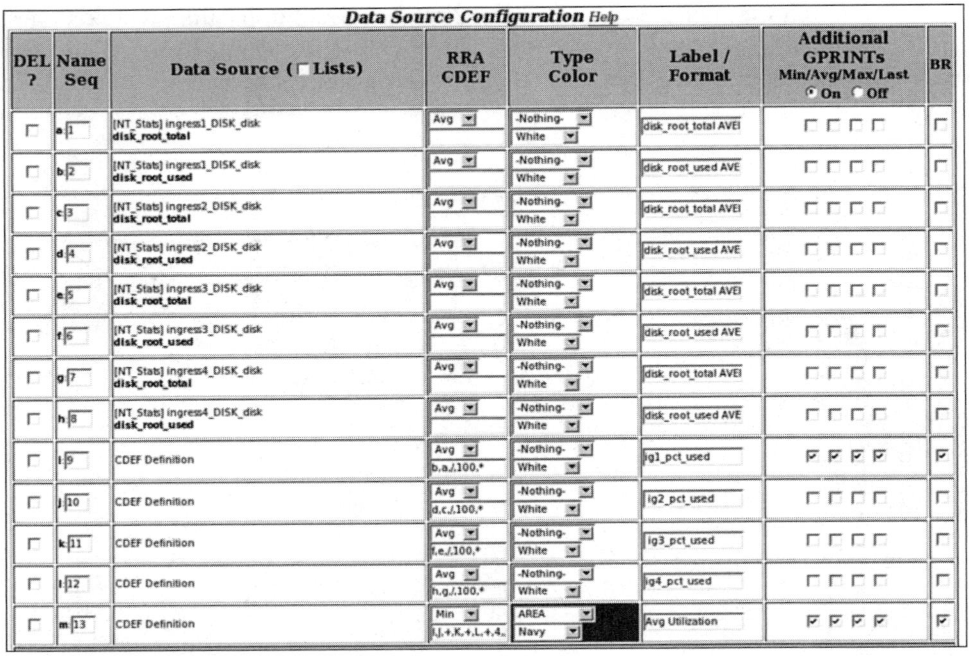

Data Source Configuration Help

DEL ?	Name Seq	Data Source (☐ Lists)	RRA CDEF	Type Color	Label / Format	Additional GPRINTs Min/Avg/Max/Last (◉ On ○ Off)	BR
☐	a 1	[NT_Stats] ingress1_DISK_disk **disk_root_total**	Avg	-Nothing- White	disk_root_total AVEI	☐ ☐ ☐ ☐	☐
☐	b 2	[NT_Stats] ingress1_DISK_disk **disk_root_used**	Avg	-Nothing- White	disk_root_used AVE	☐ ☐ ☐ ☐	☐
☐	c 3	[NT_Stats] ingress2_DISK_disk **disk_root_total**	Avg	-Nothing- White	disk_root_total AVEI	☐ ☐ ☐ ☐	☐
☐	d 4	[NT_Stats] ingress2_DISK_disk **disk_root_used**	Avg	-Nothing- White	disk_root_used AVE	☐ ☐ ☐ ☐	☐
☐	e 5	[NT_Stats] ingress3_DISK_disk **disk_root_total**	Avg	-Nothing- White	disk_root_total AVEI	☐ ☐ ☐ ☐	☐
☐	f 6	[NT_Stats] ingress3_DISK_disk **disk_root_used**	Avg	-Nothing- White	disk_root_used AVE	☐ ☐ ☐ ☐	☐
☐	g 7	[NT_Stats] ingress4_DISK_disk **disk_root_total**	Avg	-Nothing- White	disk_root_total AVEI	☐ ☐ ☐ ☐	☐
☐	h 8	[NT_Stats] ingress4_DISK_disk **disk_root_used**	Avg	-Nothing- White	disk_root_used AVE	☐ ☐ ☐ ☐	☐
☐	i 9	CDEF Definition	Avg b,a,/,100,*	-Nothing- White	ig1_pct_used	☑ ☑ ☑ ☑	☑
☐	j 10	CDEF Definition	Avg d,c,/,100,*	-Nothing- White	ig2_pct_used	☐ ☐ ☐ ☐	☐
☐	k 11	CDEF Definition	Avg f,e,/,100,*	-Nothing- White	ig3_pct_used	☐ ☐ ☐ ☐	☐
☐	l 12	CDEF Definition	Avg h,g,/,100,*	-Nothing- White	ig4_pct_used	☐ ☐ ☐ ☐	☐
☐	m 13	CDEF Definition	Min I,J,+,K,+,L,+,4,.	AREA Navy	Avg Utilization	☑ ☑ ☑ ☑	☑

Figure 7.12 The drraw CDEF configuration interface.

With Nagios, NG, RRDTool, and drraw, you have all the pieces of the puzzle you need to create great-looking time-series visualization. Now take a look at some other ways to visually represent information and examine some of the reasons you might need to do so.

Management Interfaces

In systems monitoring circles, terms such as Dashboard and Management Interface are thrown around quite a bit, and they mean vastly different things to different people. This section is not here to strictly define what a management interface is or even to teach you how to build one, but it should help you toward building what you need, using some interesting tools.

Time-series graphs and the Nagios Web interface are sufficient to provide systems administrators the visibility they need, in my experience, but the needs of the organization do not necessarily end with those of its sysadmin. For this reason, the data consumer should dictate the definition of the management interface, be it anything from an emailed report to an alternative Web interface written in (gasp) Flash. Hopefully, this section will point you toward some tools that will be useful to you in meeting the specialized needs of your data consumers.

Know What You're Doing

Before you start designing custom interfaces and dashboards, I would highly recommend you read up on what good data visualization is and especially what it isn't. There are many ways to get it wrong and only a few to get it right. I highly recommend Edward Tufte's book, *The Visual Display of Quantitative Information*. I'll give you a few tips to get you started, but I'm certainly no expert, so be sure to do your homework before you get started.

First, avoid pie charts. Although adored by marketing folks, pie charts are awful for data visualization for several reasons. Primary among these is that humans are notoriously bad at interpreting angles. (3D effects on pie charts only make things worse.) Given two similar values in a pie chart, most people won't register the difference unless you point it out to them or publish values in the legend labels. Secondly, pie charts have no frame of reference, which means that people can glean only the actual value each slice represents by reading it in a label. Finally, pie charts have no obvious beginning or end, which makes it difficult for people to know where to focus their attention.

Anything you can visualize with a pie chart is better visualized with a bar or point chart. These provide a frame of reference on two axes and communicate data more effectively to humans, in general. If you absolutely have to use a pie chart, do not compare more than a few values and be sure to colorize in such a way that the slices have a high contrast.

Bar charts are especially good at depicting categorical information, so if you have information that fits nicely into categories, use a bar chart and arrange the data such that the largest values are furthest to the left. Point charts or line charts are better for depicting time-series data. The time-series data graphed in Figures 7.13 and 7.14 give a good example of how much clearer point graphs are when information is depicted as a function of time.

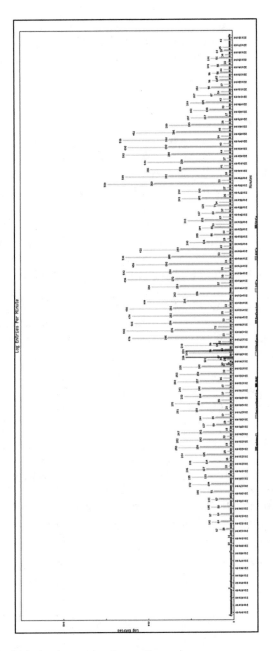

Figure 7.13 Bar charts don't depict time-series data well.

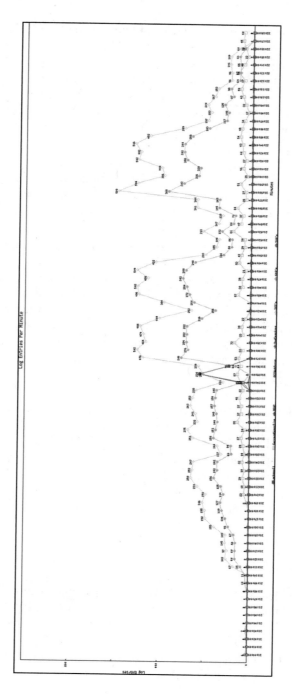

Figure 7.14 Point charts are much cleaner when time is involved.

Try to think about your graphics in terms of maximizing for information per pixel. You know you are doing things correctly if you are packing large amounts of data into small areas. Fancy effects, such as 3D, should be avoided for this reason. 3D effects usually take up more space and rarely add useful information. They also have a habit of obfuscating the useful information that remains. Silly widgets, such as thermometers, speedometers, or any other '"ometers," should be avoided for the same reason. These things take up a lot of space to communicate a single value.

You should attempt to keep your graphs as uncluttered as possible, so that they stand on their own without requiring extra explanation. If the graphs are large and there is space, label the individual points for clarity. Axis labels should convey the units they express, and titles should be carefully thought out, short, and descriptive.

Of course, all of this highbrow advice goes out the window when your marching orders are to provide whiz-bang displays with little or no substance. Many a well-built monitoring system has been scrapped in favor of a kludgy black box with neat-o graphics that impressed the execs. Because the well-being of your hard-won monitoring solution may one day rest on your ability to come up with something other than line graphs, my last piece of advice to you is not to be a visualization elitist. Don't be afraid to throw a speedometer or two around, if for no other reason than to prove you can. By all means, guide and educate the people who will use the dashboard, but always remember that the data consumer defines the management interface.

Some of the tools that follow can provide the eye-candy so coveted by the upper echelons, but all of them (well, most of them) can also be used to create interesting visual displays that are very useful in a pragmatic sense. The art, or science, of data visualization is growing very quickly, especially in the area of IT security, where visualization may be the only hope for good real-time, enterprise wide event correlation in the absence of true AI. The tools referenced herein should not be considered a comprehensive list. They represent only the tip of the iceberg and, by the time you read this, chances are the iceberg will have grown considerably.

RRDTool Fetch Mode

Just when you thought you were done with RRDTool, you must make one last foray. Because much of the historical data you need to visualize resides in your RRDs, you need a way to query and extract it. RRDTool, in fetch mode, can give you raw data dumps for a given period of time. To use it, provide RRDTool the name of the RRD, the CF you are interested in, and the time range in epoch seconds. For example, to get the last 10 minutes of data from the server1_load.rrd, you could type

```
rrdtool fetch server1_load.rrd AVERAGE -s `date -d "10 minutes ago" +%s`
  -e N
```

Listing 7.9 contains the output from this fetch command. As you can see, the data from fetch mode requires some processing.

Listing 7.9 *Output from RRDTool fetch command.*

```
              avg1min              avg5min               avg15min
1158207000:  1.9546666667e-01  1.1120000000e-01  3.4666666667e-02
1158207300:  7.8000000000e-02  1.0040000000e-01  4.5066666667e-02
1158207600:  nan nan nan
```

Two polling intervals have happened in the last 10 minutes. Depending on when you launch the command, the last polling interval (N) may not have happened yet, so these values are nan'd (Not A Number). The values are in scientific notation. You can use the bc math language in shell to convert these values to numbers that you can use with visualization tools. Listing 7.10 is the shell script I use to process and extract the data from a fetch command.

Listing 7.10 *A shell script to parse the output from the fetch command.*

```sh
#!/bin/sh

#loop across the lines that actually have values
grep '^[0-9]' | grep -v 'nan' |while read i
do
    #extract each element of the line
    for h in 'echo $i'
    do
        #if this element is data then convert it
        if echo $h | grep -q 'e'
        then
            value='echo "scale=10; $h" \
                | sed -e 's/\([0-9]\)e+*/\1^/' | bc'
            out="$out $value"
        #otherwise if it's a timestamp then reset out
        elif echo $h | grep -q '[0-9]:'
        then
            out=$h
        fi
    done
    echo $out
done
```

You can pipe the output from a fetch command straight into the shell script in Listing 7.10, and you will get back just the data that matters, converted from scientific notation into real values.

Fetching is fine if you need every data point for your intended purpose, but if you plan to do things like averaging the data, or otherwise munge (perform transformation operations on the datasets) it together after you fetch it, you would probably save yourself a lot of time and CPU cycles by letting RRDTool do it for you. An oft-unspoken detail about RRDTool in graph mode is that the graph element definitions are optional.

In other words, RRDToolgraph doesn't necessarily have to generate graphs. It can be used from the command line to derive data for other purposes, such as sending it to external graphing tools. RRDTool performs math on internal data very quickly, so it will be much faster at doing the math for you than exporting the data to an external program.

Say, for example, you had a graphical widget, such as a speedometer, and you wanted it to depict the average system load for the server in Listing 7.9 for the last 10 minutes. You could use RRDTool fetch, parse the data with the shell script in Listing 7.10, further parse the data to extract just avg5min, then, add the values up and divide by 2, but that's far more crunching than you need to do. Instead, use something similar to Listing 7.11, which is an RRDTool graph command that simply asks RRDTool to average the metric for you and to print it to stdout.

Listing 7.10 *A shell script to parse the output from the fetch command.*

```
rrdtool graph /dev/null --start=end-600 \
'DEF:foo=server1_load.rrd:avg5min:AVERAGE'\
'PRINT:foo:AVERAGE:%lf' \
| tail -n1
```

The GD Graphics Library

If you wondered, the bar and point charts in Figure 7.13 and Figure 7.14 were created with the GD Library. GD is an open source graphics library designed to make it easy to create images programmatically. It is implemented as a C library, but wrappers exist for Perl, Python, Ruby, and most other interpreted languages.

GD is especially good at creating instrumentation widgets, such as speedometers. Figure 7.15 is a simple gauge created with the Perl GD::Dashboard module.

Figure 7.15   A gauge created with GD::Dashboard.

GD also has excellent built-in charting and graphing capabilities. As mentioned previously, the graphs in Figures 7.11 and 7.12 were created with GD; specifically, Perl's GD:: Graph module. RRDs are good for dynamic data that is constantly streaming in, but GD is good in data analysis situations in which the data is static, such as one-time log analysis or creating one-off graphs for presentations. Speaking of presentations, Figure 7.16 shows off some of the whiz-bang 3D capabilities of GD using the GD::Chart Perl module. The GD library can be obtained from www.boutell.com/gd/. The various Perl modules are all available from www.cpan.org.

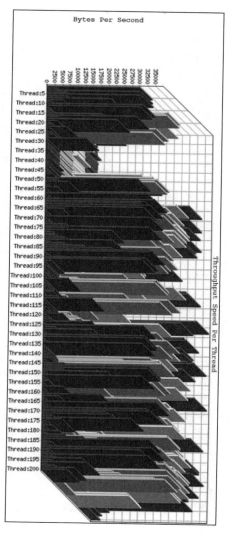

Figure 7.16 A 3D bar graph depicting execution time per thread from a Web server performance test, created with GD::Chart.

NagVis

Second to shiny little widgets, interactive maps seem to be the most requested form of management interface. These are, literally, maps with little blinking lights on them, such as the kind you see if you've ever taken a tour of a power station or water treatment plant. NagVis, a PHP tool available from www.nagvis.org, can use Nagios status data to animate status indicators on a graphic, such as a map flowchart or network diagram.

NagVis is easy to install and has a definition syntax similar to Nagios itself. Simply download NagiVis, untar it, and place the nagvis folder inside your Nagios share folder. When there, the package should work out of the box. Figure 7.17 is a map of moderately sized corporate email infrastructure. In the NagVis map file, you define which Nagios services to map to which status indicators. When the service is okay, according to Nagios, its status indicator is green. If a service goes into a warning state, NagVis changes its status indicator appropriately, and so on. With animated GIFs, the status indicators can even be made to blink.

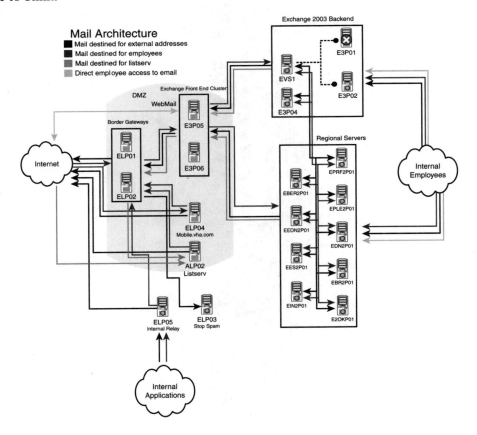

Figure 7.17 NagVis network diagram of email architecture.

Each green status indicator links back to the Nagios status detail page for the service to which it refers. NagVis even provides mouseovers, so when you point at a status indicator, you get some information about the service from Nagios. In Figure 7.15, all of the hosts are alive except for E3P01 in the upper-right-hand corner. NagVis works with any static image, so you can get as creative as you want. Figure 7.18 is a map in the geography sense of the word.

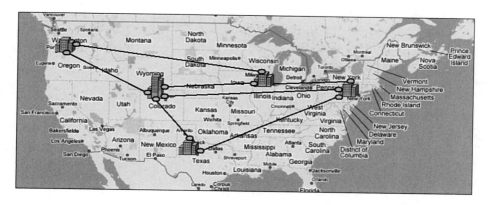

Figure 7.18 NagVis interactive map.

GraphViz

GraphViz is an open source tool for programmatically creating graphs that represent structural information such as networks and flow charts. It does the same sort of thing Visio does, only programmatically instead of interactively. GraphViz is implemented as a textual language called dot. You create a text file, similar to source code, in the dot language, and call one of several GraphViz interpreters to compile it into an image. Each interpreter uses a different layout algorithm, and because of this, there are subtle differences in the syntax they each support.

GraphViz diagrams are excellent when you want to show relationships between a large number of entites. It is already a very popular tool in the sysadmin and security communities because it works well for log analysis. Figure 7.19 is a very simple GraphViz diagram that was generated from an NMap scan of three hosts.

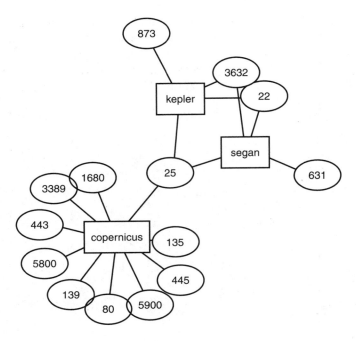

Figure 7.19 GraphViz diagram of open ports from NMap data.

GraphViz makes up for many of the shortcomings of the Nagios statusmap.cgi, but it is also good at modeling data from log files and RRDs to spot strange behavior, or cliques. For example, plotting a GraphViz diagram of hosts with CPU, Network, and Memory utilization statistics causes the boxes that use more CPU than memory to cluster together in a group.

In practice, most people don't actually type out the dot files required to create an image. Rather, most people use dot file creation utilities and GraphViz wrappers to do the dot file and image creation. The previous graph was actually created from a Perl script I wrote using the GraphViz Perl module.

If writing graphing engines is not your bag, I point you to the excellent shell-based GraphViz wrapper, Afterglow, which was written by Raffael Marty. Afterglow can be used from the command line and lets you easily define colorization mappings and filters. For example, it's possible to tell Afterglow to draw only hosts that have three or more outbound connections. Afterglow's syntax allows you to quickly draw and redraw graphs by simply altering arguments on the command line; even if you do write code, it's worth checking out. Figure 7.20 is a GraphViz diagram created with Afterglow.

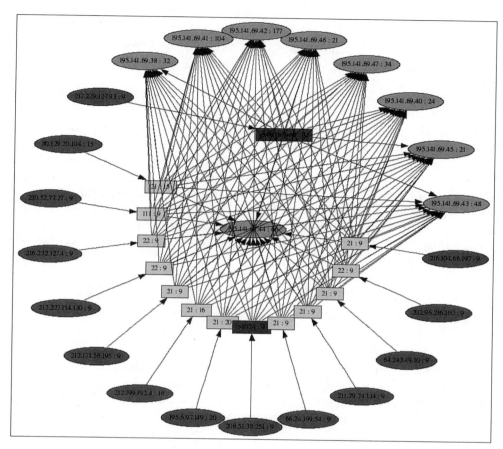

Figure 7.20 Afterglow-generated GraphViz diagram.

Sparklines

Sparklines are a concept introduced by Edward Tufte in his recent book, *Beautiful Evidence* (find the Sparklines chapter online at www.edwardtufte.com/bboard/q-and-a-fetch-msg?msg_id=0001OR&topic_id=1). Sparklines, in Tufte's words, are "intense, simple, word-sized graphics." They are drawn in one of two ways: as a miniature line graph or a miniature bar graph. Sparklines are intended by Tufte to be viewed in the context of some text, as sort of an inline footnote. Figure 7.21 shows the page hits per day of a Web site for the last three months.

Figure 7.21 Web-a page hits per day Sparkline.

The beginning and ending points are marked with a red dot and labeled. The highest and lowest points on the graph are also labeled. Sparklines are a fantastic idea for people who build monitoring dashboards of any type. I think they make a perfect replacement for "ometers" because they display much more information in the same amount of space, fit perfectly in HTML tables, and have a spiffy EKG-like feel. (For a definition of Electrocardiogram.) see http://en.wikipedia.org/wiki/Electrocardiogram.) The bar graph Sparklines are equally interesting for depicting the history of Boolean states. For example, the bar graph Sparkline in Figure 7.22 is the availability of the HTTP service on a Web server for the past few months.

Figure 7.22 Web-a service availability Sparkline.

There are a few Sparklines implementations out there. The most popular is the Sparkline PHP Library, available from www.sparkline.org. Figures 7.21 and 7.22 were created with a Python script called sparkplot.py, which is available from http://agiletesting.blogspot.com/2005/04/sparkplot-creating-sparklines-with.html.

As described in Chapter 4, "Configuring Nagios." allows you to specify per-service graphics in the Web interface. Sparklines are a perfect fit for this space, giving you a short history for each service inline in the user interface. Figure 7.23, for example, has a Sparkline under the fully qualified domain name of the server in the status detail CGI screen of Nagios.

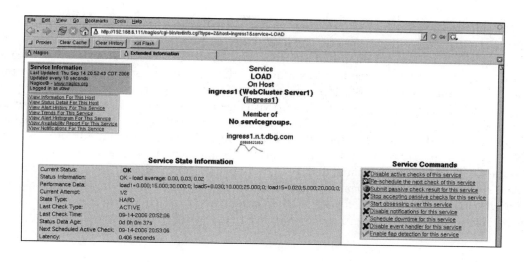

Figure 7.23 Sparkline embedded into the Nagios Web interface.

Force Directed Graphs with jsvis

The problem with static graphics is fitting everything in. Tools such as GraphViz and LGL (see http://apropos.icmb.utexas.edu/lgl/) use complex layout algorithms that maximize for the most efficient use of space while maintaining readability, but large graphs can still become cluttered, limiting their usefulness. If you've ever wished you could interact with a network graph in real-time, then jsvis might be for you.

Written by Kyle Scholz, jsvis is a freely-available JavaScript applet that implements force directed graphs in a Web interface. If you've ever used the visual thesaurus (www.visualthesaurus.com/), you are familiar with the concept. Force directed graphs are very much like GraphViz diagrams that you can interact with. If the graph contains so many servers that they are obscuring each other, for example, you can move the nodes you want to examine into view.

I think force directed graphs have huge potential in a systems monitoring context. Far less complex and more organic than 3D visualization, they are simply the best way I've seen to model a large number of network nodes in a small space. Kyle's blog contains the code, interactive samples, and even a tutorial to get you started coding. I highly recommend a visit: www.kylescholz.com/blog/2006/06/force_directed_graphs_in_javas.html.

Animation is certainly the next step in data visualization for monitoring systems and intrusion detection and prevention. The integration of NetFlow, data into routers and network gear, has accelerated the use of animated visualization tools. NetFlow is a Cisco standard to depict network traffic flows as a unidirectional sequence of packets that share the same source and destination IP address, source and destination port, and IP protocol. Current open source NetFlow analysis tools exist to visualize these network flows in real-time or as historical data in a forensics context. The gpl cube of potential doom is located at www.kismetwireless.net/doomcube/, NvisionIP is located at http://security.ncsa.uiuc.edu/distribution/NVisionIPDownLoad.html, and xovi is located at http://www.doxpara.com/?q=node/1133. As the trend toward the animated display of monitoring data continues, I expect to see many more solutions such as jsvis being integrated into Web interfaces. This is undoubtedly a good thing for those who struggle for visibility in complex systems. If you are building custom management interfaces, there's no reason you can't get ahead of the power curve today with jsvis.

CHAPTER 8

Nagios Event Broker Interface

In this chapter, you delve into the inner workings of Nagios by exploring the Nagios Event Broker. The Event Broker is new to the 2.0 kernel series, and it is definitely the most powerful interface available to Nagios; however, actually wielding it requires some modest knowledge of C programming. Don't let that scare you, however; if you possess even a passing familiarity of C, the information presented in this chapter should get you well on your way to extending Nagios's functionality to your heart's content.

Function References and Callbacks in C

If C programming isn't something you do often, you may not have ever used function pointers. If you are adept at C, feel free to skip this section. Function pointers are equivalent to variable pointers, except they point to a memory address that corresponds to a function instead of a variable of some type. If you understand pointers, they work the exact same way and their syntax is what you would expect, but they are rarely covered in C programming books. I think this is because it's hard to come up with simple examples in which they might be useful. This is a shame, because they enable some elegant software engineering in larger C programs, such as Nagios.

Nagios uses function pointers often to implement callbacks. Callbacks are functions that take pointers to other functions as initialization arguments. When interesting events occur,

Nagios can use the passed function pointers to call back to event handlers that are interested in that particular type of event. But before we get into all of that, take a look at Listing 8.1, which outlines the use of a function pointer.

Listing 8.1 *Using a function pointer.*

```
void main(){

/*  **********************************************
    Here we have two functions, one that converts Celsius
            to Fahrenheit and one that does the opposite.
            ********************************************** */

    int c2f( int c ) { return (9/5)*c+32; }
    int f2c( int f ) { return (5/9)*(f-32);}


/*  **********************************************
    The convert function acts as an interface to
    the actual math functions. It takes a function
    pointer as one of its init arguments.
            ********************************************** */

    int convert(int input, int (*fPointer)(int)){
            return fPointer(input) ;

}

/*  **********************************************
    Now we can call the convert function
    whenever we want, and we can tell it which
    conversion to do by passing it a pointer to
    either f2c or c2f, like below.
            ********************************************** */
void Go(){
            int result=convert('72',&f2c);

}
}
```

So, you can see why nobody teaches you this in a programming book. Using normal conditional logic, such as a switch or if/else loop, is a much more straightforward way to choose between f2c and c2f. In this example, and probably any other simple example you can think of, there are better ways to do things than using function pointers. Function pointers begin to shine, however, when things get a bit more complicated. The primary magic you need to understand to write NEB modules is the convert function declaration line:

```
int convert(int input, int (*fPointer)(int)){
```

The first argument is a normal integer called input, but the second argument is strange indeed: int (*fPointer)(int). If you try to parse it as a variable argument, it doesn't make any sense, but this isn't a variable argument; it's actually a minifunction declaration inside the convert declaration. So, in plain English, the convert function takes two arguments. The first is an int called input, and the second is a pointer called fPointer, which points to another function that takes a single int as an argument and returns an int. If the fPointer function took an int and a float, the declaration would look like the following:

```
int convert(int input, int (*fPointer)(int,float)){
```

The convert function just turns around and calls whichever conversion function to which it is passed a pointer. Passing a function pointer to convert is just like passing any other pointer. You simply use the & operator to pass the memory address that corresponds to the conversion function you want to use. In Listing 8.1, the f2c conversion is used, so you pass &f2c (the address of f2c) to convert. If you don't understand it, no worries; I recommend checking out www.newty.de/fpt/intro.html.

The NEB Architecture

As depicted in Figure 8.1, the Event Broker itself is a software layer between Nagios and the NEB modules. Nagios notifies the Event Broker of interesting events. The Event Broker's job is to figure out which modules, if any, are interested in the events and to create and pass out memory handles to the modules, which the modules can use to get work done.

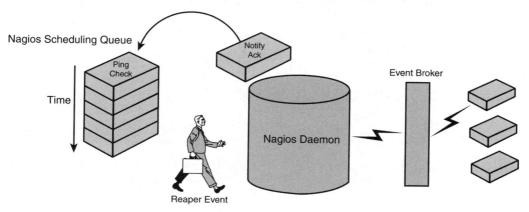

Figure 8.1 The NEB architecture from the perspective of the Event Broker.

NEB modules are shared libraries written in either C or C++. The NEB module registers for the types of events it is interested in and provides function pointers to functions that presumably do things with the events they receive. Each NEB module is required to have an entry and exit function and, beyond that, can do anything it wants. The interesting thing about this architecture is that Nagios globally scopes almost everything (see the Nagios web site, the source of this information). According to Ethan Galstad, Nagios' creator, this is by design. Ethan says, "There are a whole number of things that I would like to see Event Broker do. Essentially, I would like to allow Event Broker modules to override most of the internal login the daemon when it comes to host-service checks, notifications, flap detection, logging, executing external commands, etc. This will allow people to do a number of neat things that would otherwise require extensive rewriting of the Nagios daemon." Thus, from the perspective of the NEB module, the architecture looks more like the one shown in Figure 8.2.

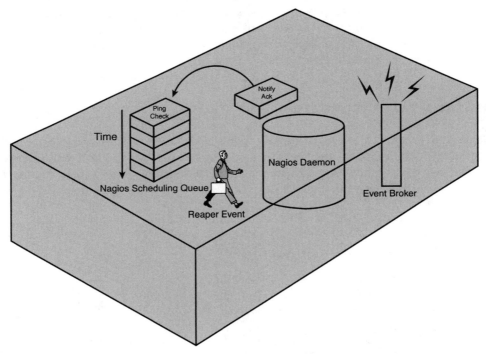

Figure 8.2 The NEB architecture from the perspective of an NEB module.

Because almost all of the interesting functions and structs are globally scoped—if Nagios' execution pointer is in the module's address space—the module has the power to change anything it wants to change about the entire runtime environment. It can insert and remove events from the scheduling queue and it can turn on or off notifications. In summary, anything that can be changed at runtime can be changed by the module. You might think that the module would have a limited opportunity to do these things because Nagios runs only its callbacks when interesting events to which it subscribes happen, but because the functions to insert events in the queue are globally available, the module can, conceivably, schedule its own callback routines in a timed fashion when it is first initialized.

In Nagios 2.3.1, there are 31 total callback types, although some of them are reserved for future use. These constants are defined in nebcallbacks.h, in the includes directory of the tarball. Table 8.1 lists the callback type constants.

Table 8.1 *NEB Callback Types*

NEBCALLBACK_RESERVED0	NEBCALLBACK_DOWNTIME_DATA
NEBCALLBACK_RESERVED1	NEBCALLBACK_FLAPPING_DATA
NEBCALLBACK_RESERVED3	NEBCALLBACK_PROGRAM_STATUS_DATA
NEBCALLBACK_RESERVED4	NEBCALLBACK_HOST_STATUS_DATA
NEBCALLBACK_RAW_DATA	NEBCALLBACK_SERVICE_STATUS_DATA
NEBCALLBACK_NEB_DATA	NEBCALLBACK_ADAPTIVE_PROGRAM_DATA
NEBCALLBACK_PROCESS_DATA	NEBCALLBACK_ADAPTIVE_HOST_DATA
NEBCALLBACK_TIMED_EVENT_DATA	NEBCALLBACK_ADAPTIVE_SERVICE_DATA
NEBCALLBACK_LOG_DATA	NEBCALLBACK_EXTERNAL_COMMAND_DATA
NEBCALLBACK_SYSTEM_COMMAND_DATA	NEBCALLBACK_AGGREGATED_STATUS_DATA
NEBCALLBACK_EVENT_HANDLER_DATA	NEBCALLBACK_RETENTION_DATA
NEBCALLBACK_NOTIFICATION_DATA	NEBCALLBACK_CONTACT_NOTIFICATION_DATA
NEBCALLBACK_SERVICE_CHECK_DATA	NEBCALLBACK_CONTACT_NOTIFICATION_METHOD_DATA
NEBCALLBACK_HOST_CHECK_DATA	NEBCALLBACK_ACKNOWLEDGEMENT_DATA
NEBCALLBACK_COMMENT_DATA	NEBCALLBACK_STATE_CHANGE_DATA

These callback types cover every type of event that can happen in Nagios. An NEB module may register to receive information about any or all of these event types. After it initializes all the modules, the Event Broker waits for events matching the type subscribed to by the module and, upon receiving one, gives the module information about the event and a handle to the relevant data structures.

For example, if the module registered for EXTERNAL_COMMAND_DATA, the Event Broker would notify it every time an external command was inserted into the command file. A handle to a struct that defined the command would accompany the notification. The module can inspect and optionally change any of the information in the command struct or even delete it altogether. But enough talk about the architecture; the best way to learn about the NEB is to see how these modules work in practice.

Implementing a Filesystem Interface Using NEB

This section walks through a simple NEB module, which implements a filesystem status interface to Nagios. The basic idea behind the filesystem interface is to provide an interface that makes it easy to write shell scripts to do things, such as check the status of a particular service on a certain host, or output a list of all the services that are not okay. Wouldn't it be nice if the shell script could grep across a filesystem instead of parsing logs or web pages? If you could tell Nagios to write a file for each service containing the service's current status code, you could do something such as this:

```
cat /var/lib/nagios/status/host24/ssh
```

If you got back a 0, you would know that the SSH service on host24 was okay. This also makes it trivial to get summaries of the entire environment with commands, such as the following:

```
grep -rl 2 /var/lib/nagios/status/
```

Though the following could be solved with a global event handler, it is a good NEB example. This command gives a list of all the services that were in a 2 (critical) state. This is exactly the kind of problem that NEBs were designed for. First, you want Nagios to notify you of service status events. When you get them, you write them out to files. The module in Listing 8.2 borrows heavily from a blog post by Taylor Dondich from Groundwork, which no longer appears to be online. It is a fully functional NEB module that implements the filesystem interface described previously.

Listing 8.2 *A NEB module that implements a filesystem interface.*

```
#ifndef NSCORE
#define NSCORE
#endif

/* include the needed Event Broker header files */
#include "../include/nebmodules.h"
#include "../include/nebcallbacks.h"
#include "../include/nebstructs.h"
#include "../include/broker.h"

/* include some Nagios stuff as well */
#include "../include/config.h"
```

(continues)

```c
#include "../include/common.h"
#include "../include/nagios.h"
#include "../include/objects.h"

/*declare the handler function to make this example easier to
write about*/
int handle_service_status(int , nebstruct_service_status_data *);

// specify Event Broker API version (required)
NEB_API_VERSION(CURRENT_NEB_API_VERSION);

// our module handle
void *basic_module_handle=NULL;

/* this function gets called when the module gets loaded by
the Event Broker*/
int nebmodule_init(int flags, char *args, nebmodule *handle) {

    basic_module_handle = handle;

write_to_logs_and_console("Loading FS Module...",
                    NSLOG_INFO_MESSAGE,TRUE);

neb_register_callback(NEBCALLBACK_SERVICE_STATUS_DATA, handle,
                    '1', (void *)&handle_service_status);

    write_to_logs_and_console("Done",NSLOG_INFO_MESSAGE,TRUE);

    return 0;
}

// this is our unloading function, which gets called by the neb
int nebmodule_deinit(int flags, int reason){

write_to_logs_and_console("Unloading FS Module...",
                    NSLOG_INFO_MESSAGE,TRUE);

    return 0;
}

/*this function handles service status updates from the
Event Broker*/
int handle_service_status(int neb_event_type,
                    nebstruct_service_status_data *ds){

    //get a handle to the service struct
    service *svc = ds->object_ptr;

    //create some name buffers for various output
    char outbuf[100];
    char host_path[100];
    char service_path[10 0];
```

(continues)

Listing 8.2 *A NEB module that implements a filesystem interface. (Continued)*

```
    //create a logging string and write it out
    sprintf( outbuf,"Caught status code: '%i' from host '%s' for
            service %s", svc->current_state, svc->host_name,
            svc->description );

write_to_logs_and_console( outbuf , NSLOG_INFO_MESSAGE, TRUE );

    //create the host and service path strings
    sprintf( host_path,"/usr/share/nagios/status/%s", svc->host_
name);

sprintf( service_path,"/usr/share/nagios/status/%s/%s",
        svc->host_name, svc->description);

    //create the directory
    mkdir( host_path, S_IRWXU|S_IRGRP|S_IXGRP|S_IROTH|S_IXOTH );

    //write the file
    FILE *outfile=fopen(service_path,"w");
    fprintf(outfile,"%i:%i",svc->current_state,svc->state_type);
    fclose(outfile);
    return 0;
}
```

To compile this, you need access to the headers that come in the include directory of the Nagios tarball. Grab and extract the current tarball, and then run configure and make all. After this is done, you can create a new directory for your module in the root of the tarball directory. Place this file in there as something such as fs.c and compile it into a shared lib with the following:

```
gcc -shared fs.c -o fs.o
```

Decide on a decent location for NEB modules for your particular distro packaging and copy the object file there. Finally, tell Nagios to load the module. Do this by adding the following line to your nagios.cfg:

```
broker_module=/path/to/your/modules/fs.o
```

Of course for Nagios to actually load the module, you need to have compiled Nagios with Event Broker support. See Chapter 4, "Configuring Nagios," for details on how to do this. If all goes well, you should see something similar to the following in your nagios.log when you start up Nagios.

```
[1156799404] Loading FS Module...
```

Next let's look at the code starting at the top, with the include statements in Listing 8.3.

Listing 8.3 *Includes.*

```
/* include the needed Event Broker header files */
#include "../include/nebmodules.h"
#include "../include/nebcallbacks.h"
#include "../include/nebstructs.h"
#include "../include/broker.h"

/* include some Nagios stuff as well */
#include "../include/config.h"
#include "../include/common.h"
#include "../include/nagios.h"
#include "../include/objects.h"
```

The first section of headers includes the data structures and functions necessary to interact with the Event Broker. These encompass functions such as neb_register_callback for subscribing to interesting events and structs such as nebstruct_service_status_data, which contains the notification data handed down from the Event Broker for a service status event. The second section of headers describes core Nagios functions and structs, so things such as service_struct, which define a Nagios service, and write_to_logs_and_console, which is a function for...well, writing messages to the logs and console.

If you plan on writing an Event Broker module, you have to poke around in most of these headers, but even if you don't plan on writing a module, take a look. Nagios is one of the most nicely written C programs you can work with. The function and variable names are self-documenting, the comments are terse, descriptive, and liberally dispersed, and the application is well engineered.

After the include statements is a declaration for the handler function. I declared it at this point in the program so that I wouldn't have to write about it yet, so ignore it for now. The next relevant section is in Listing 8.4.

Listing 8.4 *Some required parts.*

```
/* specify Event Broker API version (required) */
NEB_API_VERSION(CURRENT_NEB_API_VERSION);

// Our module handle
void *basic_module_handle=NULL;
```

The NEB_API_VERSION macro is designed to ensure that the module runs under the version of the NEB API that it is compiled to run on. All NEB Modules are required to include this line. The void pointer declaration is a globally scoped handle that eventually refers to the memory address of the module. It's declared here so that it can be referenced in a global context. Later, when you start registering for callbacks (as in listing 8.5), you will use this handle to tell the event broker how to find you.

Listing 8.5 *The init function.*

```
/* this function gets called when the module gets
loaded by the Event Broker*/
int nebmodule_init(int flags, char *args, nebmodule *handle) {

    basic_module_handle = handle;

write_to_logs_and_console("Loading FS Module...",
                      NSLOG_INFO_MESSAGE,TRUE);

neb_register_callback(NEBCALLBACK_SERVICE_STATUS_DATA, handle,
                  '1', (void *)&handle_service_status);

    write_to_logs_and_console("Done",NSLOG_INFO_MESSAGE,TRUE);

    return 0;
}
```

Every NEB module is required to have an entry function and an exit function. Listing 8.5 is the entry function for our module. As you can see, it returns an exit code in the form of an int and takes three arguments. The first argument, an int called flags, is meant to give you the context in which the module is initialized. The second argument is a string pointer called args. It is possible to pass arguments to your module in the nagios.cfg file by adding them to the end of the module name in the broker_module directive. For example, our current filesystem module hard codes its base directory as /var/lib/nagios/status, but you can pass the directory name as an argument to the module with the following definition in the nagios.cfg.

```
broker_module=/path/to/your/modules/fs.o \
base=/usr/lib/nagios/status
```

To keep the example source code simple, I did not do this; but had I specified it as an argument, I could have parsed it out with the args pointer in the init function. The third argument is a pointer of type nebmodule that points to a struct, which defines the module. In short, this is a handle that uniquely identifies the memory address for our module. The nebmodule struct is defined in nebmodule.h. If you are curious about what a module consists of, Listing 8.6 contains the definition.

Listing 8.6 *The nebmodule struct.*

```
/* NEB module structure */
typedef struct nebmodule_struct{
    char                *filename;
    char                *args;
    char                *info[NEBMODULE_MODINFO_NUMITEMS];
    int                 should_be_loaded;
    int                 is_currently_loaded;
#ifdef USE_LTDL
    lt_dlhandle         module_handle;
    lt_ptr              init_func;
    lt_ptr              deinit_func;
#else
    void                *module_handle;
    void                *init_func;
    void                *deinit_func;
#endif
#ifdef HAVE_PTHREAD_H
    pthread_t           thread_id;
#endif
    struct nebmodule_struct *next;
        }nebmodule;
```

Like I said, Nagios is a nifty C program. There are many interesting tidbits of information you can query about your own module. Other functions may want to know some of this information. So, the first thing to do in the init function is to cache a copy of your own memory handle with the following line.

```
basic_module_handle = handle;
```

Then, start dereferencing information about yourself, if desired. For example, if you wanted to know your thread ID, you could do something such as the following:

```
pthread_t t_id=handle->thread_id
```

After you have a copy of your handle, write some output to the console and log files to let the outside world know that you are alive and functional. This is done by the write_to_logs_ and_console function, which is defined in nagios.h. This function takes three arguments; the first is a string that points to the message. The second is a constant that defines the type of message; there are several of these, which are also specified in nagios.h. The one I use is for informational messages. The last argument is a Boolean that toggles console output, so if this is true, the message goes to the console and the logs.

With the next line, register with the Event Broker to receive events:

```
neb_register_callback(NEBCALLBACK_SERVICE_STATUS_DATA, handle,
                      '42', (void *)&handle_service_status );
```

The neb_register_callback function is defined in nebcallbacks.h. The definition looks like this:

```
int neb_register_callback(int callback_type, void *mod_handle,
                          int priority, int (*callback_func)
                          (int,void *));
```

The neb_register_callback takes four arguments. The first is the constant describing what types of events you are interested in. The second is a handle, which the Event Broker may use to find your module in the event that the broker needs to send you a notification." The third is a priority number. In general, when more than one module registers for the same type of event, they are executed in the order they are loaded and by the Broker on startup. You can override this behavior by specifying a priority number.

The last argument to neb_register_callback is a function pointer, as described in section "Function References and Callbacks in C." The function pointer must point to a subroutine that returns an exit code in the form of an int and accepts two arguments. The first of these is a constant specifying the event type; yes, once again, one of the constants specified in Table 8.1. The second is a void pointer, which is discussed shortly. So, this last argument to neb_register_callback is the function to which the Event Broker will actually send the event. It is the event handler.

But why would the event handler need to be passed the event type? The event handler function should be able to infer the event type, because the events were specified at the same time that the handler was defined. In the example, the event handler was written to specifically handle the one type of event that it registered for, but this isn't necessarily a requirement. The nice thing about being passed back the event type constant is that it enables the module to register for more than one type of callback and handle each type it registers for with a single event handler function.

What is the null pointer? To answer this, look at what the Event Broker does when it makes the callback. Consider the code in Listing 8.7 from broker.c in the base directory of the tarball.

Listing 8.7 *The Event Broker sending data.*

```
/* sends program data (starts, restarts, stops, etc.)
to broker */
void broker_program_state(int type, int flags, int attr,
                          struct timeval *timestamp){
    nebstruct_process_data ds;

    if(!(event_broker_options & BROKER_PROGRAM_STATE))
        return;

    /* fill struct with relevant data */
    ds.type=type;
    ds.flags=flags;
    ds.attr=attr;
    ds.timestamp=get_broker_timestamp(timestamp);

    /* make callbacks */
    neb_make_callbacks(NEBCALLBACK_PROCESS_DATA,(void *)&ds);

    return;
        }


/* send timed event data to broker */
void broker_timed_event(int type, int flags, int attr,
                        timed_event *event,
                        struct timeval *timestamp){
    nebstruct_timed_event_data ds;

    if(!(event_broker_options & BROKER_TIMED_EVENTS))
        return;

    if(event==NULL)
        return;

    /* fill struct with relevant data */
    ds.type=type;
    ds.flags=flags;
    ds.attr=attr;
    ds.timestamp=get_broker_timestamp(timestamp);

    ds.event_type=event->event_type;
    ds.recurring=event->recurring;
    ds.run_time=event->run_time;
    ds.event_data=event->event_data;

    /* make callbacks */
    neb_make_callbacks(NEBCALLBACK_TIMED_EVENT_DATA,
                       (void *)&ds);

    return;
        }
```

There's a pattern here. You can see two functions, which represent two different types of events (again, defined by the constants in Table 8.1) being sent out by the Broker. In each case, the Broker first populates a struct called ds with data relevant to the type of event it is about to send and then, after the ds struct is populated, it uses the neb_make_callbacks function to send the event-type constant and a pointer to the ds struct. The Broker does this same exact thing for every type of event in Table 8.1, so the null pointer the event handler function receives is the ds struct that the broker populates. This data is specific to each type of event; for example, when the broker makes a callback to the modules interested in timed events, the ds struct is of type nebstruct_timed_event_data.

After the init function in Listing 8.5 registers for events of type SERVICE_STATUS_DATA, it writes the word "done" to the logs and exits with a 0, the universal sign that everything's okay. The deinit function that follows init in the example in Listing 8.2 is also required, but it doesn't bear much of an explanation. It receives some constants that specify the reason the module is unloaded and provides you an opportunity to do some cleaning up before the module goes "bye-bye."

Now look at the event handler function in Listing 8.8. Most of the guts of the program reside there.

Listing 8.8 *The event handler function.*

```
int handle_service_status(int neb_event_type, nebstruct_service_
status_data *ds){

    //get a handle to the service struct
    service *svc = ds->object_ptr;

    //create some name buffers for various output
    char outbuf[100];
    char host_path[100];
    char service_path[100];

    //create a string with some logging info
    sprintf( outbuf,"Caught status code: '%i' from host '%s' for
            service %s", svc->current_state, svc->host_name,
            svc->description );

//write it out to the logs
write_to_logs_and_console( outbuf , NSLOG_INFO_MESSAGE, TRUE );

    //create the host and service path strings
    sprintf( host_path,"/usr/share/nagios/status/%s",
            svc->host_name );
    sprintf( service_path,"/usr/share/nagios/status/%s/%s", svc-
>host_name, svc->description);

    //create the directory                              (continues)
```

Listing 8.8 *The event handler function.* *(Continued)*

```
mkdir( host_path, S_IRWXU|S_IRGRP|S_IXGRP|S_IROTH|S_IXOTH );

//write the file
FILE *outfile=fopen(service_path,"w");
fprintf(outfile,"%i:%i",svc->current_state,svc->state_type);
fclose(outfile);
return 0;
}
```

As stated earlier, the event handler is passed by two arguments: the event type constant and a reference to the ds struct containing information about the specific type of argument. But what will the ds struct contain for events of type SERVICE_STATUS? Let's take a look at the relevant code snippet in Listing 8.9, from the broker.c.

Listing 8.9 *The broker's make_callback code for SERVICE_STATUS_DATA.*

```
/* sends service status updates to broker */
void broker_service_status(int type, int flags, int attr,
                           service *svc,
                           struct timeval *timestamp){
    nebstruct_service_status_data ds;

    if(!(event_broker_options & BROKER_STATUS_DATA))
        return;

    /* fill struct with relevant data */
    ds.type=type;
    ds.flags=flags;
    ds.attr=attr;
    ds.timestamp=get_broker_timestamp(timestamp);

    ds.object_ptr=(void *)svc;

    /* make callbacks */
    neb_make_callbacks(NEBCALLBACK_SERVICE_STATUS_DATA,
                       (void *)&ds);

    return;
        }
```

The first thing to note is the following line:

```
nebstruct_service_status_data ds;
```

This tells us that the ds struct for the event is of type nebstruct_service_status_data. The struct appears to have five elements: type, flags, attr, a timestamp, and a void pointer to svc, which is a struct describing a Nagios service. Check out nebstructs.h (Listing 8.10) for a description of the struct.

Listing 8.10 *The nebstruct_service_status_data struct.*

```
/* service status structure */
typedef struct nebstruct_service_status_struct{
    int          type;
    int          flags;
    int          attr;
    struct timeval  timestamp;

    void         *object_ptr;
        }nebstruct_service_status_data;
```

You have three ints, a timeval struct, and a pointer to the service itself. The service pointer sounds interesting. Considering all the cool stuff the module struct contains, the service struct must have several goodies. This leads to Listing 8.11, which is the service_struct definition (formatted into two columns to save space) from objects.h.

Listing 8.11 *The service_struct def from nagios.h.*

```
/* SERVICE structure */
typedef struct service_struct{
    char    *host_name;
    char    *description;
        char    *service_check_command;
    char     *event_handler;
    int    check_interval;
    int      retry_interval;
    int    max_attempts;
    int      parallelize;
    contactgroupsmember *contact_groups;
    int    notification_interval;
    int      notify_on_unknown;
    int    notify_on_warning;
    int    notify_on_critical;
    int    notify_on_recovery;
    int      notify_on_flapping;
    int      stalk_on_ok;
    int      stalk_on_warning;
    int      stalk_on_unknown;
    int      stalk_on_critical;
    int      is_volatile;
    char    *notification_period;
    char    *check_period;
```

(continues)

Listing 8.11 *The service_struct def from nagios.h. (Continued)*

```
    int      flap_detection_enabled;
    double   low_flap_threshold;
    double   high_flap_threshold;
    int      process_performance_data;
    int      check_freshness;
    int      freshness_threshold;
    int      accept_passive_service_checks;
    int      event_handler_enabled;
    int   checks_enabled;
    int      retain_status_information;
    int      retain_nonstatus_information;
    int      notifications_enabled;
    int      obsess_over_service;
    int      failure_prediction_enabled;
    char     *failure_prediction_options;
#ifdef NSCORE
    int      problem_has_been_acknowledged;
    int      acknowledgement_type;
    int      host_problem_at_last_check;
#ifdef REMOVED_041403
    int      no_recovery_notification;
#endif
    int      check_type;
    int   current_state;
    int   last_state;
    int   last_hard_state;
    char    *plugin_output;
    char    *perf_data;
        int      state_type;
    time_t   next_check;
    int      should_be_scheduled;
    time_t   last_check;
    int   current_attempt;
    time_t   last_notification;
    time_t  next_notification;
    int      no_more_notifications;
    int      check_flapping_recovery_notification;
    time_t   last_state_change;
    time_t  last_hard_state_change;
    time_t  last_time_ok;
    time_t  last_time_warning;
    time_t  last_time_unknown;
    time_t  last_time_critical;
    int      has_been_checked;
    int      is_being_freshened;
    int      notified_on_unknown;
    int      notified_on_warning;
    int      notified_on_critical;
    int      current_notification_number;
    double   latency;
    double   execution_time;
```

(continues)

Listing 8.11 *The service_struct def from nagios.h. (Continued)*

```
    int     is_executing;
    int     check_options;
    int     scheduled_downtime_depth;
    int     pending_flex_downtime;
    int     state_history[MAX_STATE_HISTORY_ENTRIES];     /* flap
detection */
    int     state_history_index;
    int     is_flapping;
    unsigned long flapping_comment_id;
    double  percent_state_change;
    unsigned long modified_attributes;
#endif
    struct service_struct *next;
    struct service_struct *nexthash;
    }service;
```

Wow, jackpot! The service struct has everything you might hope to know about a service and then some. In addition, the nifty Event Broker hands over a pointer, straight to the service to which the event is currently in reference. So, getting back to Listing 8.8, the first thing the event handler function does is grab a type of specific handle to the service pointer for convenient dereferencing:

```
service *svc = ds->object_ptr;
```

Then, because you mix and match output from various sources, you can create a few output buffers. I can't wait to dereference something from my cool new service handle, so the next line is

```
sprintf( outbuf,"Caught status code: '%i' from host '%s' for
service %s", svc->current_state, svc->host_name, svc->description
);
```

This builds a string suitable to output to the logs. After you write this out, you create two more strings, which you can use to create the fs interface. The first dereferences the hostname to which the service refers. Use this to create the directory for the service. The second string dereferences the service description, which you use for the filename:

```
sprintf( host_path,"/usr/share/nagios/status/%s", svc->host_name);
sprintf( service_path,"/usr/share/nagios/status/%s/%s",
  svc->host_name, svc->description);
```

After this is done, you can create the directory, write the file, and then you are done:

```
//create the directory
mkdir( host_path, S_IRWXU|S_IRGRP|S_IXGRP|S_IROTH|S_IXOTH );

//write the file
FILE *outfile=fopen(service_path,"w");
fprintf(outfile,"%i:%i",svc->current_state,svc->state_type);

fclose(outfile);
```

Notice that the actual contents of the file are two numbers separated by a colon. With that great service struct, I couldn't resist pulling out an extra tidbit of information. This is the state_type, which is an int that specifies whether the service is in a hard state (0) or a soft state (1). So, if ping on host15 was in a hard critical state, then the contents of the file /var/lib/nagios/status/host15/ping are 2:0.

Although it compiles and works, this module has some big problems. It doesn't do things, such as check whether the directory creations and file writes succeed, and it can be far more efficient about making system calls. For example, you can dereference last_state and compare it with current_state to determine if it is worth opening the file. In fact, subscribing to state change events is probably more efficient, but in the interest of keeping the example as straightforward as possible, a lot of important functionality has been omitted.

The goal of this chapter was to get you excited about the Event Broker interface and its capabilities. The Nagios community needs creative people to contribute interesting modules. If you have an idea for a useful module, I hope this chapter gave you a head start. I can't wait to use your module when you are done.

Configure Options

This appendix contains a full list of options for the Nagios 2.5 configure script. You can use these options to customize the Nagios installation as described in Chapter 3, "Configuring Nagios."

Table A.1 *Options to the Configure Script*

Option	Long Name	Description
-h	—help	Displays help text and exit.
-V	—version	Displays version information and exit.
-q	—quiet	Do not print checking messages.
-n	—no-create	Do not create output files.
—srcdir=DIR	—srcdir=DIR	Look for the sources in DIR.

Table A.2 *Installation Directories*

Option	Description	Default Location
—prefix=PREFIX	Installs architecture-independent files in PREFIX	/usr/local/nagios
—exec-prefix=EPREFIX	Installs architecture-dependent files in EPREFIX	PREFIX
—bindir=DIR	User executables	EPREFIX/bin
—sbindir=DIR	System admin executables	EPREFIX/sbin
—libexecdir=DIR	Program executables	EPREFIX/libexec
—datadir=DIR	Read-only, architecture-independent data	PREFIX/share
—sysconfdir=DIR	Read-only, single-machine data	PREFIX/etc

Table A.2 *Options to the Configure Script* (continued)

Option	Description	Default Location
—sharedstatedir=DIR	Modifiable architecture-independent data	PREFIX/com
—localstatedir=DIR	Modifiable single-machine data	PREFIX/var
—libdir=DIR	Object code libraries	EPREFIX/lib
—includedir=DIR	C header files	PREFIX/include
—oldincludedir=DIR	C header files for non-gcc	/usr/include
—infodir=DIR	Information documentation	PREFIX/info
—mandir=DIR	Manual documentation	PREFIX/man

Table A. 3 *Optional Features*

Feature	Description	Default Setting
Statusmap	Compilation of statusmap CGI	Enabled
Statuswrl	Compilation of statuswrl	Enabled
DEBUG0	Shows function entry and exit	Disabled
DEBUG1	General information messages	Disabled
DEBUG2	Shows warning messages	Disabled
DEBUG3	Shows scheduled events (service and host checks, and so on)	Disabled
DEBUG4	Shows service and host notifications	Disabled
DEBUG5	Shows SQL queries	Disabled
DEBUGALL	Shows all debugging messages	Disabled
nanosleep	Uses nanosleep (instead of sleep) in event timing	Disabled
event-broker	Integration of event broker routines	Enabled
embedded-perl	Embedded Perl interpreter	Disabled
Cygwin	Building under the CYGWIN environment	Disabled

Note: To enable FEATURE, use –enable-FEATURE. To disable FEATURE, use —disable-FEATURE.

Table A.4 *Optional Packages*

Package	Description	Default Value
—with-nagios-user=<user>	Sets user name to run Nagios	Nagios
—with-nagios-group=<grp>	Sets group name to run Nagios	Nagios
—with-command-user=<user>	Sets user name for command access	Nagios
—with-command-group=<grp>	Sets group name for command access	Nagios
—with-mail=<path_to_mail>	Sets path to equivalent program to mail	Auto-detected
—with-init-dir=<path>	Sets directory in which to place init script	Auto-detected
—with-lockfile=<path>	Sets path and filename for lock file	PREFIX/var/nagios.lock
—with-gd-lib=DIR	Sets location of the gd library	Auto-detected
—with-gd-inc=DIR	Sets location of the gd include files	Auto-detected
—with-cgiurl=<local-url>	Sets URL for CGI programs (do not use a trailing slash)	http://localhost/nagios/cgi-bin/
—with-htmurl=<local-url>	Sets URL for public html	http://localhost/nagios/
—with-perlcache	Turns on caching of internally compiled Perl scripts	Disabled

nagios.cfg and cgi.cfg

Intended as an addendum to Chapter 4, "Configuring Nagios," this appendix contains complete lists of all the configuration options in the nagios.cfg and cgi.cfg files. Most descriptions are from the sample configuration files. Sample files may be built by running the install-config target, as described in Chapter 3, "Installing Nagios."

Table B.1 *nagios.cfg*

Option	Description
log_file	The main log file where service and host events are logged.
cfg_file	Used to specify an object configuration file containing object definitions that Nagios should use for monitoring.
cfg_dir	Used to specify a directory that contains object configuration files that Nagios should use for monitoring.
object_cache_file	Determines where object definitions are cached when Nagios starts or restarts.
resource_file	An optional resource file that contains $USERx$ macro definitions.
status_file	Where the current status of all monitored services and hosts is stored.
nagios_user	Determines the effective user that Nagios should run as.
nagios_group	Determines the effective group that Nagios should run as.
check_external_commands	Specifies whether or not Nagios should check for external commands.

(continues)

Table B.1 *nagios.cfg (continued)*

Option	Description
command_check_interval	Interval at which Nagios should check for external commands.
command_file	File that Nagios checks for external command requests.
comment_file	File that Nagios uses for storing host and service comments.
downtime_file	File that Nagios uses for storing downtime data.
lock_file	File that Nagios uses for storing its PID number when it's running in daemon mode.
temp_file	Temporary file that is used as scratch space when Nagios updates the status log, cleans the comment file, and so on.
event_broker_options	Controls what (if any) data gets sent to the event broker. Currently either 0 (nothing) or −1 (everything).
broker_module	Specifies an event broker module that should be loaded by Nagios at startup.
log_rotation_method	Log rotation method that Nagios should use to rotate the main log file. Values are as follows: n = None (don't rotate the log) h = Hourly rotation (top of the hour) d = Daily rotation (midnight every day) w = Weekly rotation (midnight on Saturday evening) m = Monthly rotation (midnight last day of month)
log_archive_path	Directory where rotated log files should be placed.
use_syslog	Specifies if logs also go to the syslog daemon. 0 = no, 1 = yes.
log_notifications	Specifies if notifications are logged. 0 = no, 1 = yes.
log_service_retries	Specifies if service check retries are logged. 0 = no, 1 = yes.
log_host_retries	Specifies if host check retries are logged. 0 = no, 1 = yes.
log_event_handlers	Specifies if event handlers are logged. 0 = no, 1 = yes.

(continues)

Table B.1 *nagios.cfg (continued)*

Option	Description
log_initial_states	Specifies if the result of an initial host or service check should be logged. (This is helpful for long-term log analysis.) 0 = no, 1 = yes.
log_external_commands	Specifies if external commands are logged. 0 = no, 1 = yes.
log_passive_checks	Specifies if passive checks are logged. 0 = no, 1 = yes.
global_host_event_handler	Specifies a command to be run for every host state change.
global_service_event_handler	Specifies a command to be run for every service state change.
service_inter_check_delay_method	Method that Nagios should use when initially "spreading out" service checks when it starts monitoring, as described in Chapter 2, "Theory of Operations."
max_service_check_spread	Specifies the amount of time (in minutes) from the start time that an initial check of all services should be completed.
service_interleave_factor	Determines how service checks are interleaved, as described in Chapter 2.
host_inter_check_delay_method	Determines how host checks are interleaved, as described in Chapter 2.
max_host_check_spread	Specifies the amount of time (in minutes) from the start time that an initial check of all hosts should be completed.
max_concurrent_checks	Maximum number of service checks that can be run in parallel at any given time.
service_reaper_frequency	Frequency (in seconds!) with which Nagios will reap check results, as described in Chapter 2.
auto_reschedule_checks	Specifies if Nagios will attempt to automatically reschedule active host and service checks to "smooth" them out over time (experimental). 0 = no, 1 = yes.
auto_rescheduling_interval	How often (in seconds) Nagios will attempt to automatically reschedule checks (experimental).
auto_rescheduling_window	Defines the "window" of time (in seconds) that Nagios will look at, when automatically rescheduling checks (experimental).
sleep_time	The time (in seconds) to sleep between checking for system events and service checks that need to be run.

(continues)

Table B.1 *nagios.cfg (continued)*

Option	Description
service_check_timeout	Specifies the length of time (in seconds) Nagios allows service check commands to execute before killing them off.
host_check_timeout	Specifies the length of time (in seconds) Nagios allows host check commands to execute before killing them off.
event_handler_timeout	Specifies the length of time (in seconds) Nagios allows event handler commands to execute before killing them off.
notification_timeout	Specifies the length of time (in seconds) Nagios allows notification commands to execute before killing them off.
ocsp_timeout	Specifies the length of time (in seconds) Nagios allows obsessive-compulsive service processor commands to execute before killing them off.
perfdata_timeout	Specifies the length of time (in seconds) Nagios allows perfdata commands to execute before killing them off.
retain_state_information	Specifies if Nagios saves state information for services and hosts before it shuts down. 0 = no, 1 = yes.
state_retention_file	File that Nagios should use to store host and service state information.
retention_update_interval	Determines how often (in minutes) Nagios automatically saves retention data during normal operation. 0 = no, 1 = yes.
use_retained_program_state	Specifies if Nagios sets program status variables based on the values saved in the retention file. 0 = no, 1 = yes.
use_retained_scheduling_info	Specifies if Nagios retains the scheduling information (next check time) for hosts and services based on the values saved in the retention file. 0 = no, 1 = yes.
interval_length	Defines the interval length used in various other time-based directives, as described in Chapter 2.
use_aggressive_host_checking	Specifies if to use aggressive host checking. 0 = no, 1 = yes.
execute_service_checks	Globally toggles service checking. 0 = no, 1 = yes.
accept_passive_service_checks	Specifies if Nagios accepts passive service checks. 0 = no, 1 = yes.

(continues)

Table B.1 *nagios.cfg (continued)*

Option	Description
execute_host_checks	Specifies if Nagios actively runs host checks (normally disabled, as described in Chapter 2). 0 = no, 1 = yes.
accept_passive_host_checks	Specifies if Nagios accepts passive host checks 0 = no, 1 = yes.
enable_notifications	Globally toggles notifications. 0 = off, 1 = on.
enable_event_handlers	Globally toggles notifications. 0 = off, 1 = on.
process_performance_data	Specifies if Nagios processes performance data returned from service and host checks. 0 = no, 1 = yes.
host_perfdata_command	Specifies the short name of a command definition that defines a program to be run after every host check for the purpose of handling performance data.
service_perfdata_command	Specifies the short name of a command definition that defines a program to be run after every service check for the purpose of handling performance data.
host_perfdata_file	Specifies a file used to store host performance data.
service_perfdata_file	Specifies a file used to store service performance data.
host_perfdata_file_template	Template that defines what and how data is written to the host perfdata file.
service_perfdata_file_template	Template that defines what and how data is written to the host perfdata file.
host_perfdata_file_mode	Determines if the host performance data file is opened in write (w) or append (a) mode.
service_perfdata_file_mode	Determines if the service performance data file is opened in write (w) or append (a) mode.
host_perfdata_file_processing_interval	Defines how often (in seconds) the host performance data files are processed using the commands defined below.
service_perfdata_file_processing_interval	Defines how often (in seconds) the service performance data files are processed using the commands defined below.
host_perfdata_file_processing_command	Specifies a command that is used to periodically process the host performance data files.
service_perfdata_file_processing_command	Specifies a command that is used to periodically process the service performance data files.
obsess_over_services	Toggles if Nagios obsesses over service checks and run the ocsp_command defined below. 0 = no, 1 = yes.

(continues)

Table B.1 *nagios.cfg (continued)*

Option	Description
oscp_command	Command run for every service check that is processed by Nagios for various reasons, such as distributed monitoring scenarios.
check_for_orphaned_services	Determines if Nagios periodically checks for orphaned services. Orphaned service checks are checks that have been executed and removed from the scheduling queue for which no status has been returned. 0 = no, 1 = yes.
check_service_freshness	Toggles if Nagios periodically checks the "freshness" of service results. This is used primarily for passive checks. 0 = no, 1 = yes.
service_freshness_check_interval	Specifies how often (in seconds) Nagios checks the "freshness" of service check results.
check_host_freshness	Toggles if Nagios periodically checks the "freshness" of host results. This is used primarily for passive checks. 0 = no, 1 = yes.
host_freshness_check_interval	Specifies how often (in seconds) Nagios checks the "freshness" of host check results.
aggregate_status_updates	Toggles if Nagios aggregates host service and program status updates. Updates normally happen immediately, which can cause high CPU loads in large environments. 0 = no, 1 = yes.
status_update_interval	Defines the frequency (in seconds) that Nagios periodically dumps program, host, and service status data.
enable_flap_detection	Toggles if Nagios attempts to detect host and service "flapping." Flapping occurs when a host or service changes between states too frequently. 0 = no, 1 = yes.
low_service_flap_threshold	Defines thresholds used by the flap detection algorithm.
high_service_flap_threshold	Defines thresholds used by the flap detection algorithm.
low_host_flap_threshold	Defines thresholds used by the flap detection algorithm.
high_host_flap_threshold	Defines thresholds used by the flap detection algorithm.
date_format	Defines how dates display.
us	(MM-DD-YYYY HH:MM:SS)
euro	(DD-MM-YYYY HH:MM:SS)
iso8601	(YYYY-MM-DD HH:MM:SS)

(continues)

Table B.1 *nagios.cfg (continued)*

Option	Description
strict-iso8601	(YYYY-MM-DDTHH:MM:SS)
p1_file	The location of the p1.pl script, which is used by the embedded Perl interpreter.
illegal_object_name_chars	Defines the characters that are not allowed to be used in hostnames, service descriptions, or names of other object types.
illegal_macro_output_chars	Defines the characters that will be stripped from macros before the macros are used in command definitions. The following macros are stripped of the characters you specify:
	$HOSTOUTPUT$
	$HOSTPERFDATA$
	$HOSTACKAUTHOR$
	$HOSTACKCOMMENT$
	$SERVICEOUTPUT$
	$SERVICEPERFDATA$
	$SERVICEACKAUTHOR$
	$SERVICEACKCOMMENT$
use_regexp_matching	Toggles if regular expression matching takes place in the object configuration files, as described in Chapter 4, "Configuring Nagios." This option enables only regex matching for strings that contain * or ?. 0 = no, 1 = yes.
use_true_regexp_matching	Toggles if true regular expression matching takes place in the object configuration files. 0 = no, 1 = yes.
admin_email	The administrator's email address.
admin_pager	The administrator's pager address/number.
daemon_dumps_core	Toggles if Nagios is allowed to generate .core files. 0 = no, 1 = yes.

Table B.2 *cgi.cfg*

Option	Description
main_config_file	Specifies the location of nagios.cfg.
physical_html_path	Specifies the path where the HTML files reside.
url_html_path	Specifies the portion of the URL that corresponds to the physical location of the Nagios HTML files. If you access the Nagios pages with a URL like http://www.localhost.com/nagios, this value should be /nagios.
show_context_help	Toggles if a context-sensitive help icon will be displayed for most of the CGIs. 0 = no, 1 = yes.
nagios_check_command	Specifies the full path and filename of the program used to check the status of the Nagios process. A check_nagios command is included in the plugins tarball for this purpose.
use_authentication	Toggles if the CGIs uses authentication when displaying host and service information. 0 = don't use authentication, 1 = use authentication.
default_user_name	Specifies a default username that can access pages without authentication.
authorized_for_system_information	A comma-delimited list of all usernames that have access to viewing the Nagios process information, as provided by the Extended Information CGI (extinfo.cgi) (as described in Chapter 4).
authorized_for_configuration_information	A comma-delimited list of all usernames that can view *all* configuration information (as described in Chapter 4).
authorized_for_system_commands	A comma-delimited list of all usernames that can issue shutdown and restart commands to Nagios via the command CGI (cmd.cgi) (as described in Chapter 4).
authorized_for_all_services	A comma-delimited list of all usernames that can view information for all services that are being monitored (as described in Chapter 4).
authorized_for_all_hosts	A comma-delimited list of all usernames that can view information for all hosts that are being monitored (as described in Chapter 4).
authorized_for_all_service_commands	A comma-delimited list of all usernames that can issue service-related commands via the command CGI (cmd.cgi) for all services that are being monitored (as described in Chapter 4).
authorized_for_all_host_commands	A comma-delimited list of all usernames that can issue host-related commands via the command CGI (cmd.cgi) for all hosts that are being monitored (as described in Chapter 4).

(continues)

Table B.2 *cgi.cfg (continued)*

Option	Description
statusmap_background_image	Specifies an image to be used as a background in the statusmap CGI.
default_statusmap_layout	Specifies the default layout method the statusmap CGI should use for drawing hosts.
	0 = User-defined coordinates
	1 = Depth layers
	2 = Collapsed tree
	3 = Balanced tree
	4 = Circular
	5 = Circular (Marked Up)
default_statuswrl_layout	Specifies the default layout method the statuswrl (VRML) CGI should use for drawing hosts.
	0 = User-defined coordinates
	2 = Collapsed tree
	3 = Balanced tree
	4 = Circular
statuswrl_include	Specifies additional, user-created objects to include in the VRML CGI.
ping_syntax	Specifies what syntax should be used when attempting to ping a host from the WAP interface (using the statuswml CGI).
refresh_rate	Defines the refresh rate (in seconds) used by the CGIs.
host_unreachable_sound	Specifies an optional audio file that should be played in your browser window when a host becomes unreachable.
host_down_sound	Specifies an optional audio file that should be played in your browser window when a host goes into a critical state.
service_critical_sound	Specifies an optional audio file that should be played in your browser window when a service goes into a critical state.
service_warning_sound	Specifies an optional audio file that should be played in your browser window when a service enters a warning state.
service_unknown_sound	Specifies an optional audio file that should be played in your browser window when a service enters an unknown state.
normal_sound	Specifies an optional audio file that should be played in your browser window when nothing is broken and everything is fine.

Command-Line Options

This appendix contains command-line options for the Nagios binary and as several frequently used plugins in the plugins tarball.

Nagios

Nagios Binary

Syntax

```
/path/to/nagios [option] <main_config_file>
```

Discussion

The Nagios binary normally starts by way of an init script; however, it can be called from the command line and provides two interesting and useful modes when accessed in this manner.

Table C.1 *Nagios Command-Line Options*

Option	Description
-h	Display help text.
-d	Daemon mode. Launch Nagios in the background as a daemon.

(continues)

Table C.1 *Nagios Command-Line Options (continued)*

Option	Description
-s	Scheduling information mode. Displays projected or recommended scheduling information, based on the current data in the configuration file.
-v	Verification mode. Reads all data in the configuration files and performs a sanity check. (Handy for verifying your configuration data after you make a change and before you start Nagios.)

Plugins

By nature, all plugins may be executed directly from the command line. The first law of plugins is that they share an -h switch. The -h switch displays information about the plugin and how it works. All plugins are self-documenting, in this respect.

Most plugins support warning and critical thresholds; these are nearly always specified by way of -w and -c, respectively. Some thresholds may be specified as a range of numbers. Where this is true, the range is represented as a pair of colon-separated numbers with the minimum value on the left and the maximum value on the right (min:max). Some plugins require both numbers in the range to be specified, whereas others allow you to specify one half of the pair; for example "4:" to mean "at least 4."

check_ping

Syntax

```
Check_ping –H <host_address> -w <wrta>,<wpl>% -c <crta>,<cpl>%
   [-p packets] [-t timeout] [-L] [-4|-6]
```

Discussion

Use the systems ping command to check connection stats for a remote host. Warning and critical thresholds are given as a combination of roundtrip time (in milliseconds) and packet loss (as a percentage).

Table C.2 *Check_ping Options*

Option	Description
-h	Displays help text.
-V	Displays version information.

(continues)

Table C.2 *Check_ping Options (continued)*

Option	Description
-4	Uses Ipv4 pings.
-6	Uses Ipv6 pings.
-H	Specifies the target hostname.
-w	Specifies the warning threshold.
-c	Specifies the critical threshold.
-p	Specifies number of packets to send (default: 5).
-L	Generates HTML output 1.30. Copyright (c) 1.
-t	Specifies the timeout limit (in seconds).

Example

```
check_ping -H bart -w 700,20% -c 1200,50%
```

check_tcp

Syntax

```
check_tcp -H host -p port [-w <warning time>] [-c <critical
time>][-s <send string>] [-e <expect string>] [-q <quit
string>][-m <maximum bytes>] [-d <delay>] [-t <timeout seconds>]
[-r <refuse state>] [-M <mismatch state>] [-v] [-4|-6] [-j]
[-D <days to cert expiry>] [-S <use SSL>]
```

Discussion

The check_tcp plugin opens a TCP connection to the specified port on the specified host. It is capable of interacting with text-based protocols and supports SSL. Check_tcp provides performance data back to the Nagios daemon.

Table C.3 *Check_tcp Options*

Option	Description
-h	Displays help text.
-V	Displays version information.
-H	Targets hostname or IP address.
-p	Targets port number (the default is none).
-4	Uses IPv4.

(continues)

Table C.3 *Check_tcp Options* *(continued)*

Option	Description
-6	Uses IPv6.
-s	Specifies a string to send to the serve.
-e	Specifies a string to expect in server response.
-q	Specifies a string to send server to initiate a clean close of the connection.
-r	Specifies how to treat TCP refusals (okay, warn, or crit). This is useful for, as an example, verifying firewall rules. (The default is crit).
-M	Specifies what to do when expected string mismatches with returned string (okay, warn, or crit [default: warn]).
-j	Hides output from TCP socket. This is useful for keeping sensitive information out of the Nagios Web interface.
-m	Closes connection once more than this number of bytes are received.
-d	Seconds to wait between sending string and polling for response.
-D	Minimum number of days an SSL certificate has to be valid.
-S	Toggles the SSL for the connection.
-w	Warning timeout (in seconds).
-c	Critical timeout (in seconds).
-t	Timeout (in seconds [default: 10]).
-v	Prints verbose output.

Examples

Simple port 80 query:

```
check_tcp -H bart -p 80
```

SMTP hello:

```
check_tcp -H bart -p 25 -s 'helo homer.skeptech.org' -e '250 bart.
skeptech.org' -q 'quit'
```

check_http

Syntax

```
check_http -H <vhost> | -I <IP-address> [-u <uri>] [-p <port>]
  [-w <warn time>] [-c <critical time>] [-t <timeout>] [-L]
  [-a auth] [-f <ok | warn | critcal | follow>] [-e <expect>]
  [-s string] [-l] [-r <regex> | -R <case-insensitive regex>]
  [-P string] [-m <min_pg_size>:<max_pg_size>] [-4|-6] [-N]
  [-M <age>] [-A string] [-k string]
```

Discussion

Check_http attempts to open an HTTP connection with the host. Successful connections return okay, refusals and timeouts return critical, and other errors return unknown. Successful connections that return unexpected messages or text result in warning. If you are checking virtual servers that use host headers, you must specify the fully qualified domain name of the target host.

Table C.4 *Check_http Options*

Option	Description
-h	Prints detailed help screen.
-V	Prints version information.
-H	Hostname argument for servers using host headers (virtual host). Appends a port to include it in the header (such as example.com:5000).
-I	IP address or name (uses numeric address, if possible, to bypass DNS lookup).
-p	Port number (default: 80).
-4	Uses IPv4 connection.
-6	Uses IPv6 connection.
-S	Connects via SSL.
-C	Minimum number of days a certificate has to be valid. (When this option is used, the URL is not checked.)
-e	String to expect in first (status) line of server response (default: HTTP/1.) If specified, skips all other status line logic (ex: 3xx, 4xx, 5xx processing).
-s	String to expect in the content.
-u	URL to GET or POST (default: /).
-P	URL encoded HTTP POST data.

(continues)

Table C.4 *Check_http Options (continued)*

Option	Description
-N	Don't wait for document body: Stop reading after headers. (Note that this still is an HTTP GET or POST, not a HEAD).
-M	Warn if document is more than SECONDS old. The number can also be of the form 10m for minutes, 10h for hours, or 10d for days.
-T	Specifies content-type header media type when POSTing.
-l	Allows regex to span newlines (must precede -r or -R).
-r	Searches page for regex STRING.
-R	Searches page for case-insensitive regex STRING.
-a	Username:password on sites with basic authentication.
-A	String to be sent in HTTP header as User Agent.
-k	Any other tags to be sent in HTTP header, separated by semicolon.
-L	Wraps output in HTML link (made obsolete by urlize).
-f	How to handle redirected pages (okay, warn, critical, or follow).
-m	Minimum page size required (bytes): maximum page size required (bytes). For example, 20:150 for a page between 20 and 150 byte.
-w	Response time to result in warning status (seconds).
-c	Response time to result in critical status (seconds).
-t	Seconds before connection times out (the default is 10).
-v	Shows details for command-line debugging (Nagios may truncate output).

Examples

Simple HTTP connect:

```
check_http www.google.com
```

SSL-enabled check

```
check_http -S mail.google.com
```

Connect via SSL, present a "howdy" cookie, and search the site for the word login.

```
check_http -S -k 'Cookie: howdy=itsMeDave' -r 'login'
   mail.google.com
```

check_load

Syntax

```
check_load -w WLOAD1,WLOAD5,WLOAD15 -c CLOAD1,CLOAD5,CLOAD15
```

Discussion

The check_load plugin checks the utilization triplet on the local host. For remote hosts, it is launched via NRPE or check_by_ssh. Critical and warning thresholds are given as utilization triplets separated by commas. For an in-depth discussion of utilization triplets, see Chapter 6, "Watching."

Table C.5 *Check_load Options*

Option	Description
-h	Print help text.
-V	Print version text.
-w	Warning threshold triplet.
-c	Critical threshold triplet.

Example
```
check_load -w 15 10 5 -c 30 20 10
```

check_disk

Syntax

```
check_disk -w limit -c limit [-p path | -x device] [-t timeout]
   [-m] [-e] [-v] [-q]
```

Discussion

The check_disk plugin checks the amount of used disk space on a mounted file system and generates an alert if free space is less than one of the threshold values. Thresholds are given as either percentages or static amounts of disk space. The space units are definable to kilobyte, megabyte, gigabyte, or terabyte. The default unit is the megabyte. Check_disk works on device files and network file systems as well as mount point paths. Checks of network file system mounts may be suppressed with the -l option.

Table C.6 *Check_disk Options*

Option	Description
-h	Print detailed help screen.
-V	Print version information.
-w	Exit with WARNING status if less than INTEGER—units of disk are free.
-w	Exit with WARNING status if less than PERCENT of disk space is free.
-c	Exit with CRITICAL status if less than INTEGER—units of disk are free.
-c	Exit with CRITCAL status if less than PERCENT of disk space is free.
-C	Clear thresholds.
-u	Choose bytes, kB, MB, GB, TB (the default is MB).
-k	Same as --units kB.
-m	Same as --units MB.
-l	Only check local file systems.
-p	Path or partition (may be repeated).
-x	Ignore device (only works if -p unspecified).
-X	Ignore all file systems of indicated type (may be repeated).
-M	Display the mountpoint instead of the partition.
-e	Display only devices/mountpoints with errors.
-w	Response time to result in warning status (seconds).
-c	Response time to result in critical status (seconds).
-t	Seconds before connection times out (the default is 10).
-v	Verbose output.

Example:
Check all locally-mounted partitions:

```
Check_disk -l -w 10% -c 5%
```

Check /var and /etc only.

```
Check_disk -w 10% -c 5% -p /var -p /etc
```

check_procs

Syntax

```
check_procs -w <range> -c <range> [-m metric] [-s state] [-p ppid]
   [-u user] [-r rss] [-z vsz] [-P %cpu] [-a argument-array]
   [-C command] [-t timeout] [-v]
```

Discussion

Check _procs generates WARNING or CRITICAL states if the specified metric is outside the required threshold ranges. Many metrics are supported, including

- PROCS—Number of processes (default)
- VSZ—Virtual memory size
- RSS—Resident set memory size
- CPU—Percentage CPU
- ELAPSED—Time elapsed in seconds

Additionally, filters may be applied to the process list to narrow the search results. The filters and metrics combine to enable complex process query functionality. Thresholds are specified as min:max ranges. Only one half of the range is required.

Table C.7 *Check_procs Options*

Option	Description
-h	Display help text.
-w	Generate warning state if metric is outside this range.
-c	Generate critical state if metric is outside this range.
-m	Specifies the metric, one of:
	PROCS—Number of processes (default)
	VSZ—Virtual memory size
	RSS—Resident set memory size
	CPU—Percentage cpu

(continues)

Table C.7 *Check_procs Options (continued)*

Option	Description
ELAPSED—Time elapsed in seconds	
-t	Timeout value (the default is 10).
-v	Be verbose.
-s	Filter for processes possessing the given status flag (see the ps manual page for valid flag types for your OS) (statusflag).
-p	Filter for children of the given parent process ID (ppid).
-z	Filter for processes using more than the given virtual memory size (vsz).
-r	Filter for processes using more than the given resident set memory size (rss).
-P	Filter for processes using more than the given percent processor utilization (pcpu).
-u	Filter for processes owned by the given username or UID (user).
-a	Filter for processes with args that contain the given string (arg).
-C	Filter for exact matches of the given command (command).

Examples

Critical, if not one process with command name Nagios. Critical, if < 2 or > 1024 processes.

```
check_procs -c 1:1 -C nagios
```

Warning alert, if > 10 processes with command arguments containing /usr/local/bin/perl and owned by root.

```
check_procs -w 10 -a '/usr/local/bin/perl' -u root
```

Alert, if the virtual memory size of any processes over 50K or 100K.

```
check_procs -w 50000 -c 100000 --metric=VSZ
```

Alert, if CPU utilization of any processes over 10% or 20%.

```
check_procs -w 10 -c 20 --metric=CPU
```

INDEX

THIS BOOK IS SAFARI ENABLED

INCLUDES FREE 45-DAY ACCESS TO THE ONLINE EDITION

The Safari® Enabled icon on the cover of your favorite technology book means the book is available through Safari Bookshelf. When you buy this book, you get free access to the online edition for 45 days.

Safari Bookshelf is an electronic reference library that lets you easily search thousands of technical books, find code samples, download chapters, and access technical information whenever and wherever you need it.

TO GAIN 45-DAY SAFARI ENABLED ACCESS TO THIS BOOK:

- Go to **http://www.prenhallprofessional.com/safarienabled**
- Complete the brief registration form
- Enter the coupon code found in the front of this book on the "Copyright" page

If you have difficulty registering on Safari Bookshelf or accessing the online edition, please e-mail customer-service@safaribooksonline.com.

PRENTICE
HALL

Also of Interest from Addison-Wesley and Prentice Hall

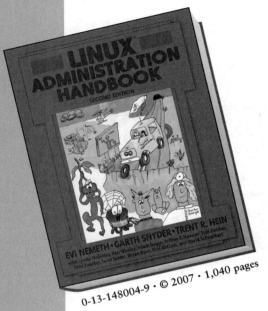

0-13-148004-9 · © 2007 · 1,040 pages

Linux® Administration Handbook, Second Edition

By Evi Nemeth, Garth Snyder, and Trent R. Hein

Since 2001, *Linux Administration Handbook* has been the definitive resource for every Linux® system administrator who must efficiently solve technical problems and maximize the reliability and performance of a production environment. Now, the authors have systematically updated this classic guide to address today's most important Linux distributions and most powerful new administrative tools.

The authors spell out detailed best practices for every facet of system administration, including storage management, network design and administration, web hosting, software configuration management, performance analysis, Windows interoperability, and much more. Sysadmins will especially appreciate the thorough and up-to-date discussions of difficult topics such as DNS, LDAP, security, and the management of IT service organizations.

0-321-49266-8 · © 2007 · 848 pages

The Practice of System and Network Administration, Second Edition

By Tom Limoncelli, Christine Hogan, and Strata Chalup

The industry standard for best practices in system administration, updated to address today's challenges

This book revolves around six key principles of site design and support practices: simplicity, clarity, generality, automation, communication, and basics first. It examines the major areas of responsibility for system administrators within the context of these principles. The book also discusses change management, server upgrades, maintenance windows, and service conversions. Chapters are divided into "The Basics" and "The Icing." "The Basics" discusses the essentials that sysadmins have to get right to avoid problems and added work down the road. "The Icing" deals with the cool things that sysadmins can do to be spectacular, but should only attempt once they've mastered the basics. This new edition has been updated to reflect the changing IT landscape, and another five years of experience in the trenches. A lively, witty style and the use of anecdotes and case studies taken from the authors' personal experience all contribute to make this book an effective, instructive, and yet entertaining read.

PRENTICE HALL

Visit us online for more information about these books and to read sample chapters:

www.awprofessional.com

www.prenhallprofessional.com